T5-DGB-756

The COMPLETE IDIOT'S GUIDE TO

Buying and Upgrading PCs

by Shelley O'Hara

alpha
books

A Division of Macmillan Publishing USA
A Prentice Hall Macmillan Company
201 W. 103rd Street, Indianapolis, IN 46290

To my mother, Darlene Ball, who made me believe I could do anything.

©1995 Alpha Books

International Standard Book Number: 1-56761-583-X
Library of Congress Catalog Card Number: 94-79735

97 96 95   8 7 6 5 4 3 2 1

Interpretation of the printing code: the rightmost number of the first series of numbers is the year of the book's printing; the rightmost number of the second series of numbers is the number of the book's printing. For example, a printing code of 95-1 shows that the first printing of the book occurred in 1995.

Screen reproductions in this book were created by means of the program Collage Plus from Inner Media, Inc., Hollis, NH.

Printed in the United States of America

Publisher
Marie Butler-Knight

Product Development Manager
Faithe Wempen

Acquisitions Manager
Barry Pruett

Managing Editor
Elizabeth Keaffaber

Production Editor
Phil Kitchel

Copy Editor
Audra Gable

Cover Designer
Scott Cook

Designer
Barbara Kordesh

Illustrator
Judd Winick

Indexer
Brad Herriman

Production Team
*Gary Adair, Don Brown, Angela Calvert, Dan Caparo, Brad Chinn, Kim Cofer,
Dave Eason, Jennifer Eberhardt, Rob Falco, David Garratt, Erika Millen,
Cheryl Moore, Beth Rago, Karen Walsh, Holly Wittenberg, Robert Wolf*

*Special thanks to C. Herbert Feltner for ensuring
the technical accuracy of this book.*

Contents at a Glance

Contents

THIS HERE COMPUTER WAS USED BY A LITTLE OLD LADY FROM PASADENA, **AND** SHE ONLY KEPT FOOD RECIPES IN IT.

NO FOOLIN'?

Introduction

A few years ago, I went around to a number of stores to see what it would be like to buy a computer. At one major department store, I asked a saleswoman about the computers on display. She picked up the mouse, held it in the palm of her hand, and pointed it at the computer. "See, you point like this," she said, while pressing the mouse button about 15 times. When I asked her what programs came with the computer, she said, "Oh, some have DOS, and some have 1-2-3."

Wrong, wrong, wrong. At first I thought perhaps she had stumbled over from the lingerie section and was covering for the "real" salesperson who might be at lunch. But, no, she was the real salesperson. Yikes! How can you be expected to buy a computer when the salespeople know even less than you do?

So I opened up a computer magazine and read a review. Here's a quote from an article on microprocessors:

Developers will love it, particularly because several major compiler vendors are creating cross-compilers that will enable the development of x86-compatible applications on the image RISC-station hardware.

Say *what*? How are you going to buy a computer when the computer magazines don't make any sense? Where's the help you need?

Right here.

This Book Can Help

Instead of overwhelming you with technical specifications and technobabble, this book explains in clear, easy-to-understand terms the critical decisions you make when buying a computer. You understand the components you need to purchase, and you understand what the technical specifications *really* mean to you, the user and buyer. It doesn't have to be so difficult.

You don't have to be an expert on how a washing machine works to wash some clothes. You don't have to know how an internal combustion engine works to drive a car. Likewise, you don't have to be an expert on how a computer works to use the computer. You just need to know enough to make a good purchase decision. You just need this book.

How to Use This Book

This book is set up to lead you through the purchase process. Here's how it's organized.

Part 1: Initial Decisions

When you purchase a car, your decision is affected by what you want to do with the car: who will ride in it, where you'll drive, and so on. If you have a family of seven, a convertible two-seater Mustang isn't going to work very well for the family car. If you want a car to impress the opposite sex, you probably won't be looking at a family wagon with a built-in baby seat and wood paneling.

Similarly, when you purchase a computer, the first thing you should think about is what you want to do, who will use the computer, and where. Part 1 helps you understand exactly what you want from the computer, so that you can match your needs with the perfect PC (personal computer).

Part 2: Hardware

Once you know what you want to do, you can start your shopping list. What components do you need? What are the important factors for selecting each component? Part 2 answers these questions. You'll read about the different pieces and parts that make up a PC, and you'll learn how to make sense out of all the advertised specs such as 486DX2/50MHz.

Part 3: Extras

One of the coolest things about the PC is its flexibility. Depending on the equipment you have, you can use the PC to type letters, record sounds, watch TV, print newsletters, and more. Because each person wants to do something different with the PC, it's hard to predict what equipment each person needs (beyond the basic components). Part 3 of this book explains some of the extra equipment you may want to think about.

Part 4: Making the Purchase

Once you know what you need, you just have to close your eyes and jump. Go out there and buy the PC. There's never been a better time to purchase a computer; prices are dropping, and there's a great selection. Part 4 helps you make the final purchase decision and gives you some advice on where to shop.

Part 5: Upgrading

The more you use your PC, the more you'll crave all the latest equipment for it. What makes the PC so great is that you can easily add equipment (well, semi-easily). Replacing some components can add new features and make the computer more powerful. Part 5 of this book covers the upgrades you may want to consider.

Special Reminders

As you use the book, pay attention to these icons, which are used to help you make sense of the information.

Want the background information, the nitty-gritty technical details? Look for these boxed elements to provide more detailed information on a concept, feature, or component.

Want to decode a mysterious term? Look for these boxed elements that give you easy-to-understand definitions of technical terms.

Want a shortcut or tip? Look for these boxed elements to find the fastest way, the best bargain, or other tip information.

Watch out! These boxed elements warn you of common mistakes and pitfalls.

Good luck and happy shopping!

Acknowledgments

A special thanks to Faithe Wempen, Product Development Manager. So many of the ideas, suggestions, and even words in this book are actually Faithe's. She's always in the background of a book, but she deserves a place in the spotlight for all her work.

Thanks also to Barry Pruett, my favorite acquisitions guy; to Audra Gable, copy editor; to Phil Kitchel, production editor; to Martha O'Sullivan, the perfect assistant; and to Herb Feltner, technical editor. Finally, thanks to Marie Butler-Knight, publisher.

About the Author

Shelley O'Hara is a free-lance writer in Indianapolis. She has written over 30 computer books, including *The 10 Minute Guide to Buying a Computer, Excel for Windows Cheat Sheet, Word 6 for Windows Cheat Sheet,* and the best-selling *Easy* series. O'Hara has a B.A. in English from the University of South Carolina and an M.A. in English from the University of Maryland.

Trademarks

All terms mentioned in this book that are known to be trademarks have been appropriately capitalized. Alpha Books cannot attest to the accuracy of this information. Use of a term in this book should not be regarded as affecting the validity of any trademark or service mark.

Part 1
Initial Decisions

Want a quick summary of the decisions you need to make when purchasing a computer? Then step right up. In this quickie part, you can read the least you need to know (conveniently placed in Chapter 1). You see what's possible in the wonderful wacky world of computing, and you get a quick understanding of what makes PCs different. (After all, they do look a lot alike. Why is one $1,200 and another that looks practically identical $3,600?)

After you read these key chapters, you'll know exactly what you want, which is the first step in making a smart purchasing decision.

WE GOT A MODEM, A CD-ROM DRIVE, SOUND CARD, A LASER PRINTER, A SECOND HARD DRIVE, WE'RE HOOKED UP TO INTERNET, A FLOPPY DISK DRIVE, A SCANNER, FOUR INTEGRATED SOFTWARE PACKAGES, AN ADJUSTABLE KEYBOARD, AND SOME THIRTY GAME PROGRAMS. WE JUST DON'T HAVE A COMPUTER...

BLEW BILLY'S COLLEGE FUND.

VICTIMS OF BARRY PRUETT, BEST COMPUTER SALESMAN IN NORTH AMERICA...

Chapter 1

The Least You Need to Know

Want to know the most important things to remember when buying a PC? Then this chapter is for you. Here you'll get a bite-sized rundown on the critical decisions you need to make.

1. Know Thyself

The most important thing you need to know when buying a PC is what you want to do with it. That's *your* unique contribution to this book. Armed with that information, you can make a good, solid decision.

You should start by thinking about what you expect: the benefits you hope to gain and the activities you want to do. Do you want to save money? Save time? Get more organized? Do you want to write letters? Create floor plans? Balance your budget? Learn to play the piano? Make a list of everything you hope to accomplish with a PC. Once you have this list, you can find a system that will exactly match your needs. You can read more about figuring out your needs in Chapter 2.

2. Pick a Processor

The most important component of the PC is the microprocessor (processor, for short), a little electronic chip that functions as the computer's brain. This chip is the biggest factor in determining the speed, power, and performance of the whole computer system.

3. Go for the Memory

The next important consideration when purchasing a PC is how much memory it has. Memory is the computer's working area, so the more memory your computer has, the more it can do, and the faster it can do it.

Memory is measured in kilobytes (one thousand bytes, abbreviated K or KB) and megabytes (one million bytes, abbreviated M or MB). The minimum amount of memory you should consider is 8MB, but 16MB is better if you can afford it. You should also ask what the computer's maximum memory capacity is, in case you want to add more later. You can find more about memory in Chapters 6 and 25.

4. For Hard Disks, Bigger Is Better

Memory is only a temporary work area. You also need a permanent place to keep your programs and data when you're not working with them. Hence, you need a hard disk.

The most important consideration when selecting a hard disk is capacity. How much storage space do you have? The capacity is measured in megabytes (M or MB) or gigabytes (one billion bytes, abbreviated G or GB).

How big should you go? Once again, get the largest capacity you can afford. At the minimum, I would recommend a 300MB hard drive. (For more information on hard disks, see Chapter 7.)

5. Floppy Disks Aren't So Hard

How do programs get onto your hard disk? They don't just jump onto it by themselves—you have to transfer them from a floppy disk. That means your computer needs at least one floppy disk drive. Floppy drives come in two different sizes: 5 1/4-inch (older, less popular) and 3 1/2-inch (current standard).

If you need to share data with someone who has only a 5 1/4-inch disk drive, or if you have old programs or data on 5 1/4-inch disks yourself, get both. Otherwise stick with just the 3 1/2-inch drive. Floppy drives are covered in more detail in Chapter 8.

6. Seeing Is Believing: Pick a Good Monitor

Every time you use the computer, you'll be staring at the monitor, the TV-like part of the system. Therefore, you want to get a good quality monitor that doesn't make your eyeballs ache after 10 minutes.

You have a lot of choices to make in this area. Monitors come in different sizes, follow different standards, and can display images in varying degrees of quality or complexity. As for size, the standard 14-inch monitor will work for most users. In higher-end systems, you may find a 15-inch monitor included, which is a nice bonus. For special purposes, such as intense graphics work or desktop publishing, you may want to invest in an even larger monitor, a 17-inch or more.

Resolution refers to the number of individual dots (*pixels*) that form the picture on the screen. The current standard for monitors is SuperVGA (abbreviated SVGA). SVGA monitors have a *resolution* of up to 1,024 × 768. The first number (1,024) is the number of pixels the monitor can display horizontally; the next number (768) is the number of pixels the monitor can display vertically.

Actually, resolution is a bit more complicated than that, and you also have to worry about the number of colors and the refresh rate. Let's hold off on all that until Chapter 9.

7. Seeking Input: Mouse and Keyboard

The most basic way to enter information and control a computer is with a keyboard. Keyboard keys are arranged like a typewriter's keys, with special function keys around the outside edges.

Since most keyboards have the same keys, the "touch" of a keyboard is the most important factor to consider. Pick a keyboard and try it out. How do the keys feel? Do you have to press very hard to depress the key? Do the keys make a loud noise when you press them?

Nowadays, most computers also come with a mouse, which provides another way to control the computer. It's a little device about the size and shape of a bar of soap, with a "tail" (cord) that connects to your computer. You roll it across your desktop to control an on-screen pointer. Microsoft Windows and other graphics-based programs are much easier to use if you have a mouse.

The best test of a mouse is *you*. Does it feel comfortable in your hand? Does it move smoothly? You'll learn more about mice in Chapter 10.

8. Printing It Out

Most computer buyers buy a printer to go with the system. Without one, you can't show your work to anyone who isn't standing right there at your monitor.

There are lots of different kinds of printers. You can select a low cost (low quality) dot-matrix printer, a middle range inkjet printer, or a top-of-the line laser printer, depending on your printing needs. Chapter 14 will help you make your printing choice.

9. Making Movies, Playing Games—Jamming with Multimedia

In the last couple of years, there has been an explosion of multimedia hardware and software. *Multimedia* (as its name implies) is the combination of different media (sound, text, and graphics). For example, when you look up the entry for "brown bear" in an electronic encyclopedia, you can read about the brown bear, see a video clip of the brown bear catching fish in a stream, and hear the brown bear roar. The visual and audio data make this encyclopedia entry much more interesting than one with some text and a black and white line drawing of a bear.

To use multimedia on your PC, you need a CD-ROM drive, a sound card, and some speakers. There are minimum standards for each of those items, which you'll learn about in Chapter 12. Most new computers sold today include these elements. However, you can add these components later if you prefer; most computer stores sell easy-to-install multimedia upgrade kits. Installing the components is covered in Chapter 24.

10. Leave Room for Growth

Just as you should always wear pants with an expandable waistline on Thanksgiving, you should always leave room for your PC to expand. Right now you may be happy with its features, but next month or next year you may want to add something. To keep your computer from being obsolete, leave some room for expansion.

First, be sure you have extra expansion slots. When you add a new component to the PC, that component is usually a circuit board (sometimes called a "card") that you snap into an open expansion slot in the PC. Video cards, sound cards, some types of mice, some types of modems, and some hard disk controllers require expansion slots. Your PC will come with some slots already filled, but it should also have several extra slots to plug in next year's latest and greatest gadget.

 All expansion slots are not created equal! There are 8-bit, 16-bit, and 32-bit slots, as well as special local-bus (high-speed) slots for special devices. Make sure you know what kind of slots you have. You'll learn everything you want to know about expansion slots in Chapter 11.

Second, make sure you have extra drive bays. A drive bay is like a little shelf inside the PC. You can use this area to insert extra drives, such as another hard or floppy drive, a tape backup unit, a CD-ROM drive, and so on.

For information on expansion slots, see Chapter 11. For an understanding of what you can add, see Chapters 12 (sound cards and CD-ROM), 15 (Fax/Modem), 16 (other drives), and 17 (gadgets, such as TV receiver boards).

11. Do Your Research

This book will help you come up with the "ideal" computer system for you, but it can't make the purchase for you. Once you decide what you want, you'll have to do the legwork to find out where you can get the best deal. Chapters cover where to shop and how to compare brands.

12. Make Your PC Better

Granted, a PC is an investment of time and money, but I think once you start using the PC, the investment will quickly pay off. You're going to love having a PC (most of the time!). There's so much exciting technology available, you'll be amazed.

The drawback to all that advancing technology is that yesterday's PC is quickly out of style. How can you avoid this problem? First, buy a good PC to start with. Second, consider making some upgrades. You can upgrade many of the components: get a new monitor, add a second hard disk, add more memory, and replace the microprocessor. Part 5 of this book explains some of the changes you may want to consider making.

Chapter 2

A Tour of the Software

In This Chapter

➤ Discovering what you can do with a PC

➤ Understanding the operating system

➤ Making your software shopping list

There are many, many reasons to consider purchasing a PC. If you watch the TV ads, you may have been told that a PC can do just about anything: answer your phone, do your household budget, play chess with you, teach little Millie about the solar system, and pick your lottery numbers. It's all true! So what are you waiting for?

Well, you may be overwhelmed by all the possibilities. Don't feel bad—you're not alone. Very few people use a computer to do *everything* you see on TV. (Yes, I know, the guy in the infomercial said that by the year 2000, everyone would be mowing their lawn by computer, but he's just trying to scare you into buying his product.) Besides that, there are probably a lot of really useful things you could do with a computer that you haven't even seen on TV yet—but you'll learn about them in this chapter.

Welcome to the Wide World of Software

If you go out to buy a PC with no idea of what you want to do with it, you probably won't make a very good decision. So step 1 is answering this question: *What do you want to do?* Before you can answer that question, you need to know *what your choices are.* That's where this section comes in. It explains the many types of things you can make your PC do.

There's a lot more software out there than I can possibly show you in one chapter. Browse in a software store or pick up a computer magazine and flip through the ads to find out what else is available.

The key to making the PC do anything is *software*. Software is the magic that turns your PC into a PGA tournament golf course or a financial wizard or an art easel. When you want to do something with the PC, you have to use the right software for that task.

You need only take a quick look through a computer magazine or browse through a software store or catalog to be astounded by all the software possibilities. You can plan your garden, play Solitaire, create a newsletter, figure out a budget, balance your checkbook, learn Spanish, fly a plane, and even do things you wouldn't want your mother to know about, all with your computer.

What follows is a tour of this wide world of software. So that you don't get lost, I'm going to break down the various types of software into neighborhoods or "districts" that we'll explore individually. Enjoy the tour!

The Business District

The business district is the home of the software commonly used in business. If you're buying a computer for your business or to do work at home, you'll most likely be interested in the following types of programs:

Software Type	Description
Word Processing	You can think of a word processor as a fancy type-writer. You use it to create memos, letters, reports, flyers, brochures, and so on. You can check your spelling, change the appearance of your document, insert pictures, easily make changes, and more.

Software Type	Description
Spreadsheet	Think of this type of program as a financial wizard. You can use it to create budgets, do sales forecasts, amortize a loan, and so on. To really save time, you can create formulas that are updated automatically if you change any of the data in the formula. You can also create charts and manage data lists.
Database	This type of program is like a big Rolodex, only much more powerful. You can keep track of people (clients, vendors, associates), events (such as sales transactions), and items (such as inventory). You can sort the data, find data quickly, query for particular information, create reports, and so on.
Presentation	You use this type of program to create slides, transparencies, and handouts that you can use to make presentations. If you have the right equipment, you can hook the computer up directly to a TV or slide projector and show the presentation through your computer.
Mail	Electronic mail (e-mail) programs let you send and receive messages on your computer. You have to be connected to a network, be a member of an online service, or otherwise be connected with the outside world in order to send and receive messages.

Because these types of programs are commonly used in businesses, many software companies sell them in a bundle; that is, several pieces of business software are packaged as one product. For example, Microsoft sells Office, which includes Word (word processor), Excel (spreadsheet), Access (database), PowerPoint (presentation program), and in some cases Mail (a mail program). When you buy Office, you get all the applications in that bundle.

With fax machines, answering machines, voice mail, and e-mail (electronic mail), you may find that you don't ever have to speak to a live person again. You can just exchange messages until eternity.

11

Industrial District

Some software is industry-specific. For example, if you're an architect, you might use a computer-aided drawing and drafting (CAD) program to create blueprints. If you're an accountant, you could buy an accounting program to do the bookkeeping for your office.

If you will use all of the business programs, consider a bundle. Buying a bundle is much cheaper than purchasing the programs individually.

If you're a photographer, you could get a program that enables you to manipulate photos (put the family dog's face on your sister's face in the family Christmas photo). Practically every industry has its own specific software.

Here's an important thing to note: for every professional-quality CAD or accounting or graphics program, there are scores of simple, limited programs aimed at the amateur. These programs aren't necessarily bad—they're just basic. Whereas a simple $30 CAD program might be fine for the guy who just wants to fool around with some floor plans, a professional architect will want more sophisticated software. The same is true with all the other industries. Ask other professionals in your industry what software they recommend. Depending on the industry, you may not be able to find the best programs in stores; you may have to special-order them.

Residential Area

More and more people have PCs in their homes nowadays, and seeing the potential for big money, software makers have turned their attention to this market. There's a ton of stuff out there marketed expressly for the casual, at-home PC user.

Even if you know which program you want, it's still a good idea to ask other people in your field what software they use. This will give you an idea of the products that are out there.

As for the basics, home PC users want the same things that everyone else does. They want a simple operating system, like Windows. They want good word processing software for their correspondence, a decent spreadsheet program, and maybe a database.

But home users also want programs designed specifically for their domestic needs—and software makers have complied. You can get a checkbook program (the most popular is Quicken) that will not only balance your checkbook but also help you keep track of a budget, do your taxes, remind you to pay your mortgage, and more. You can buy software for home inventory, home repair, cooking, genealogy, and more. For almost any home-related task, you can find a computer program to do it. (Well, computers can't clean your house—yet—but watch for that in the future.)

Schools and Playgrounds

A computer can be for fun as well as for business! You'll find a huge variety of software in the education and recreation category. You can drive a race car, fight dragons, investigate crimes, play chess, design the ultimate basketball team, play a round of golf with Jack Nicklaus or a game of bridge with Omar Sharif, and lots more.

In the education arena, you can learn to type, teach your child to read, learn a foreign language, look up information in an encyclopedia, learn algebra, study for SATs, and more. If you have children, the computer can be a great educational tool for teaching many different subjects. And if you are a kid at heart, you'll be thrilled with the education and recreation software that is available.

> If it's home software you want, pick up a copy of *The Home Computer Companion* by Clayton Walnum and John Pivovarnick (Alpha Books). It has reviews (with pictures) for over 150 software programs, including home helpers, educational programs, games, and word processors—the whole range of programs that a home user might want.

Construction Zone

The final type of software is called utility software. These are programs that let you tweak, fine-tune, and troubleshoot your computer system.

Believe it or not, utility software is not just for computer geeks who love to play around with their settings. Utility programs can improve the speed of your hard disk, find and remove dreaded computer viruses, salvage deleted files, and do multiple other wonders you never thought possible.

> When buying educational software, check the age range of the program. Little four-year-old Mikey won't get much out of a program designed for 8–12 year olds.

Utility programs aren't on most beginners' "must-have" lists, but after you have been using your computer for a while, you may want to check one out. If you have Dos 6.0, you'll have some utility programs.

The Telephone Company

If you want to use your computer and a modem to hook up to other computers and networks, you need a communication program. You can fax a recipe to your sister in Illinois, for example, or send a file to a friend in South Carolina. The details of telecommunication are explained in Chapter 15.

The Fine Arts District

Fancy yourself an artist? Want to design your dream house or teach a seminar? Want to create a newsletter for New Age Disciples? There are all kinds of graphics programs that you can use to create and display artistic endeavors. You can use paint and draw programs to create artwork. You can use computer-aided drawing programs (CAD) to create blueprints. If you need to display a series of slides, you can create a presentation using a presentation program. Desktop publishing programs are ideal for working with the layout of documents—for creating newsletters, brochures, and other types of documents.

Local Government: The Operating System

The fun parts of any city are the various districts where you can do things: business, industrial, residential, and so on. The not-so-fun, but necessary, part of the city is the local government: the police, the garbage collectors, the city council.

It's the same way with your computer. The fun part of using a computer is the application software—the garden planner, the race car simulator, the tax calculator. (Well, the last one probably isn't too fun unless you're an IRS auditor.)

However, in addition to fun stuff, you have some not-so-fun software called *operating system software*. The operating system keeps the computer running smoothly; it manages your files, runs your programs, and cleans up the streets at night. All computer systems need an operating system.

The good news is that all computers come with an operating system, so you don't have to buy one. The bad news is that the operating system is usually the hardest part of your computer to understand. Don't fret, though. This quick primer tells you the key things to remember about operating systems.

What an Operating System Does

Your operating system can't do flashy things like answer your phone or display a photo, but there are several things it can do really well. For one thing, your operating system is a skilled translator. Your computer can't speak English, and you can't speak Computer. That leaves the two of you with a pretty big communication gap. The operating system takes the commands that you enter and translates them into a language that the computer hardware can understand. For instance, you tell the operating system that you want to delete a file, and the operating system relays that request to the hard disk, which wipes out the file for you.

The operating system is also an efficient file clerk, keeping track of where you store all your programs and data. When you type and save a letter, the operating system files the letter away. When you want to see the letter again, the operating system pulls the file for you. Sure, the word processor may be the program that actually edits the letter, but it relies on the operating system to tell it where the file is stored.

Finally, you can think of the operating system as a traffic cop. When you are using the PC, there's a lot of work going on inside that little box: a program zipping in and out of memory, a data file being opened and closed, a request for more information interrupting it all. Someone has to organize all this traffic, and the operating system does just that. It makes sure programs don't collide and data doesn't get misplaced.

DOS is the Boss

Most computers come with a copy of DOS, the most common operating system. (They're up to version 6.22 at this writing.) DOS stands for Disk Operating System and rhymes with *loss*. That's appropriate because you may feel like a loser when you try to use DOS. It's rather cryptic, to say the least. Here's what you see when you use DOS:

The DOS prompt.

Not very intuitive is it? Remind you of a big black hole? DOS uses a *command line interface*, which means that to get the computer to do anything you have to type a command. Not only that, but you have to type the command in the exact format DOS expects. If you don't get the command right, DOS spits back some unfriendly error message like **Bad command or filename** and makes you try again.

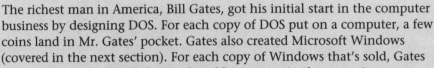

The richest man in America, Bill Gates, got his initial start in the computer business by designing DOS. For each copy of DOS put on a computer, a few coins land in Mr. Gates' pocket. Gates also created Microsoft Windows (covered in the next section). For each copy of Windows that's sold, Gates receives a few more sawbucks. He has parlayed his success in the operating system arena to the software arena and beyond. With an estimated 150 million PCs out there, you can see how he became the richest man in America.

Luckily, you only use DOS if you have DOS-based programs. Newer computers come with Windows-based programs, and Windows is a lot easier to use.

Windows Is Supposed to Make It Easy

To make the computer easier to use, the makers of DOS developed an additional program to use with DOS. This program, called Microsoft Windows, is an operating environment that sits on top of DOS. DOS is still there, but you don't have to deal with its ugliness. Instead you see little pictures, called *icons*. You move the on-screen pointer to the icon or command you want instead of typing a command. Much simpler, eh? This kind of environment is known as a GUI, or *graphical user interface*.

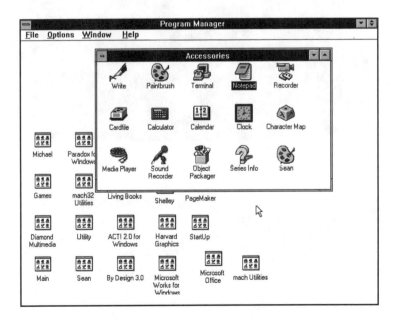

Windows displays little pictures (called icons) that enable you to start programs, work with files, and so on.

16

Some salespeople will tell you that Windows is an operating system and that you don't need DOS if you have Windows. That's not true. All IBM-compatible PCs need DOS to operate. Windows is an optional tool that you lay on top of DOS to make it easier to use.

This is going to change, however, when the new version of Windows comes out (probably late in 1995). Rumor has it that this new version of Windows will render DOS as we know it unnecessary.

Most new computer systems sold today come with Windows. If yours doesn't, you can purchase Windows separately. Windows is not necessary, strictly speaking, but you really ought to have it because most of the best new software coming out these days has to be run from within Windows.

There are other operating systems, such as OS/2, which was created and marketed by IBM. (Seen their latest marketing blitz for the version called Warp?) Although they make Warp sound cool, it's not as popular as Windows. As a first-time buyer, it's better to stick with the masses.

> If you're playing around with a computer and you wonder whether or not it has Windows, try typing **WIN** and pressing **Enter** from the DOS prompt. If it has Windows installed, Windows will start.

Making Your Software Shopping List

Well, we've come full-circle. Now that you have some idea of what's available, you can start to answer that question: *What do I want to do?* This section helps you summarize your choices, provides some buying tips, and explains how to decode software requirements.

Your Software Wish List

Are you getting excited about all the possibilities yet? Good. Because it's time to make some choices. Use the checklist that follows to record your responses. If you know the name of the exact program you want, go ahead and write it in the right-hand column of the checklist.

> **GUI** Stands for graphical user interface and is pronounced "gooey"—as in gooey chocolate chip cookies.

1. In the Need Now column, mark the software types that you absolutely need. Don't be greedy—yet. Stick to the ones that are absolutely critical.

2. Think about the other people who will use your PC. What software will these people need? Check these programs too.

3. Okay, now it's time to dream about the software you would like to have. You don't have to purchase this software immediately, but you will at least have some idea of what you intend to add later. Mark these in the Want Later column.

Type of program	Need Now	Want Later	Software Program
Word processing	❏	❏	_____
Spreadsheet	❏	❏	_____
Financial	❏	❏	_____
Database	❏	❏	_____
Integrated	❏	❏	_____
Paint	❏	❏	_____
Draw	❏	❏	_____
CAD	❏	❏	_____
Presentation	❏	❏	_____
Desktop publishing	❏	❏	_____
Communication	❏	❏	_____
Games	❏	❏	_____
Educational	❏	❏	_____
Utility	❏	❏	_____

Software Buying Tips

You can end up spending as much on software (maybe more!) as you do on the computer system. When buying software, hold onto your pocketbook or wallet and consider the following tips:

➤ When shopping for a PC, budget some money for software. You don't have to buy all the software you need at once, but you'll need at least a few good programs to get you started.

➤ Some new computers come bundled with software. If you need the software, that's great! However, don't get trapped into paying more for a computer that comes with "free" software that you'll never use.

➤ Most programs have hardware requirements; to run the software, you have to have the particular equipment the software demands. We'll talk more about this momentarily.

➤ Most programs require a particular operating system. For instance, you have to run Windows programs from within Windows. (You can run most DOS programs in either DOS or Windows.) When you are shopping for application software, make sure you purchase the type of program for your type of system.

At first, you may be so enthralled with all the possibilities that you end up with a shopping list three blocks long. Listen to the cash register—Cha-Ching! Really, now, I don't think that Pro Golf game is critical to your business day. You can always go back for what you *want* after you have a little more experience with the computer.

Check the software box carefully! Sometimes software that is deeply discounted at a store will be usable only on some less-popular operating system, such as Apple IIe, Commodore, or Amiga. Make sure the box says IBM-compatible.

Decoding the Software Requirements

When you shop for software, read the "fine print" on the software box. This fine print explains what equipment you need to run the program. Programs require a certain type of processor, a certain amount of memory, a certain amount of hard disk space, and a certain type of monitor. The program may also have other requirements, such as a mouse or a sound card. The software box should list all the required equipment.

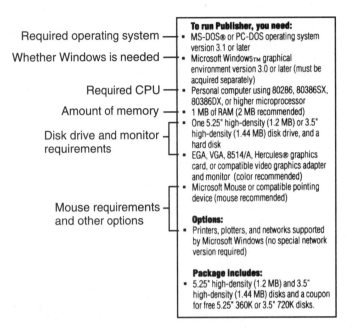

Required operating system — **To run Publisher, you need:**
- MS-DOS® or PC-DOS operating system version 3.1 or later

Whether Windows is needed —
- Microsoft Windows™ graphical environment version 3.0 or later (must be acquired separately)

Required CPU —
- Personal computer using 80286, 80386SX, 80386DX, or higher microprocessor

Amount of memory —
- 1 MB of RAM (2 MB recommended)

Disk drive and monitor requirements —
- One 5.25" high-density (1.2 MB) or 3.5" high-density (1.44 MB) disk drive, and a hard disk
- EGA, VGA, 8514/A, Hercules® graphics card, or compatible video graphics adapter and monitor (color recommended)

Mouse requirements and other options —
- Microsoft Mouse or compatible pointing device (mouse recommended)

Options:
- Printers, plotters, and networks supported by Microsoft Windows (no special network version required)

Package includes:
- 5.25" high-density (1.2 MB) and 3.5" high-density (1.44 MB) disks and a coupon for free 5.25" 360K or 3.5" 720K disks.

The software package lists what you need to run the application.

Watch out for minimum system and recommended system requirements. Sometimes a manufacturer will list the minimum requirements, but getting the program to run well with those minimum specs will be difficult. Think about those "one-size-fits-all" T-shirts. If you've ever seen 250-pound Aunt Lulu in her one-size-fits-all T-shirt, you know it's not pretty. If you see two sets of guidelines, you should be sure your system meets the recommended system requirements.

When you get into specialized software (a CAD program, for example), the requirements may be more steep. In this case, check the requirements carefully.

If you take my advice in this book, you'll end up with a computer system that will run most popular business applications, so you don't have to fret too much about matching system specs. You may want to review the requirements of a program anyway, though, to get used to the way the specs are presented.

The Least You Need to Know

When buying a new computer system, keep in mind that you will need to buy software to run on the computer—in fact, running software is the whole point of buying the computer in the first place!

➤ You can find software to do just about any task you have in mind. Review magazines or software catalogs to get an idea of the different software that's available. Then make a list of the software you need.

➤ All computers require an operating system, and usually the operating system is included as part of the system. The most popular operating system is MS-DOS.

➤ Because DOS is so difficult to use, many computers also have an operating environment called Microsoft Windows. This program sits on top of DOS and lets you issue commands by selecting little pictures instead of by typing. Using Windows is much easier than using DOS.

➤ Software requires certain hardware equipment to operate properly. When you are purchasing software, review the software requirements, which are usually listed on the software box.

HMMMN...

Chapter 3

PCs at a Glance

In This Chapter

➤ Defining hardware

➤ Understanding what makes one PC different from another

➤ Picking winning lottery numbers (just kidding)

Are you excited by all the possibilities? Shivering with anticipation? Can't wait to buy a PC? That's good—but hold onto your wallet until you finish the book, or you may come away with the wrong PC for your needs.

Or maybe you're on the other side of the spectrum, shivering not with anticipation but in dread of making all those complicated decisions. Well, I can't say that I blame you for being anxious. Buying any complex piece of electronic equipment can be daunting. There are so many choices! But if you read this book carefully, you'll minimize your chances of making expensive mistakes.

Buying a computer is a lot like buying a car: there are standard equipment items, luxury extras, and pushy salespeople trying to get you to buy the most expensive one on the lot. In this chapter, you'll learn the basic parts of a PC and what differentiates one PC from another, so that even the most crafty salesperson won't be able to fool you into buying a car without wheels.

What Is Hardware?

When you hear the word "hardware," you may think of nuts and bolts and hammers and nails. You may think of Tim Taylor's "Tool Time." Well, yes, that's one meaning of the word.

When people talk about hardware in reference to computers, though, it means something different. Computer hardware is the physical equipment that makes up the computer system. When you buy a computer, you are buying hardware. It may come with some software too, but the hardware is what you're shelling out the bucks for.

The two meanings of the word **hardware** are no doubt related because when you can't get the computer to work, you will feel like taking the hardware (as in hammer) to the hardware (as in computer).

No matter what type of computer you purchase, you will at least have the following minimum hardware pieces:

➤ system unit

➤ monitor

➤ keyboard

➤ mouse

These items are the "standard equipment" of the PC. If any of these pieces aren't included, your computer won't run as advertised.

The System Unit (a.k.a. "The Box")

The large box-like piece is the system unit. It stores the circuit boards and silicon chips that make up the computer. All of the electronic wizardry that makes the computer operate goes on inside this box.

Here's a quick tour of the system unit:

Item	Description
Motherboard	The motherboard is a big, flat circuit board that covers the entire floor of the PC casing. All the other components hook into it, including the microprocessor and the memory.
Microprocessor	The microprocessor is the "brain," the main chip in the computer. You'll learn about it in Chapter 5.

Item	Description
Memory	Memory is the computer's workspace. It's covered in Chapter 6.
Hard disk	A hard disk stores your programs and data. Think of it as a big electronic filing cabinet. To find out the skinny on hard disks, see Chapter 7.
Floppy disk	Without a floppy disk, you wouldn't have any way to get programs and data onto the hard disk. The floppy disk and all its wonders are covered in Chapter 8.
Power supply	The power supply converts electricity from your wall socket into power that the PC can use. It looks like a silver box and is described in Chapter 11.
Other circuit boards	You will most likely have other circuit boards inside the system unit that add other functions. For example, you might have a circuit board called a fax/modem that lets you use your PC as a fax machine.

You can choose from various sizes and styles of system unit cases. You can buy one that sits on the desk or one that stands on the floor. You can buy one that is connected to the monitor or one that is separate. Chapter 12 discusses different box styles.

The Monitor (a.k.a. "The TV-Looking Thing")

The piece of hardware that looks like a TV is called a *monitor*, because you use it to monitor what's going on with your computer. (Clever name, eh?) On the monitor, you can see your input (what you type on the keyboard or select with the mouse) and the output (the computer's response to it). The monitor is hooked to a circuit board in the system unit by a cable. We'll talk more about monitors in Chapter 9.

System unit cases are not interchangeable; once you buy a PC with a certain case style, you're stuck with that case style until you buy a different PC. That's because each motherboard is designed to fit a certain case style.

 You may wonder whether you can actually watch TV using the monitor. If you had asked that question a few years ago, people would have thought you were an idiot. Now, though, you can watch TV on your monitor if you have a special circuit board. Gadgetry for watching TV on your PC is covered in Chapter 17.

The Keyboard (a.k.a. "The Typewriter-Like Thing")

The keyboard is what you use to type commands and enter information. All keyboards have the same set of keys, but they may be arranged slightly differently on some models. The keys may also have a different feel from model to model. Chapter 11 explains the keyboard in more detail.

The Mouse (a.k.a. "The Soap on a Rope")

The mouse looks like a bar of Dove soap connected to your computer with a tail. (If you really want it to look like a mouse, you can buy a ridiculous mouse cover that adds a furry suit and ears to the mouse.) Mice and other spin-offs of them are the topic of Chapter 11.

What Makes One PC Different from Another?

When you go out shopping for a car, you can easily see the differences between models. You probably wouldn't confuse a Jaguar with a wood-panelled station wagon. By looking at the cars, you can probably guess which ones have the most power and which ones cost the most money. You can also most likely guess their purpose. The Jaguar, for example, is for helping some middle-aged man with a receding hairline deal with his mid-life crisis, and the station wagon is for hauling around Tommy and his soccer team.

On the other hand, when you go shopping for a PC, you will probably notice that most PCs look the same. They all have the same bland rectangular system unit and the same swirling demo program running on the monitor. Each one has a keyboard with 101 keys and a 2-button mouse.

If they all look the same, you may think, "What's the big deal about picking one? Aren't they all the same?" No, they aren't. Understanding what makes one PC different from another is the key to making a successful purchasing decision. This section summarizes some of the differences.

Microprocessor: The Computer's Brain Power

The main difference between computers is the microprocessor. You can think of the microprocessor as the computer's brain. The "smarter" the brain, the faster and more powerful the computer—and the more you can expect to pay for it. When you purchase a computer, the most critical decision you make will be which microprocessor you choose. Understanding the differences among the processors is covered in Chapter 5.

Hard Disks: How Much Junk Can You Store?

Another difference in PC models is the size of the hard disk. The bigger the hard disk, the more expensive the model. When you are shopping for a PC, you will want to select the biggest hard disk you can afford. You'll be surprised at how quickly you fill up a hard disk with programs and files.

Monitors: Seeing Is Believing

If you take a close look at the monitors for different computers, you'll see that they are different. Some are bigger than others. (With monitors, bigger is better, no matter what else you may have been lead to believe.) There are other factors, too, such as the number of colors the monitor can display at once, and the resolution of the screen. Also, on some, the image is crisper—that is, it looks clearer. When you are comparing different PCs, take a look at the monitor to determine whether one system has a better monitor than another.

The Extras

When you buy a car, you can get lots of extra options: air conditioning, car stereo, air bags, refrigerator, TV, VCR. Some items you will want, such as AC if you're in AZ. Some items will be available in several models of varying quality. For example, you can get the cheap old AM/FM stereo, the middle range stereo/tape deck, or the top-of-the-line multitray CD player that comes with a faceplate that looks like the cheap old AM/FM stereo so that car thieves don't break your window and steal your top-of-the line CD player.

The same comparisons are true for a computer. There are some items that you will definitely want, and there are some items that you will want but which you can choose from several levels of products. You need to keep in mind a few points.

Some PCs come bundled with all kinds of extra equipment, such as a printer, fax machine, speakers, CD-ROM drive, and more. Face it—nothing is free. That item is there because something else was cut back, or because the price of the overall package was increased. If you were planning to buy all the bundled extras anyway, great. But if you don't need all these items, your money would be better spent on other components that you do need. Deciding what pieces you need is the focus of Part 2 of this book.

And don't forget, you can always add hardware pieces as you become more proficient with the computer. In fact, Part 5 of this book covers some of the upgrading options you can consider. When you are buying a computer, you can decide to purchase the extra equipment now or add it later.

Look for the Label: Computer Brands

The final major difference among computers is the brand of computer. There are hundreds of computer manufacturers, all with varying reputations for performance, price, and service. The best way to pick one is to read computer magazine articles that rate the companies, and then pick one that gets high ratings in all areas.

A lot of people think that because IBM is the standard that other computers are compatible with, IBMs are automatically the best computers. That's not necessarily true. IBM was just the first.

Here's a little history lesson. When personal computers were first invented, IBM dominated the mainframe (big computer) market. When IBM saw the growing interest in little computers (PCs), they quickly jumped into the market. Because they were in a hurry to capture this new market, IBM didn't have time to create the PC from scratch all by themselves, so they licensed the various components from other hardware makers. They got the microprocessor from one company, the hard drive from another, the monitor from yet a third, the operating system from another (the famous Bill Gates), and so on. IBM then assembled these pieces into a PC.

Because IBM didn't create the parts, they didn't own the trademarks and patents needed to prevent other people from creating competing machines. This left the door wide open for other companies to take the same pieces and parts and create their own PCs. The systems that the competitors made worked the same as an IBM system, so they became known as "clones" or "IBM-compatibles."

Initially, there was some variance in quality among the different compatibles. Some were as sturdy as the IBM computers themselves; others seemed to break down at the press of a button. Compatibility was also an issue. Some computers weren't 100% compatible—that is, they didn't work well with the other hardware and software designed to be used on the IBM-manufactured PC.

Today, however, there is no noticeable difference in quality among most PC manufacturers' products. In fact, some of the most highly rated PCs are *not* IBM computers. Does this mean you shouldn't buy a *real* IBM? No. It does mean that an IBM computer isn't necessarily better than a computer manufactured by another company.

> **PC**   The term PC in this book refers to all IBM and IBM-compatible computers.

You'll find that once you define the features you want, the final decision is which brand to buy. The brand matters because you'll find some manufacturers are known for reliability, some for price, some for performance. You'll have to decide which manufacturer provides the best mix of all three. The next chapter will talk a bit more about setting your priorities to get the best combination of these factors in the PC you choose.

And Then There's the Macintosh...

You may have heard of another type of personal computer called a Macintosh, or Mac for short. This type of computer is manufactured by Apple, and these are *not* IBM-compatible.

> Time for another history lesson. Around the same time IBM was creating the PC, another dynamic duo (Steve Jobs and Steve Wozniak) was creating another type of computer in their garage. (Yes! It's true. One of the great legends of computing!)

A Macintosh has the same basic hardware components as a PC: a system unit, a monitor, a keyboard, and a mouse. But the internal workings are different. Think of the Macintosh as French and the PC as English. Although the two speak a different language, you can still *say* the same things. That means you can't use software designed for the Mac on the PC or vice versa, but whatever you can do on a Mac, you can do on the PC. You just have to have the software designed for that particular type of computer.

> Gateway 2000 is an extremely popular manufacturer of PCs. They offer good performance at modest prices, and they have a reputation for excellent warranties and support. If you're willing to buy a computer by mail, consider this company. You can find their ads in most computer magazines.

Don't automatically rule out the Macintosh. It's known for its ease of use and graphics capabilities. Just like comparing French to English, it's difficult to say whether the IBM or the Macintosh is better. They're just different. There are lots of people who will argue vigorously for hours about the merits of Macintosh over PCs or vice versa. But in the end, it's all personal preference. Here are some things to consider when deciding:

➤ The Macintosh operating system has a built-in graphical interface much like Microsoft Windows for the PC. That means you don't have to deal with DOS.

➤ Most businesses use IBM-compatibles. In fact, around 80–90% of all computers sold are IBM-compatible. If you're concerned about being able to bring work home with you to a home PC, make sure you buy the same type your office uses.

➤ Macintoshes tend to be more expensive than PCs because there aren't any Macintosh-compatibles (every Mac is made by Apple itself).

Apple has just recently begun to license their technology to clone makers, so you may soon see Macintosh-compatible computers in the stores. These clones will probably be substantially cheaper than "real" Macintoshes, but it's uncertain whether the machines will have the same high-quality parts and workmanship that Apple puts into the Macintoshes they manufacture.

This book covers only IBM-compatible PCs. However, if you're interested in buying a Mac, there are many places you can turn. One of the best is *The Complete Idiot's Guide to the Mac* by John Pivovarnick, a Mac guru extraordinaire with a real sense of humor.

The Least You Need to Know

Later in the book, you'll get in-depth info about the different hardware components, but this chapter started you on your way with an overview. Here's what you learned:

➤ Hardware refers to the physical components of the PC. All computers have the bare-bones minimum of a system unit, monitor, keyboard, and mouse.

➤ The system unit houses the pieces that make up your PC's guts, such as the motherboard (which contains the microprocessor and memory). The system unit also contains disk drives, the power supply, and other circuit boards.

➤ Even though PCs may look the same, they differ in their speed and power. These factors are determined mostly by the microprocessor. PCs also differ in what extra options are included and in the manufacturer.

Chapter 4

Setting Your Priorities

In This Chapter

➤ What do you hope to gain from using a PC?

➤ Who else will use the PC?

➤ How much do you want to spend?

➤ What's important to you?

➤ Why do they always change the TV line-up just when you get used to it?

By now you should have a good idea of what you want your computer to do. The problem is, there are dozens of computers that will do everything you want. How do you pick the best one?

If the answer to this question were easy, this book would consist of one page stating the best PC for everyone. But because everyone is different (isn't that what makes life grand?), there is no single best PC. Instead, there are *lots* of best PCs, depending on your situation.

What you bring to this book, then, is your knowledge and experience of your particular circumstances. Do you want to purchase a PC for your family? Or are you buying the PC for your business? Are you wealthy and not concerned about the price? (Lucky you!) Or are you working within a budget?

This chapter helps you bring your needs into sharper focus so that when you start learning about the available options, you can easily say, "Yes, that's for me" or "No, not interested in that."

What Benefits Are You Looking For?

Besides listing what you want to do with the PC, you should also think about what you hope to gain by having a computer. Do you want to save time? Save money? Become more accurate? Organize your affairs? Educate the kids? Well, in theory anyway, a computer can help you do all those things, but let's take a realistic look at each of those goals.

Saving Time

Can the computer save you enough time that you can sit in front of the TV eating junk food and watching Ricki Lake every afternoon? Well, maybe.

The computer can do some things much faster than you can. For example, ask a computer to sort a list of 200 names, and it can do it in a single second. If you did it yourself manually, you probably wouldn't even get to the first name before the computer would be finished. Ask a computer to total a row of numbers. Again, in less than a second, the computer will be done—and it will *always* be right. Even with a calculator, you'd barely have time to peck in the first number before the PC finished.

The computer also makes it easier to reuse information. Suppose your mother makes you send out a nice holiday letter each December to your 15 maiden aunts. Instead of typing 15 individual letters, you can type one and then modify it for each of your aunts:

Dear Aunt _____:

Thank you for the fruitcake. It was _____. The tooth I chipped should be fixed up like new by early February. I was so sorry to hear about your _____ surgery. Hello to your cat _____.

Does all this time saving mean you can knock off work at 2 p.m. every day in time for Oprah? Probably not. You still need to enter the information for the computer to do its magic (total the numbers or create the "Dear Aunt" fill-in-the-blank letter).

You also will find that you lose some time tinkering around with your software. For example, you may spend three minutes composing the content of your "Dear Aunt" letter, but you may spend one hour adding different letters and shading to make the letter look nice and drawing a diagram of your chipped tooth.

Saving Money

If you think that the computer is going to save you money, guess again. It seldom works out that way.

In theory, you might save some money doing things on your PC that you used to pay someone else to do. For instance, if you paid a graphic designer to lay out your newsletter, you can do it now yourself. And you may be able to do your own taxes with some good tax software.

However, it's difficult to quantify cost savings. For one thing, you have to have the right software for each task, and software isn't cheap. Most programs cost anywhere from $30 to over $1,000. You may be able to pay someone to do what you need done for a whole year and not spend any more money than you would on the software itself.

When you first buy a computer, you are going to have to spend some time learning how to use it. At first, you may wish you had stuck with your typewriter and hand calculator. Don't worry, though—the time you invest in learning will eventually pay off.

And then there's the time you spend. How much is it worth? Do you really want to give up several hours of your working day to fiddle with the margins of a newsletter, when you can hire a graduate student to do it for $20 a month? Remember, the PC isn't going to do anything magically on its own—you're going to have to be there working with it.

Being More Accurate

Another benefit of using a PC is that your work is more accurate. For example, if you type a letter, you can have the program check the spelling or grammar and then correct any errors. If you're figuring a budget, the program can calculate the totals. A computer won't make a mistake when adding a row of numbers.

Also, the computer doesn't get tired. Even if it's 4 a.m. and you've been up all night working on a deadline, the PC won't make a bleary-eyed mistake and come up with $250,000 when the right answer is $25.

Does this mean your life will be error free? Hardly. The computer is only as accurate as the person using it. If you type 5,000 when you should have typed 5,000,000, don't count on accurate calculations. If you use "two" in a letter when you meant "too," don't count on your spell-checker to notice.

Getting Organized

When I teach a class on how to buy a computer, many class participants tell me they want a computer to "help them get organized." Getting organized can be a benefit—if you are organized to start with. If you're not, you'll probably lose your motivation to be organized when you realize how much work it is.

Forget the paperless office. If you are buying a PC to save paper, you're going to quickly find that you generate the same amount of paper—if not more. Don't throw away your filing cabinets.

For instance, if you buy a PC to keep track of your expenses for tax purposes, you have to enter each of those expenses into the computer throughout the whole year. If you don't enter any transactions until April 14, kiss your organization good-bye. On the other hand, if you faithfully enter and update your expenses, you'll be ready for tax time. Instead of walking into your accountant's office with three shoe boxes full of miscellaneous receipts, you can walk in with a printout of the expenses. (You still have to keep those receipts though!)

You can use the PC to keep track of contacts, clients, customers, expenses, orders, and other data. Keep in mind, though, that you need to be systematic in maintaining and updating this information.

New Opportunities

Besides all the basic benefits that immediately come to mind, there may be extra bonuses and opportunities for PC users. It depends on your situation, but here are some things you might not have thought of:

➤ You might be able to bring work home from the office to your PC. Doing so may provide the flexibility you need—especially if you have children.

➤ If you own a business, you can use the computer to better analyze your business. For instance, you can check out your sales data to figure out what your best-selling product is or determine which service is the most profitable.

➤ If you *want* to own your own business, you can use the PC to get started. Many successful home-based businesses start with an idea and a PC.

➤ If you are retired, are a homemaker, have children, or have some free time away from work, you can use the PC to learn new things. Learn a foreign language. Teach yourself how to fly using a flight simulator. Master chess. Explore geography. All these things are possible with a PC.

Educating the Kids

Unless Junior can create artwork on the PC by the time he's two years old, you may feel as if you are a bad parent. In this age of getting ahead, many parents feel as if their children should have every advantage. You may want to purchase a PC to keep your child on the fast track.

The truth is that although kids like PCs, it's not because they make them smarter or more competitive, but because there are so many cool things to do with a PC. With the right software, children are *tricked* into learning new things while having fun. A child can learn about geography while playing Where In the World Is Carmen Sandiego?, learn how to recognize words and letters by playing with Broderbund's Little Monster at School Living Book, and learn about math by playing MathBlasters. You shouldn't buy a PC for Junior so that he'll get ahead; you should buy one because he'll enjoy it. Plus, if you get a PC for Junior, then he can teach you how to use it!

Who Is It for, Anyway?

Another thing to think about when buying a PC is who else will use the PC. Just you? You and your spouse? You and your children? Your dog? Your nieces and nephews? Your neighbor's kids?

If more than one person will use the PC, you need to consider the needs of the other users. For example, will your dog require a special keyboard? Will your neighbor's kids need high-quality stereo speakers for playing Dungeons and Dragons? Will Granny require a modem so that she can keep in touch via PC with the other members of her windsurfing club?

Modem A piece of hardware that enables your computer to connect to other computers through your phone lines.

The safest way to make sure each person is covered is to make a list of all the people who will use the PC. Be sure to include each person's needs in your shopping list.

Where Will You Use It?

Also think about where you will use the PC. Do you need to take the PC on the road? If so, you may want to consider a portable computer (as covered in Chapter 13). Will you keep the PC in your home office? If so, do you have room for a big desktop model, or are you short on space? If you are short on space, you may want to consider one of the slimline models. The style of the case is the topic of Chapter 12.

You should visualize where you will place the PC and know in advance where each component will sit. Doing so will help you make such decisions as which case style is best for you.

How Much Do You Want to Spend?

You might think that this section will tell you to draw up a budget on a PC and stick to it. Wrong.

When you are creating your budget, be sure to include some money for furniture on which to set up the new computer system. Furniture and other accessories are covered in Chapter 18.

You couldn't have picked a better time to purchase a PC because prices continue to drop. By shopping around, you can get a great deal. To find out the best places to shop, review Chapters 19 and 20.

Of course, money is always important. But it's not a good idea to let your budget dictate the type of computer you purchase. Suppose that you budget $1,500 for a computer to start a desktop publishing service out of your home. You purchase a complete system (computer, monitor, printer, sound system, and software) for $1,500 and consider yourself on your way to a successful business.

But when you try to use your computer, you find out that your system isn't powerful enough to run the desktop publishing program you need. The printer you bought is okay for drafts, but you need a higher quality printer for your final printouts. The computer came with a sound card and speakers, but you don't really use them; a scanner would have been more useful. Your bargain system suddenly doesn't seem like such a bargain.

It's better to come up with the system that does what you want to do, and then see how much that setup is going to cost. If the price is too high, you can then decide whether to spend the extra money or cut back on a component.

For instance, in the desktop publishing business scenario, you may find that the complete system you want costs $3,000. You may decide to pay the additional amount to get this system, or you may decide not to purchase all the items at once. For example, you may decide that you can do without the scanner until you get the business off the ground.

What's Most Important to You?

Another factor in your personal assessment is what is most important to you. Take a moment to consider what you want in your PC by reading the following list and checking whichever items are important to you.

❑ I want the most powerful PC.

❑ I want the most affordable PC.

❑ I want the PC that is easiest to use.

❑ I want a PC that isn't going to break.

❑ I want a PC that looks nice.

Did you check them all? That's okay, because ideally you would want the most powerful, cheapest, easiest to use, most reliable, and most attractive PC. The PC you purchase, however, is probably going to be a balance of the preceding. The following list explains:

➤ **Power**   By power, I mean the speed and capabilities of the PC. And you can never have too much power. But as mentioned in the next chapter, the more powerful the computer, the more expensive it will be. Unless you aren't concerned about money, you are most likely going to have to balance power with affordability.

➤ **Affordability**   You can probably find a PC for under $1,000, if not cheaper. But buying a cheap PC is going to be frustrating if that PC can't do what you want it to do. Instead of focusing on price, focus on what you want to do. Then shop for the best deal on a PC that will do just that.

➤ **Ease of use**   All IBM-compatible computers operate basically the same way, so you won't find too great a difference in ease of use. You may find, though, that some computers are easier to set up or easier to upgrade (add new components to). When you are comparing brands, you can use ease of use to help you break ties between two or more models.

➤ **Reliability**   One of the differences you will find when selecting a particular brand of PC is that some are more reliable than others. Checking out the warranty and reliability of the PC is covered in Chapter 20.

➤ **Look and feel**   As you look at different PCs, you may find that one just *looks* better than the others. You may like the style of the case better or the feel of the keyboard. It's okay to use this factor to make your final choice—after all, you're going to have to live with it.

Go back through your checklist and prioritize what's important to you. Put a 1 next to the most important item, a 2 next to the next most important item, and so on. You can use this list later when you are narrowing down your choices.

The Least You Need to Know

"Know thyself" would be a good motto to follow when purchasing a computer. The more you consider what you want to do and what you expect to gain, the better you will be at finding a computer that will match your needs exactly.

➤ Potential benefits of using a PC include better accuracy and increased opportunity. Saving time and getting organized are also benefits, but will depend on what you do with the time you save and how organized you are to start with.

➤ If more than one person will use the PC, be sure to consider that person's needs when you are creating your shopping list. Also think about where you will use your PC.

➤ When you are thinking about how much to spend, think about what you need first. Then find a system to match. If the system you need costs more than you wanted to spend, consider spending a little extra or cutting back on some of the extras.

➤ Ideally, you want the most powerful, most affordable, most reliable, and easiest-to-use PC. Realistically, you are going to have to balance these factors, deciding which is most important to you.

Part 2
Hardware

Put on your hard hat and prepare for the nitty gritty on hardware in this part. When you hear hardware, you may think of hammers, nails, and circular saws. You may think of row after row of gadgets. But that's a different kind of hardware.

Computer hardware includes the physical pieces that make up a PC: the boxy-like thing called the system unit or system case, the TV-like thing called the monitor, and the typewriter-like gadget called the keyboard. The hardware, basically, is the PC. So to make a smart purchasing decision, you have to dissect the PC hardware and see what makes it tick. This section explains why one PC is faster, smarter, or more powerful than another.

After reading this part, you'll know exactly the type of system that is best for you.

Chapter 5

The Power of the Processor

In This Chapter

➤ What is a processor?

➤ Figuring out what the processor name means

➤ Determining how fast the chip is

➤ Different standards and manufacturers of chips

➤ Upgrading a chip

Although most computers look similar, they can vary greatly in power and performance. Why? Because inside each computer is a little processor chip—about the size of a cracker—that controls the whole show, and different models of computers have different types of processors.

Therefore, the main decision to make when deciding which PC to buy is which processor you want. How do they differ? Which one is the best? Read on, my friend, to find out.

What Is a Processor?

As I mentioned, the most important part of a computer is the processor chip, sometimes called the CPU (central processing unit) or the microprocessor. It sits on the mother–board, like a queen on a throne, ruling over everything in its sight.

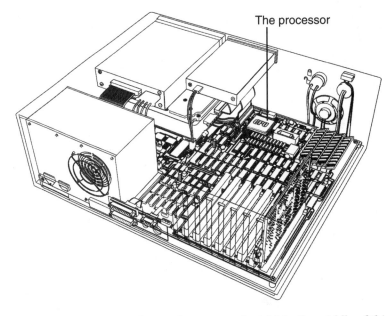

The processor

A PC's guts at a glance; the processor's right in the middle of things.

Motherboard The large green circuit board that covers the floor of the system unit. This board is a little smaller than a Monopoly board and has all sorts of electronic circuitry on it. Squint at it, and it looks like your home town as seen from an airplane window, with wiring for streets, and little subdivisions of chips, slots, and pins.

Since the processor is the main thing that distinguishes one computer from another, you'd best get to know the factors that make them different. Here's a quick overview of the three big factors:

➤ **Type of chip** If you've read any advertisements for PCs, you may have seen odd combinations of numbers and letters such as 386SX, 486DX, or P5. These codes are sort of like model numbers. More about this shortly.

➤ **Speed** Within each chip type, you can choose from several speeds. The faster the chip, the higher its price. Check out the section entitled "How Fast Can She Go?" later in this chapter to find out how to pick an appropriate speed.

➤ **Bus** The bus isn't technically part of the processor—it's part of the motherboard. The bus is the highway along which data travels between the processor and the other areas of the motherboard. The wider the bus, the more data that can travel at once. Check out the section entitled "Getting on the Bus" for more info.

Decoding Processor Names

Processor chips are named with numbers. The higher the number, the more powerful the chip. Here is a breakdown of the different chips:

Chip	Pronunciation	Description
80286	two eighty-six	Used in the AT computers introduced in 1984; now obsolete.
80386	three eighty-six	Introduced circa 1988; borders on obsolete.
80486	four eighty-six	Introduced circa 1991; this chip was the top-of-the line until the Pentium was introduced.
Pentium	Pent-ee-umm	This is the current top-of-the-line chip and is used in the most expensive computer systems.

A long time ago (back in the early '80s) there were two other processor types: 8088 and 8086. They were used in the original IBM PC and IBM PC XT. However, they've been obsolete for so long you'll probably never encounter them when shopping for a new computer.

Why isn't the Pentium called a 586? Intel, the manufacturer of most microprocessor chips, used to have a monopoly on PC chips, until a startup company called AMD introduced its own 386 chip. Intel tried to sue AMD for using the name 386, but lost. When Intel introduced the 586, they used a new, *trademarked* name: Pentium. Some people still refer to the chip as a 586, though.

When a new chip is introduced, it becomes the king of the hill—the most powerful and most expensive. The chip that *was* the king becomes the next powerful and drops in price, and the chip that was second drops to third and borders on obsolescence. Most cost-conscious buyers buy on the second tier (the second most powerful chip). That means if you were buying a new chip today, you would want at least a 486, no less.

One of the founders of the first microprocessor company came up with "Moore's Law." This law states that the number of transistors that can be built on a computer chip will double every 18 months. That means that every 1 1/2 years, a new computer is introduced that is twice as powerful as its predecessor. The new chip not only works faster (because it has more power), but also usually incorporates new technology that enhances the performance. There's work going on right now for the next generation of chip, called the P6, which will someday put the Pentium to shame.

SX, DX, Etc.

The next part of the equation for chip names is the suffix. (Remember English class? A suffix is something added to the end of another word. You can thank Mrs. Pickard, my 6th grade English teacher, for that.) After a chip name, you may see the suffix SX or DX. Generally speaking, DX is better than SX. You can think of SX as the "standard" chip and DX as the "deluxe" chip.

Standard and deluxe? What exactly does that mean? Well, it means different things in different chip types. In 386 chips, a 386SX has a 16-bit bus (like a 16-lane highway) connecting the processor to the other parts of the computer, and the 386DX has a 32-bit bus (like a 32-lane highway). More about buses later in the chapter. In 486 chips, the 486DX chip has a built-in math coprocessor and the 486SX does not. I'll explain math coprocessors in the next section.

DX2? What Does the 2 Mean?

Don't fall into the trap of waiting for the prices to fall—take it from me. When I bought my latest PC, it was in the second tier of power and performance. This PC now costs considerably less than what I paid for it; but if I wanted to purchase a second-tier PC *today*, I'd pay about what I paid for *my* second-tier system two years ago. This means you should just jump in and buy a PC now!

From its day as king of the hill to the day it borders on obsolescence, a chip type has a life of 3–4 years. During its life, the chip's manufacturers look for ways to improve it to keep it competitive. Enter the X2, X3, and X4 chips.

If you see a 2 after SX or DX, it means the chip runs at twice the speed of that particular chip in its original form. (The next section explains how speed is measured.) If you see a 3 or 4, it means the speed is tripled. Don't let the 4 fool you—it's not quadruple speed. IBM planned to come out with the first 486DX3 chip, so Intel named theirs 486DX4 to trick consumers into thinking Intel's was the faster chip. Actually, both the 486DX3 and 486DX4 are triple-clocked speed, meaning the computer's internal clock is ticking three times as fast, making the processor work three times as hard.

How can one chip be twice as fast as another chip? The chip is built to perform a certain number of operations per clock tick. By making the clock tick faster, the chip works harder. That's how the chip is quicker.

The enhanced speed can be deceiving though, because only the microprocessor works faster. The other components (memory, video, bus, and so on) still operate at the original speed.

Math Coprocessors

A math coprocessor is an extra chip designed to take the load off the main processor when the computer is doing complex math calculations.

On 386 computers, the coprocessor is separate from the main processor. In most cases, when you buy a 386 computer, it doesn't even come with a coprocessor—you have to buy it separately. It's called a 387 chip.

On 486 computers, the coprocessor is built into the processor, which makes for very smooth operation. However, the coprocessor is disabled in the 486SX chips, so you don't have access to it. All Pentiums have built-in, functioning coprocessors.

Clock vs. clock All PCs nowadays come with a built-in clock/calendar feature that tells you the date and time whenever you ask. This is called a **real-time clock**, and it is NOT the same clock as the clock that regulates how fast the chip works. They're totally separate, and it's just a coincidence that they're both called "clock."

Since all 486 chips cost about the same to manufacture, why do chip makers disable the coprocessors in some of them and then sell the disabled chips as SX models at a discount? Marketing, my friend, marketing.

Legend has it that the 486SX was invented as a marketing ploy to sell at a discount a batch of 486 chips that had been manufactured wrong and had defective coprocessors. The discount chips were so popular and sold so quickly that the manufacturer started taking perfectly good 486 chips and disabling their coprocessors to keep up with the demand for 486SX chips. Go figure.

How Fast Can She Go?

If you could drive at any speed, what speed would you drive at? Probably the fastest speed possible, right? Well, computer speeds are a lot like car speeds. The higher the speed, the more attractive the chip.

Instead of miles per hour (MPH), chips are measured in megahertz (MHz). One megahertz equals one million clock ticks per second. The higher the megahertz, the faster the computer.

Within each chip type, there is a range of speeds, and the higher speed chip you get, the more expensive it will be. Here are some examples:

Chip	Speed	Think of It This Way
486SX	25, 33	School zone
486DX	25, 33, 50	School zone with a little stretch of highway
486DX2	50, 66	Highway driving
486DX4	75, 100	Highway driving with a radar detector
Pentium	60, 66, 75, 90, 100	Race track

I recommend that you buy a chip in the minimum range of 33–50MHz, and if you can afford a faster computer, buy it. Keep in mind that although 25MHz may be okay now, computers will continue to get faster and faster. You don't want to be driving a Moped on the information superhighway, do you?

Getting on the Bus

A friend of mine got up his courage to buy a PC and felt pretty confident ordering one through a mail order company—that is, *until* the mail order salesperson asked him what kind of bus he wanted. At that point, he panicked and hung up.

The more advanced the processor type, the better use it will make of its speed. For instance, a 60MHz Pentium gives faster overall performance than a 100MHz 486DX4. That's because a 486 is maxing out its capabilities at that speed, but a Pentium chip hasn't even broken a sweat yet.

So what's the deal with buses, and what do you need to know? Inside the system unit, you have the processor, memory, and various circuit boards, all plugged into the motherboard. The motherboard contains *pathways* (etched copper circuits) that connect all these components, enabling them to communicate with one another. This electronic freeway is called the *bus*. Nice metaphor, huh? Little "bus lines" run from the microprocessor to each component, connecting them.

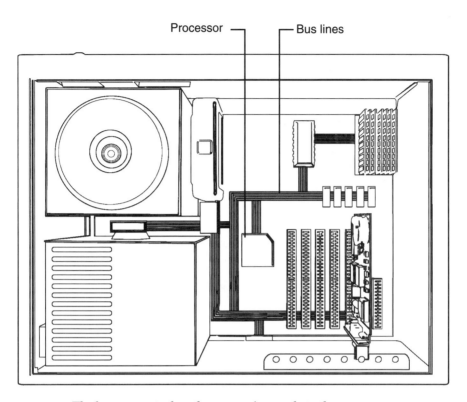

Processor — ⌐ — Bus lines

The bus connects the other expansion cards to the processor.

How Wide Is Your Bus?

If you think of the bus lines as highways, you can see that if there are more lanes on the highway, there's less chance of a traffic bottleneck. A 16-bit bus has 16 lanes, and a 32-bit bus has 32. A bus can move as many bits of data simultaneously as it has lanes: a 32-bit bus can move 32 bits of data at once.

Just like in real life, the number of lanes on the highway is not a big deal if there's not much traffic. If you don't tax your computer's processor too hard, it doesn't matter how many lanes your bus has. But come rush hour, you'll be glad for the wider road.

Bit Stands for binary digit and is the smallest bit of data on a PC. A PC uses a binary numbering system with two designations: 0 (off) or 1 (on). If you combine 8 bits, you have a byte. One typed character, for example, is a byte.

Bus width was a much bigger deal when 386 computers were popular because 386SX computers had only a 16-bit bus, while 386DX computers had a 32-bit bus. All 486 and Pentium computers have 32-bit buses.

Bus Standards

There are several types of buses. Although they all accomplish the same result—moving bits of computer data from place to place—each has its own way of getting the job done. The following table summarizes the main types you will see advertised.

Bus Type	Number of Bits	Description
ISA	16	Industry Standard Architecture. Used in 386 and some low-cost 486 computers.
EISA	32	Extended Industry Standard Architecture. Developed by a group of computer manufacturers as an improvement to ISA. Not very popular because it's rather expensive.
MCA	32	Micro Channel Architecture. Developed by IBM as an improvement to ISA. Never really caught on with other manufacturers.
VESA	32	Video Electronics Standards Association. A widely used local-bus standard in most PCs sold today.
PCI	32	Peripheral Component Interconnect. The emerging new local-bus standard that will probably replace VESA in the next few years.

On most newer computers, the motherboard has a special bus line (in addition to its 16- or 32-bit ones) for special, favored passengers that need quicker access. This special bus line is called the *local bus*, and it runs between the processor and a few privileged expansion slots on the motherboard.

For example, if you have a motherboard with a local bus, you can get a special local bus video card that fits into one of the special expansion slots and speeds up your video performance. Likewise, sometimes you can plug the hard disk controller into one of the local bus slots. For more on expansion slots, see Chapter 12.

There are two main flavors of local bus: VESA (sometimes called VL or VLB) and PCI. When you are shopping for a PC, you should purchase a VL or PCI bus computer. Because VL is a slightly older standard, it seems that the industry is gradually moving toward PCI. Therefore, PCI may be a better choice if you plan to keep your computer for many years.

Which offers better performance, VL or PCI? It's almost too close to call. Some independent magazine tests show that VL offers better performance than PCI in a 486 computer, but PCI wins in a Pentium.

Who Makes the Processor?

The largest maker of microprocessor chips is Intel, which so far has dominated the market. Recently, though, some upstart companies in the microprocessor business have been threatening Intel. AMD, Cyrix, and NexGen are all reputable companies that manufacture processor chips.

AMD gave Intel a run for their money by introducing a faster 386 chip (40MHz) than Intel's fastest one (33MHz). But then the 386 became obsolete, and the challenge went away.

This fierce competition among manufacturers is great for consumers. First, each company tries to top the other in speed, performance, and innovation. So you can expect bigger and better things from new processors each year. Second, the competition drives down the prices of the chips and ensures there's not a shortage of chips.

How is Intel responding? With a marketing blitz. You may have seen commercials for Intel on TV. Also, many computers use Intel's logo on the outside of the system box. Intel wants to make buyers aware of the leading brand name and convince new buyers that they should have—nay, *must* have—an Intel chip.

Actually, however, there's no reason to insist on an Intel chip. A recent article in *PC World* reported that there haven't been any compatibility problems with chips from other manufacturers. And some of the big hardware vendors, such as Compaq, are currently using chips from manufacturers other than Intel. However, if you do purchase a computer with a chip other than an Intel, you may want to do a little research to be sure that the company is reputable and has been in business for awhile.

Upgradable Chips—Staving Off Obsolescence

I remember when I learned that manufacturers create products to last a few years and then break. Take a toaster, for example. Sure, it may be *possible* to create an everlasting toaster; but if you only bought one toaster in your life, the toaster business would quickly be toast. Hence, after a few years, your toaster will begin to smoke and stick and spark—and make breakfast a little more exciting.

As for computers, a PC doesn't break in a few years (at least you hope not), but it does quickly become obsolete. What was once the top-of-the-line speed demon of the computer world will quickly seem like a grannymobile compared to the latest model. Wouldn't it be great if you could keep the PC and just plug in a new chip each time a new chip was introduced?

That's the idea behind upgradeable chips: you pull the old chip off the motherboard and pop the new chip on. Many new computers are advertised as upgradeable, and that's a good feature to consider. Some have a special socket called a ZIF (zero insertion force), which makes it easy to pop off the old and plug in the new. Others have an extra socket to plug the new chip into, which disables the old one automatically.

If you want to purchase an upgradeable PC, look for one that has a ZIF (zero insertion force) socket. This type of socket enables you to easily take out the current chip and insert a new one. Don't get a PC with a chip that is soldered into place.

Intel markets an OverDrive chip that lets you upgrade the speed of a 486 with a faster 486 chip. Earlier in this chapter, I told you that the 2 at the end of a model number means that the clock that controls the operations has been sped up. Well, the OverDrive chip speeds up your clock.

Intel has also promised an OverDrive chip with which you will be able to upgrade a 486 to a Pentium. That kind of OverDrive chip is a little more complicated, because it's not only speeding up the clock, but actually adding Pentium power. Such a chip may be out by the time this book goes to press.

When you're thinking about upgrading, remember the buts... (isn't there always a but?). Upgrading chips is a relatively new concept, and there are a lot of bugs still to be worked out with it. Be sure you can upgrade the chip and that you don't have to buy the upgrade from the original manufacturer only. The ins and outs of upgrading your microprocessor are covered in Chapter 27.

Making Your Decision

Now that you understand all the hoopla of the chip, you can make your decision. Here's what I recommend:

➤ If you can afford a Pentium, get one. You can get any speed you want (cost being the deciding factor); again, aim as high as you can afford. This chip will be top-of-the-line for 1995 or so, until the 686 (or whatever they decide to call it) comes out.

➤ If you can't afford a Pentium, get at least a 486DX or a 486DX2. Get the fastest chip you can afford.

➤ As for buses, you want VL or PCI. Because it's a newer technology, PCI is better if you're getting a Pentium or if you're planning to keep the computer for a long time.

Before you upgrade a processor, take a good look at the price of an entirely new PC system. You may be able to buy a whole new computer with a bigger hard disk, a better monitor, and lots of other extras for only a little more money than the upgrade chip would cost.

➤ If you want to be able to upgrade the chip on the PC, look for a PC that uses a ZIF (zero insertion force) socket.

The Least You Need to Know

Selecting the microprocessor chip is the most important decision you will make when purchasing a PC. The chip is what makes one PC faster, more modern, and more expensive than another.

➤ Chips are usually named with numbers: 286, 386, 486, and Pentium. The higher the number, the more powerful the PC. The Pentium is the king of the hill as of this writing, and the most popular chip now is the 486 because the prices are very reasonable.

➤ Sometimes you will see a suffix after the chip name. You can think of SX as standard and DX as deluxe. If you see a number after DX or SX, such as 2, 3, or 4, it means the speed of the chip has been enhanced.

➤ The speed of the chip is measured in megahertz (MHz). One megahertz is equal to 1 million clicks a second. The higher the MHz, the faster and more expensive the computer.

➤ The pathway connecting the different components inside the PC is called the bus. Buses come in different widths and conform to different standards. The two newest local bus standards are VESA (VL bus) or PCI.

➤ It is possible to upgrade the microprocessor chip. Doing so is easier if you have a ZIF (zero insertion force) socket.

Chapter 6

Memory:
The Computer's
Thinking
Capacity

In This Chapter

➤ What memory is, and why it's important

➤ How much memory is enough?

➤ Making memory work faster

➤ Understanding read-only memory (ROM)

➤ Adding memory

If the processor is the most important factor in how a PC performs, memory is a close second-place. Memory forms the computer's workspace—the larger the available pool of memory, the more work you can have going at once. Without memory, your fancy processor is useless. Even a powerful Pentium can't do much if it suffers from a lack of memory.

Tech-heads will tell you that there are two types of memory: RAM and ROM. (No, not after Romulus and Remus. They're acronyms.) RAM stands for random access memory, which is the workspace memory I just mentioned. When most people talk about their computer's memory, they mean RAM. ROM stands for read-only memory, which is the tiny bit of startup information that's permanently encoded into your computer, enabling it to start itself up each day. You won't hear non-geeks talking about ROM very often.

I know all this memory stuff can give you a headache, but hang in there, and I'll cover it as quickly as possible. In this chapter, we'll look at RAM and ROM and talk about what to look for in a new PC.

What Is ROM?

ROM is boring. Let's face that up front. All computers have ROM, but you can't do anything interesting with it. You can't even specify what kind of ROM you want to buy. It's just there.

If you have an older BIOS, you can upgrade it. On older PCs, you have to actually replace the chip. Ugh! Newer PCs have what is called flash ROM. You can upgrade this type of ROM by running a software program (much easier). That means when shopping for a PC, flash ROM is a plus.

ROM does only a few simple things, but it does them very well. ROM contains the BIOS (Basic Input Output System) and other critical information you need to start and use your computer. What's BIOS? Well, when you turn on the PC, the BIOS tells the computer what to do—how to get started. The startup routine also gives a wake-up call to all the other components. Good morning, keyboard! Hello, disk drive! Are you awake, printer?

ROM just sits there—you don't do anything with it. In fact, the information in ROM is hard-coded on the chip, so you can't even change it. You don't have to worry about the size or type of ROM chips when you purchase a computer because you don't get to choose the ROM chips that are put into the PC. You should make sure that you get a recent version of BIOS. Ask the dealer for the version date. Also, check the BIOS manufacturer to make sure they are a reputable company. (Phoenix and AMI are well-known BIOS makers.)

What Is RAM?

RAM stands for random access memory, which describes how the memory works: randomly. No, that doesn't mean the memory is scatterbrained. In this case, random is actually a good thing. RAM is a grid of little cubbyholes, each of which has a unique address. (Think of post office boxes.) When you've got data in RAM, each byte of it is stored at a particular address. "Random" means the processor can access any address just as quickly as any other address; the post office boxes on the top are just as easy to get to as the ones in the middle.

RAM is the work area where the computer holds data and instructions while you're working. For example, when you start a word processing program, the program is loaded into memory, where the microprocessor can access it quickly. Think of RAM as a desktop and the word processing program as your working materials: when you start a program, you take it off the hard disk (out of a drawer in your desk) and place it in RAM (on the top of your desk) where you can work with it. The data you create is also stored in RAM. If you type a letter to Aunt Dottie using your word processor, the letter resides in RAM as you're creating it.

> If you read techie magazines, or talk to a techie, you may hear them mention different names for RAM. **DRAM** (pronounced d-ram) is dynamic RAM, and **SRAM** (pronounced s-ram) is static RAM. You don't have to worry about the distinction.

Deciding How Much RAM You Need

Like the microprocessor, the RAM chips are plugged into the motherboard. Each chip holds a certain amount of memory, and the more memory you have, the better.

Think about your own memory. If you could remember all the state capitals, the stats of your favorite baseball teams, the key mathematic principles of calculus, and all the verses of *The Wasteland* by T.S. Eliot, as well as what you need at the grocery, you'd not only be a great Jeopardy contestant, you'd also be pretty organized. The more you can remember, the more data you have available to pop off the tip of your tongue.

> RAM is powered by electricity. When you turn off your computer, everything in RAM is —poof— gone. That's why you have to save your work to a permanent place, the hard disk. You should save often, every 5 or 10 minutes.

The same is true of computers. The more memory the computer has, the more elbow room it has to work; that is, the more room it has to store data and instructions.

How Memory Is Measured

RAM is measured in bytes. Remember that the basic numbering system used on a PC is binary, and the smallest measurement is the bit. Eight bits equal one byte, which is about one typed character. One byte isn't much when you're measuring memory (or when you're eating chocolate cream pie), so you usually measure in multiple bytes.

Measurement	Equals	Abbreviated as
kilobyte	1,000 bytes	K or KB
megabyte	1,000,000 bytes	M or MB
gigabyte	1,000,000,000 bytes	G or GB

Actually, one kilobyte is 2 to the 10th power, or 1,024 bytes, and one megabyte is 2 to the 100th power, or 1,048,576 bytes. However, it's easier to round to 1,000 and 1,000,000.

The Magic Amount of RAM for You

Although most computers today are sold with at least 4MB of RAM, you may see some older PCs that have 640KB, 1MB, or 2MB. I recommend you buy a PC with at least 8MB.

Many of the bundled systems sold as family PCs come with only 4MB of memory. This isn't really enough; you want at least 8MB. Check the system specs carefully when considering a bundled system and be sure the specs of this all-for-one PC will meet all your needs.

If you can afford more memory, get it. You can always use extra memory. You can also add memory later, as described later in this chapter and in Chapter 25.

Is there such a thing as too much RAM? Not really. But after a certain point, your computer will probably not benefit very much from more RAM. A recent test done by a computing magazine showed that a PC's performance in common applications like word processing and spreadsheets improved dramatically when upgraded from 4MB to 8MB, and improved a bit further when upgraded from 8MB to 16MB, but did not show any further improvement when upgraded to 32MB.

RAM Shopping Tips

When shopping for a PC, there are two things to watch for with RAM. One is the amount of RAM that comes with the computer (usually 4MB or 8MB). As I said earlier, it's best to get at least 8MB to start out. The other is the maximum amount of memory the computer can have. This is usually either 32MB (eight 4MB SIMMs) or 128MB (eight 16MB SIMMs).

You'll see RAM advertised something like this:

4MB expandable to 32MB

That means the system has 4MB, but you can add RAM up to a total of 32MB. Don't buy a computer that is not expandable at least to 32MB.

RAM Speed

You've probably gotten the idea that faster is better with a PC. Memory chips are measured in nanoseconds (ns). One nanosecond is one billionth of a second. Kind of unthinkable, isn't it? A good range is 70ns or faster for memory chips.

RAM Cache (or Stash the Cache)

The computer can use some tricks to make it work faster, and one such trick is a RAM cache. The definition of a cache (in a non-computer sense) is a hiding place for provisions or instruments. That's pretty much what a RAM cache is: it's a piece of RAM that's set aside as a storage spot for data that the processor frequently calls for. That way, when the processor calls for that data, the computer doesn't have to go all the way back to the hard disk to get it.

A cache, then, is a good thing, because it can significantly improve performance. You will see cache sizes advertised from 8K to 256K. The larger the cache, the more tidbits of wisdom you can sock away in the cache. Look for a cache that's at least 256K.

You can also get some of the benefits of a built-in disk cache by using software, such as SMARTDRV (which comes with Windows). The software solution provides the same benefits—stashing away key data—but your cache software may not be compatible (may not work) will all your programs. Also, the built-in cache is faster.

You Can Always Add More...

As programs become more and more complex, they make greater demands on memory. Back in the early '80s, 640KB was thought to be an ocean of memory, more than enough to run any program. Nowadays, 640KB seems more like a backyard creek.

After you have been using your PC for awhile, you might consider adding more memory to it. You normally do this by plugging memory chips onto the motherboard. (This is covered in Chapter 25, so stick around.) The most common type of plug-in chip is called a SIMM or single-inline memory module.

It's wise to buy every component of your PC with an eye toward upgrading. What I'm about to explain to you is a little bit techie, but you'll thank me later, when you go to buy more RAM for your PC.

In most computers, there are 2 RAM banks with 4 slots each. Each slot holds a SIMM (a little circuit board with memory chips on it), and each SIMM contains 256KB, 1MB, or 4MB of memory. Most motherboards don't let you mix and match SIMM types, and most require that each bank be either completely full or completely empty. That means you'll see memory in one of the following configurations in a PC:

Bank 1	Bank 2	Total Memory
256KB	Empty	1MB
256KB	256KB	2MB
1MB	Empty	4MB
1MB	1MB	8MB
4MB	Empty	16MB
4MB	4MB	32MB

Here's where the decision part comes in. If you're wavering between total memory of 4MB and 8MB, and you decide you can't afford 8MB, go with 4MB. You can always add four more 1MB SIMMs later (Bank 2 is open). Although you won't be very happy with the way your computer runs with only 4MB of RAM, at least your upgrade path is clear.

On the other hand, if you're deciding between 8MB and 16MB, keep in mind that to get 16MB, you need four 4MB SIMMs. That means that if you start out with 8MB and want to upgrade to 16MB, you'll have to scrap (or try to sell off) the eight perfectly good 1MB SIMMs that are currently filling up Banks 1 and 2 and buy all-new RAM. Ouch, that can get expensive! In a case like that, it's better to spring for the 16MB up front.

Some of the newer computers' motherboards suspend the rules about not mixing SIMM types and having to completely fill a bank. So you might find a computer that offers 8MB of RAM, but does so with 2 4MB SIMMs that half-fill Bank 1. That's a great setup because you've got loads of extra space left in the banks to add more RAM later. The ads won't tell you if the motherboard has this special feature, but a techno-savvy salesperson would know.

The Least You Need to Know

The more memory your PC has, the more room the computer has to do its work. It's like having a giant-sized desk where the computer can spread out all the instructions, scribble notes, and make chocolate chip cookies if it wants. When buying a new computer, you want to be sure to purchase one with enough memory.

➤ ROM stands for read-only memory. This type of memory is hard-coded on a chip and cannot be changed. ROM contains the instructions the computer needs to get up and running.

➤ Memory is measured in bytes: kilobytes (one thousand bytes, abbreviated KB), megabytes (one million bytes, abbreviated MB), or gigabytes (one billion bytes, abbreviated GB). You should purchase a computer with as much memory as you can afford. The bare minimum I would recommend is 8MB.

➤ To speed up the performance of memory, the computer can use a cache, a place in which it stores programs and instructions the computer anticipates that you'll need. Cache sizes are measured in kilobytes.

➤ One of the most common upgrades you will consider is adding memory. You can add memory by plugging memory chips into available slots. When shopping for a PC, make sure there are slots for extra memory on the motherboard.

Chapter 7

Your Electronic Filing Cabinet— The Hard Disk

In This Chapter

➤ Why is the hard disk so important?

➤ How big is big enough?

➤ How fast is fast enough?

➤ How the hard disk talks to other components

➤ Anatomy of a hard disk

➤ Some tips on organizing your hard disk

If memory is like the desktop (where you keep everything you're working on), a hard disk is like the drawers or filing cabinet. This is where you keep the stuff you don't currently need. As with most storage areas (the attic, closets, under the bed), the more space you have, the more stuff you can store.

So when you shop for a hard disk, the first thing you decide on is size—and the bigger the better. You also want to consider speed and such techie details as the controller type—all of which is covered in this chapter.

What Does a Hard Disk Do?

Do you need a hard disk? Absolutely. Without a hard disk, you'd have nowhere to keep your programs and data. A computer without a hard disk is like a house with no closets, or a desk with no drawers.

 You can run some programs directly from the floppy disks they came on, but most have to be installed on your hard disk. You do this by running a program called SETUP or INSTALL from the diskettes.

Programs enable your computer to do different things: calculate a budget, write the next blockbuster book, and compose award-winning songs. Programs come on CDs or floppy disks (covered in the next chapter), and you *install* them from the floppy disk onto the hard disk. Then when you want to use the program, you start up the program from the hard disk.

When you start the program, the processor copies the instructions from the hard disk to memory, where you do your work. When you want to keep a permanent copy of your work in that program, you instruct the program to save, and the processor copies the data from memory to the hard disk. When you finish working in the program, you exit the program, and all traces of the program and your data are cleared from memory. Make sense now?

Hard Disk and Memory Aren't the Same

Many people confuse a hard drive with memory. Both are measured in bytes (or, more commonly, megabytes), and techie types throw around cryptic talk like, "Yeah, this one came with 16 meg and a 500 meg disk." But don't let the techno-twaddle confuse you; hard disks and memory are really quite separate.

Memory, as you learned in Chapter 6, is only a temporary holding spot, like a desktop. When you want to work on something, you get the stuff you need out on the desktop. You can only fit so much on the desktop, so you put away what you don't need. Think of a hard drive as a big drawer or filing cabinet where you keep things you aren't working on right now.

As you can see, it makes sense to have a lot more drawer space than desktop space. Most home computers sold today have 50–80 times as much disk space as memory space. For example, you might see a computer advertised with 8MB of memory and 550MB of hard disk.

Size Matters—And So Does Performance!

There are some basics you need to know about hard drives. Controller type is a biggie, and we'll cover that in a moment. But first, let's look at the two most obvious distinguishing factors of a drive: size and speed.

Bigger Is Always Better

Like memory, hard drives are measured in bytes: megabytes (M or MB) and gigabytes (G or GB). You want the biggest hard drive you can afford. I recommend a hard disk in the 340–400MB range at a minimum, even if you don't think you'll use that much disk space. Trust me—you will.

If you need more space later, you can add extra hard drives inside or outside the system unit. Adding another hard disk is covered in Chapter 23.

Faster Than a Speeding Disk??

As I said before, the hard disk is like an electronic file drawer. When you want to get something from that drawer, two things have to happen. The data has to be found, and the data has to be copied from storage to the working area. A hard drive is rated by the speeds at which it performs these two operations: the average *access time* (how fast the disk can find the data) and the *data transfer rate* (how fast the disk can move the data to memory).

To squeeze more room out of your PC, consider using a special utility program, such as Stacker or DriveSpace, that enables you to fit more data on your same old hard disk. Chapter 21 discusses these programs in detail.

When you are reviewing specs, you will often see the access time advertised. This speed is measured in milliseconds (ms). The lower the number, the faster the drive. Speeds range from 20ms to 10ms. You'll be okay as long as the drive you get is in this range, but don't accept a drive with an access time higher than 20ms.

Once the data is found, it can be moved into memory. This measurement is called the data transfer rate, and is measured by how much data can be moved in a second. The more data that can be moved, the faster the rate. For example, 700KB per second is slower than 800KB per second. For your shopping guidelines, consider 700KB per second as the lowest number (the slowest data transfer rate) you will accept.

The Lowdown on Hard Disk Controllers

When you hear the term controller, you might wonder why the hard disk needs to be controlled. Does it get out of hand? Drive too fast? Smoke? Only sometimes.

The hard disk is actually made up of several pieces: the hard disk itself, the controller, and a data cable that connects the drive and the controller. The job of the controller is to act as a translator, handling conversations between the processor and the hard disk. Controllers vary in how they look, how they are hooked up to the processor, and what standard they follow.

What Does a Controller Look Like?

Many controllers look like an ordinary expansion card: a flat green board that's plugged into an expansion slot in the motherboard and covered with all kinds of electronic circuitry. A data cable or controller connector connects the electronic card to the drive, or the controller is built onto the motherboard.

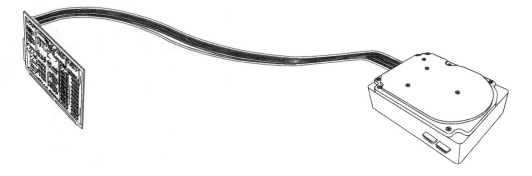

The hard disk is connected to the controller with a data cable.

On some newer systems, the disk drive controller is built into the hard disk. You still have the data cable, but this cable plugs into a small chip and connector, which fits onto the motherboard.

Making the Connection

On systems where the disk drive controller is an expansion card, any disk drive requests are sent between the motherboard and the hard disk through a controller cable. That's the long way through the neighborhood, and it takes quite a few milliseconds to get there.

A shorter (and faster) path hooks the controller to the local bus or directly to the motherboard, which enables the processor and hard disk to communicate much faster. (For an explanation of local bus, see Chapter 5.)

Different Types of Controllers

In addition to the style and type of connection, there are different types of controller standards, again identified by mysterious acronyms. (In the early days of computing, a committee would get together with a box of Scrabble letters to name a new device or standard. They'd shake out a few letters and make up words to fit the letters. Sounds believable, doesn't it?) The following table explains each controller type.

An **expansion card** adds features to the PC, such as sound, a fax, and network capabilities. Other features, such as the video and the mouse, may also be connected to an expansion card. This electronic card is flat and green and is sometimes called an expansion board or just a board.

Type of Controller	Stands for	Description
EIDE	Enhanced IDE	Latest type of controller. This type of controller can transfer data twice as fast as an IDE controller, and you can connect with several other types of drives (CD-ROM, tape, or hard drives).
IDE	Integrated Device Electronics	Most popular type of controller. Acceptable high-speed transfer.
SCSI	Small Computer Systems Interface	Acceptable high-speed controller. This type of controller enables you to chain (connect) different devices together. More expensive.
ESDI	Enhanced Small Device Interface	Slower data transfer rate. Was popular, but now not widely accepted.
ST-506	Seagate Technology something or other	Out-of-date standard.

Which one is the best? The most popular controller type is IDE. You can't go wrong with this type of controller. SCSI is faster, but more expensive. If you need to chain together several drives and don't mind paying more, consider a SCSI drive. The newest arrival on the controller scene is EIDE. Watch for this to take over for IDE as the most popular. If you want to be on the fast track, consider EIDE.

The Anatomy of a Hard Disk

The hard disk is housed inside the system unit (the big rectangular computer casing), so you can't see or touch it. The only indication of its presence is the disk activity light on the front of the computer, which flashes when the drive is working. You may also hear the drive spinning. Even if you take the lid off the system unit and look inside, you won't see any of the interesting parts of your hard disk; it's sealed inside a little rectangular box, about the size of a sandwich.

If you are curious to know what the hard disk looks like and the way the disk works, read the following section. Otherwise, just skip it—it won't really enrich your life to know this stuff.

What Does a Hard Disk Look Like?

A hard drive is actually a set of platters stacked on top of each other and sealed in a case. The case is the only part you'll ever see, because the platters are permanently sealed inside to keep out dust.

The platters are made of a magnetic recording material. Imagine them looking like a phonograph record. (Remember those?) Each platter is divided into tracks and sectors; the tracks are circles around the disk (like grooves in a record), and the sectors are like pie slices from the center of the disk out.

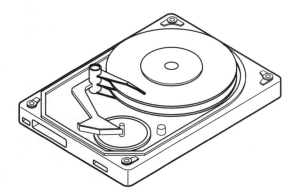

The inside of a hard drive.

The hard drive has a spindle that runs through the center of the stack of platters (just like a record player) and rotates the platters. Each platter has a read/write head (like a phonograph needle) that can be positioned precisely at any position on the platter.

The platters and spindles are housed in an airtight case that sits inside the PC in a *drive bay* (like a little shelf inside the system box). Other drives, such as floppy drives, live in drive bays too.

How a Hard Disk Works

When you want to store something on the disk, the spindle rotates the disk until the read/write head is positioned over a blank sector. Then the read/write head writes the information, using as many sectors as it needs. A special area of the disk called the *file allocation table* (FAT) keeps a master list of what information is stored where.

If a piece of data is so large that it won't fit in a single sector, the read/write head automatically moves to an adjacent sector to finish writing. If all the adjacent sectors are full, the read/write head finds some other open sector on the disk and continues writing there. The FAT keeps track of where each part of the data is stored so it can be pieced back together when it's needed.

> **Disk formatting** is the process of laying down the tracks and sectors. Before you use any type of disk (hard or floppy), you have to format it. Most new computers come with preformatted hard disks that are already loaded with software, so you don't have to format them. In fact, formatting them would erase all that software.

> When picking out a computer, make sure it has at least one extra drive bay. That way, you can add another drive later.

When you want to read some data from the disk, the spindle turns the disk again until the read/write head is positioned over the first sector where the data is located. Then the read/write head reads the information from the disk into memory, moving from one sector to another until all the data has been read. The FAT reminds the controller where each part of the file was originally stored, enabling it to find all the pieces.

The controller doesn't have a problem with skipping all over the disk to retrieve pieces of a file, but all that extra movement takes time. You can make your hard disk run faster by periodically running a utility program that reorganizes all the file pieces on the disk so that each file is stored in one contiguous cluster of sectors. For more info about these programs, check out Chapter 21.

The Least You Need to Know

To keep a permanent copy of your programs and data, you need a hard disk. Not all hard disks are created equal! When shopping for a PC, you should be aware of what size and type of hard disk is included with a system.

➤ Hard disks vary in the amount of data they can store (the capacity). The capacity is measured in megabytes (M or MB) or gigabytes (G or GB). You want a hard disk with at least 300MB, and an even bigger one if you can afford it.

➤ In advertisements for computers, you may see the hard disk speed rated in milli-seconds (ms). This is the average access time (how long the drive takes to access a certain area). Anything below 20ms is acceptable. You may also see the data transfer rate—a measure of how fast the disk can transfer data to memory. Look for one in the range of 700KB per second or faster.

➤ The hard disk is actually made up of the disk, the controller, and a data cable that connects the two. The most popular type of controller is an IDE controller, which is what you probably want.

Chapter 8

Data Movers: Floppy Disks

In This Chapter

➤ The anatomy of a floppy drive

➤ Why floppies are called floppies

➤ How many floppy drives do you need?

➤ Don't forget to buy some disks

After the last chapter, you may have been wondering, if the hard disk stores the programs, how did the programs get *on* the hard disk? Osmosis? Photosynthesis? And if the hard disk stores your data files, how do you get the data files *off* the hard disk, onto something you can take with you?

Enter the floppy disk drive. The floppy disk drive looks like a mail slot on the front of the computer. You insert a floppy disk and copy information from the hard disk to the floppy or vice versa.

For instance, you may need to copy a file from your work computer's hard disk to a floppy, so you can take the work home. Or, you may want to put a backup copy of an important file on a floppy disk in case (God forbid) something happens to your hard disk. You can see you need a floppy disk drive in the computer you buy. But how many, and what kind? This chapter answers these and other exciting questions.

Anatomy of a Floppy Disk Drive

Floppy disk drives live inside the system unit in a drive bay (like a hard disk). Unlike a hard disk, though, the floppy disk and the floppy drive are separate. As you may remember from Chapter 7, a hard disk's drive and disk are a single unit, permanently sealed together in a case. A floppy drive is different: the drive itself is permanently installed in the computer, but the disk is removable.

The Drive Itself

There are two sizes of drives, each of which has a corresponding size disk. You use 5 1/4-inch disks in 5 1/4-inch drives, and you use 3 1/2-inch disks in 3 1/2-inch drives.

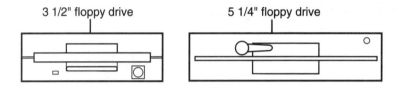

Two sizes of floppy drives.

Most 5 1/4-inch drives have a latch. You insert the disk into the computer and then flip the latch. The 3 1/2-inch disks don't have a latch. When you insert this type of disk, an eject button pops out of the drive. You can eject the disk by pressing this button. (Some of the newer 5 1/4-inch drives have a button instead of a latch.)

How Floppy Drives Work

When you want to copy data from the floppy disk to the hard disk, you start by inserting the disk into the drive. (Always insert the disk label-side up, with the label end out.) Then a spindle clamps down on the disk and makes the disk spin, just like on a hard disk.

The computer reads a floppy disk in basically the same way it reads a hard disk. (See, now aren't you glad you read Chapter 7 first?) The actual disk (inside the plastic jacket) is divided into tracks and sectors by a process called formatting. To find a particular piece of information, the disk heads consult the file allocation table (FAT). Then the disk read/write head moves to the location where the data is stored and reads data from the disk.

A Floppy Disk Lineup

The second half of the floppy disk drive equation is the actual floppy disk. Each type of floppy drive uses a matching type of floppy disk: 3 1/2-inch drives use 3 1/2-inch disks, and 5 1/4-inch drives use 5 1/4-inch disks. (Brilliantly logical, isn't it?)

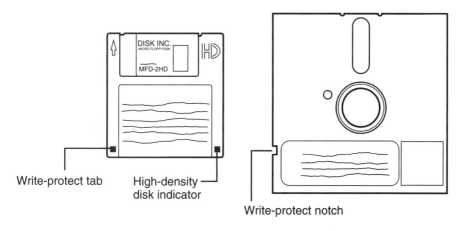

Write-protect tab   High-density
                     disk indicator
Write-protect notch

Disks come in two sizes: 3 1/2-inch and 5 1/4-inch.

The 5 1/4-inch disk is, well, floppy. This disk has a big hole in the center. The 3 1/2-inch disk isn't so floppy; it's actually encased in a hard plastic coat, making it, well, hard. It's still a floppy disk, but the floppy part is hidden inside the plastic coat.

Fill 'Er Up! Storage Capacity

In addition to varying in size, floppy disks vary in the amount of information they can store, or their *capacity*. The capacity is measured in kilobytes (K or KB) and megabytes (M or MB). Again, looks can be deceiving.

Take this little test. Which disk can store more information, the big 5 1/4-inch disk or the little 3 1/2-inch disk? It's a trick question because each size disk has two capacities.

Older 5 1/4-inch disks store 360KB and are known as double-density (DD) disks. You can still buy these disks in stores, but they're not good for much. Newer 5 1/4-inch disks store 1.2MB and are known as high-density (HD) disks. Most of the 5 1/4-inch disks you see in stores today are HD.

> Don't make the mistake of thinking that just because a 3 1/2-inch disk feels hard it is some kind of "hard disk." Your technoid friends will have a field day if you say something like, "I put the files you need on this hard disk" and then hand them a 3 1/2-inch floppy.

The original 3 1/2-inch disk was a double-density (DD) disk and stored 720KB. Again, they're still sold in stores, but unless you've got an old computer that requires them, there's no reason to bother with them. The more common high-density (HD) 3 1/2-inch disks can store 1.44MB.

This handy chart summarizes the two disk types and capacities. Use it as an easy reference.

Disk Size	Capacity	Designation
5 1/4"	360KB	DD or double-density
5 1/4"	1.2MB	HD or high-density
3 1/2"	720KB	DD or double-density
3 1/2"	1.44MB	HD or high-density

A new type of disk called an extended-density disk (ED) is also available. This type of disk can store 2.88MB of data. However, they won't work in regular floppy drives; you have to buy a special, rather expensive floppy drive to use them.

What Drive Do You Need?

How many drives do you need, and what type?

If this is your first computer purchase (and you don't have old software on 5 1/4-inch disks lying around), and you don't share data with anyone who uses 5 1/4-inch disks, you can get by with just one 3 1/2-inch high-density disk drive. Most programs sold today come on this size disk.

On the other hand, if you have programs or data on 5 1/4-inch disks, or you just want maximum flexibility, get a computer with both a high-density 3 1/2-inch disk drive and a high-density 5 1/4-inch disk drive. If you decide to get both types of drives, look for a "combo drive." In a combo drive, a single drive bay holds slots for both 5 1/4-inch and 3 1/2-inch disks, which frees up an extra drive bay so you can add other disk drives later. That's good.

A combo drive combines a 5 1/4-inch drive and a 3 1/2-inch drive into a single drive bay, saving space for other devices.

The Right Disk for the Drive

To use a disk, you have to match the disk to the right drive size. That should be pretty easy unless you are one of those people who will push and shove and mangle and strangle to fit a square peg into a round hole.

The other matching test is a little more diffi-cult. You also have to match the drive capacity to the disk capacity. Use this handy chart to figure out how to match the correct capacity to the correct drive.

What other disk drives should you consider? How about a CD-ROM, covered in Chapter 12? You may also want to think about some other drive types, discussed in Chapter 16.

Use This Type of Disk	In This Type of Drive
360KB (5 1/4")	Any 5 1/4-inch drive. However, unless you've got an old, double-density drive, don't bother with these. They're less reliable when used in a high-density drive.
1.2MB (5 1/4")	Only in high-density (1.2MB) 5 1/4-inch drives.
720KB (3 1/2")	Any 3 1/2-inch drive. There's no problem with using these in a high-density (1.44MB) drive, but there's also no reason to if your drive supports 1.44MB disks.
1.44MB (3 1/2")	Only in 1.44MB drives.

Telling the Disks Apart

When you buy a box of disks, the box should specify the disk type: HD for high-density or DD for double-density. You may also find this data on the shutter of a 3 1/2-inch disk or the label of a 5 1/4-inch disk. Also, 3 1/2-inch high-density disks usually have HD stamped on one of the corners of the disk.

But what if you don't have the box handy? Well, for 5 1/4-inch disks, there's no reliable way to tell the density except by reading the disk's label. In addition, most DD 5 1/4-inch disks have some sort of reinforcement ring around the center hole, and most HD 5 1/4-inch disks don't. However, there are exceptions to that, so don't count on the center ring as a definite way to tell the capacity.

On a 3 1/2-inch disk, it's easy to tell the density. High-density 3 1/2-inch disks have two square holes along the bottom of the disk. Double-density disks don't.

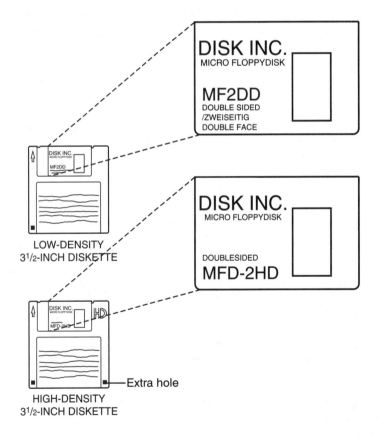

On a 3 1/2-inch diskette, look for identifying marks on the labels or disks to figure out which type of disk it is.

74

Some Quick Disk Tips

When you make that big computer purchase, don't forget to buy some disks. Here are some disk shopping and housekeeping tips:

➤ Disks come in several different brands, and most are pretty reliable. You can buy any brand you want.

➤ To prepare a disk for use, the disk has to be formatted. To save you the trouble of formatting, some disks come preformatted. These may cost a little bit more.

➤ Be sure to label your disks. There's nothing worse than trying to find a file in a huge pile of unlabelled diskettes.

➤ You may want to buy a disk organizer (usually a plastic box), which keeps all your disks neatly in one place instead of in every drawer and cabinet in your house or office.

➤ Keep your program disks in a safe place. If something happens to the copy on your hard disk, you can reinstall. Don't keep the disks in a shoe box under the sink.

➤ If you don't want you or anyone else to be able to make changes to a disk, write-protect it. A 5 1/4-inch disk has a notch on one side of the disk; you can put a piece of tape over this tab to prevent the disk from being altered. A 3 1/2-inch disk has a write-protect tab that you slide up (so that you can see through the hole) to protect the disk. Use a pencil to slide the tab.

The Least You Need to Know

When you buy a PC, you definitely want to have at least one floppy disk drive, perhaps two. Having a floppy disk drive lets you copy data or programs onto your hard disk.

➤ There are two sizes of drives, with two matching disk sizes: 5 1/4-inch and 3 1/2-inch.

➤ Each disk size has two different capacities. 5 1/4-inch disks can store 360KB (DD disks) or 1.2MB (HD disks). 3 1/2-inch disks can store 720KB (DD) or 1.44MB (HD).

➤ The most commonly used disk type is the 3 1/2-inch size. You definitely want a 3 1/2-inch disk drive. If you need to use data or programs on 5 1/4-inch disks, you may want to consider a PC with two floppy drives or a combo drive.

➤ Label your floppy disks and keep them in a safe place.

Chapter 9

Your Monitor to the World

In This Chapter

➤ The anatomy of a monitor

➤ How big of a monitor do you need?

➤ Picking the "sharpest" monitor

➤ More acronyms for monitor standards

➤ Other factors in selecting a monitor

Your monitor enables you to see what the computer is doing; it's your window to the computing scene. What's going on inside that system box? The monitor lets you know. Without the monitor, you'd have no way to see the letter you're typing, the drawing you're creating, or the alien monsters that are about to destroy you in the latest adventure game. It's pretty darned important.

Because you will stare at the monitor every time you use the PC, it's a critical component. You don't want a monitor that shakes, rattles, and rolls, and makes you seasick to watch. And you don't want a

Input device A hardware component, such as the keyboard and mouse, that you use to enter data.

Output device A hardware component, such as a monitor or printer, that displays or prints the data.

monitor that is so fuzzy that you actually see the screen better *without* your glasses. This chapter explains how to pick a good monitor and make your eyes happy!

It Takes Two: The Monitor and Graphics Card

You may hear the video card referred to as the video card, video board, or the video adapter, or some combination of video, card, board, and adapter. Some of the fancier ones are called video accelerator boards—how's that for a pretentious name?

To understand what makes one monitor better than another, take a little time to learn how the monitor works. Don't turn the page—I promise not to go into too much boring detail.

Technically, the monitor is the thing that looks like a TV. There are two other parts, though, that usually get lumped in with the monitor when you're talking about a computer's video capabilities: the video card inside the system unit and the cable that connects the monitor to the video card.

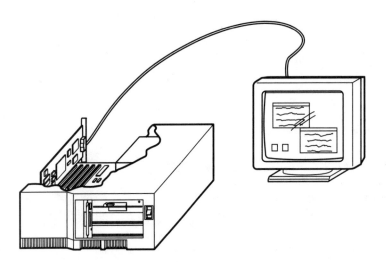

The monitor and video card work together to bring you the on-screen picture.

When you purchase a computer that includes a monitor, you get a video card and a monitor as a matched set. You can also purchase the monitor and the video card separately, if you want a better card or monitor. It's important to get a video card and a monitor that have similar capabilities, because your overall picture quality will only be as good as the weaker of the two.

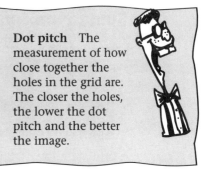

Dot pitch The measurement of how close together the holes in the grid are. The closer the holes, the lower the dot pitch and the better the image.

How a Monitor Works

Ready for a bit of techno-babble? I know it's boring, but you really need to know how a monitor works before you can make an intelligent decision about which one to buy.

When the computer wants to display something on-screen, it sends the information to the video board. The board processes the information and sends a signal to the three electron guns in the monitor. These electron guns can each "shoot" one color—red, blue, or green—in different intensities. The screen is made up of a grid of tiny holes that the beams can pass through.

All three beams align at a single, tiny spot on the screen, striking the phosphors coating the inside of the screen. When struck, the phosphors get *excited* and *glow* (no comment). The combination of glowing phosphors creates a single dot on the screen. These beams operate at an amazingly high speed, sweeping across every hole in the entire grid 60 or more times in a single second to form the complete image. (Portable computers use a different technology for displaying the image on-screen. You'll learn about it in Chapter 13.)

When you see low, low prices advertised, read the small print. Usually the monitor is not included. Also, sometimes bundled systems will have a decent system (memory, microprocessor, and so on) but a lousy monitor. Check those "bargains" carefully.

Now you're ready for any "Jeopardy" questions dealing with how a monitor works. You're also sure to win friends and liven up social functions with your knowledge of excitable phosphors. Aren't you glad you didn't skip this section?

Why Some Monitors Are Better Than Others

Knowing how the monitor works will help you understand how monitors vary—and how cheapo manufacturers will try to cut corners. Here's a quick summary of what makes monitors different:

➤ The size of the monitor

➤ The quality of the image displayed (lots of factors affect this, as you'll see)

➤ The monitor's ability to show non-interlaced images (more about that when the time comes)

➤ The monitor's standard (EGA, VGA, SuperVGA, and so on)

➤ Special features and controls

How Big Is Your Monitor?

The easiest monitor spec to understand is the size. Monitors are measured in size like TVs are: diagonally. Most monitors sold are 14-inch models. They're suitable for most applications, although a 15-inch is better, if you can get a good deal on one.

Resolution: How Sharp Is the Picture?

Think about pictures taken with two cameras: one by a four-year old with a $12 camera and one by your dad with a $2,000 camera. Which one will turn out better? (With my dad and my son, it might be a toss-up.) Sometimes a picture is fuzzy (and the people have red eyes), and sometimes the image is sharp.

If you do a lot of desktop publishing or work with graphics quite a bit, you may want to invest in a larger monitor. For example, you can get a 17-inch monitor that can display two full pages at once. Keep in mind that these monitors can be expensive.

On a computer, *resolution* is a measurement of how much of the image's detail the computer displays. Just as you can't guess who might take the best picture based on the type of camera and the photographer, you can't make the best monitor purchasing decision just from the specs.

The best way to test a monitor's quality is with your own eyes. Look at different monitors. Which one looks crisper? Which one looks blurry? Which one displays the colors more vibrantly? No amount of technical jabberwocky can replace a visual test of the monitor. Still, technical jabberwocky is what this book's all about, so the rest of this chapter will tell you why your eyes like one monitor better than another. Once you learn this, you can better judge the technical specs you see listed in catalogs or advertisements, without actually seeing the monitors.

Pixels

Pixels are cute little elves inside the computer who paint the image on your screen with magic pixel dust.

Okay, how about...*pixel* is really short for "picture element," which is the smallest unit that can be used to create an image. Each pixel has a red phosphorus dot, a green phosphorous dot, and a blue phosphorous dot, and a little bottle of Windex. As you learned earlier, sometimes the red dot gets excited and glows, sometimes the blue does, sometimes the green does, and sometimes all of them do or some do in combination. That makes the different colors.

Computer monitors measure the number of pixels or dots per inch a monitor can display horizontally and vertically. So you will see specs such as 640 × 480 or 1,024 × 768. The higher the number, the more dots per inch and the sharper the image.

Dot Pitch

When the pixels get bored, they host a ball game and pitch the dots to each other. This game is called the dot pitch. (What, you don't believe me?)

Dot pitch is a measurement of how close together the holes are that the electrons have to pass through. Dot pitch is measured in millimeters (mm): the smaller the number, the better. A measurement of .28mm is a good dot pitch for a 14-inch monitor.

Refresh Rate and Convergence

After the ball game, the pixels get tired. They all converge and are refreshed with a cooler of beer. (My version is starting to sound more interesting than the "authorized" account, isn't it?)

The *refresh rate* is actually the rate at which the electrons scan the screen horizontally and vertically. For horizontal, the rate measures how many thousands of times it scans one line, and the rate is measured in kilohertz (kHz). For example, the measurement 50kHz indicates that a monitor can redraw one screen line 50,000 times in one second.

The vertical refresh rate is a measurement of how many times it scans the entire screen; this rate is measured in hertz (Hz). The higher the hertz, the better. A good scan rate is 70Hz or more, which means the monitor redraws the screen 70 times in one second.

Convergence tests how accurately the three beams align. Ideally, they should all shoot at the same bull's-eye—that is, converge at the same point. It's difficult to get perfect convergence, though, so some monitors will look better than others. How can you test convergence? When all three dots are aligned perfectly, you should get white. So ask to see a white screen, and look for blurry spots or tinges of color. If you see just white, the convergence is all right.

In addition to these factors, you may see a monitor designated *multiscan* or *multi–frequency*. What does that mean? Well, some monitors are designed to work with one particular computer system that has a fixed frequency. Other monitors can adapt to suit any scanning frequency. These multiscan monitors will work with more than one type of standard.

Lacing Your Monitor: Interlaced vs. Non-Interlaced

After the ball game and the beer, it's time to unlace the cleats and call it a day. For shoes, lacing is good. For monitors, interlacing is bad.

Some monitors scan or redraw only every other line to save time, which is called interlacing. Interlacing can cause the screen to flicker. Non-interlaced monitors scan every line. Therefore, you want a non-interlaced monitor.

Monitor Standards: Acronyms to Go

There are several types of monitor standards. Which type do you need? Bottom line: You need SuperVGA. You can leave it at that and skip to the next section, or if you're curious, you can refer to the following table, which lists the standards from newest to oldest. Keep in mind that although a monitor meets a particular standard, it is not limited to a particular resolution. It can still display the image at more than one resolution.

Name	Description
SVGA or SuperVGA	The newest monitor standard. This type of monitor can display the same colors as the VGA and has a resolution of $1,024 \times 768$ or more. The standard varies slightly from brand to brand.
VGA (Video Graphics	This standard can display 256 colors Adapter) simultaneously out of a palette of over 200,000 colors. Resolutions range from 640×480 to 800×600.
EGA (Enhanced Graphics	This old standard (introduced in 1984) Adapter) can display 16 colors at a resolution of 640×350, or 256 colors at a resolution of 320×200.

Name	Description
Hercules	Introduced circa 1982, this standard displayed a single-color (black and white) image at a resolution of 720 × 320.
CGA (Color Graphics	This old standard (introduced circa Adapter) 1981) could display 4 colors simultaneously and had a resolution of 320 × 200 (4 colors) or 640 × 200 (2 colors).
MDA (Monochrome Display Adapter)	The oldest standard, this could display text in only one color. It could not display graphics.

Trivia time. Why did Van Suwannukul, the creator of the Hercules adapter, take the time to develop the adapter? So he could do his thesis in his native Thai alphabet.

The Colors of the Rainbow

Most monitors sold today are color monitors, and yes, you do want a color monitor. Color not only makes the display more attractive, it makes the computer easier to learn. Why? Because the software developers use color to make different elements stand out. Plus, games would be a drag without color, and most require it.

The choice of colors is called the palette and, depending on the standard, the monitor can use anywhere from 2 to 256 colors at one time. The computer uses bits to store color (as a number). In reference to the number of colors in the palette, you may hear the term 8-bit color, 16-bit color, and so on. Here's the breakdown of the number of bits and the available number of colors:

8 bits	256 colors
16 bits	65,000 colors
18 bits	250,000
24 bits	16 million colors (way more than your eye would be able to differentiate)

In some special-type applications, you may find a *paper-white* monitor. For example, high-end users of computer-aided drawing programs (CAD) may prefer a paper-white monitor.

What Else Matters When Picking a Monitor?

So, have you completed your shopping list for your monitor? To recap, you want at least a 14-inch SuperVGA monitor with a resolution of 1,024 × 768. The dot pitch should be approximately .28 mm, and the refresh rate should be 70+Hz. You also want a non–interlaced monitor. What else?

Combatting Glare and Radiation

To make the monitor as easy on the eyes as possible, manufacturers have incorporated different antiglare features. Flat screens (as opposed to curved screens) reduce glare. Some monitors also have an antiglare coating.

Also, if you are worried about emissions from the monitor causing health problems, buy a monitor that conforms to the Swedish MPR-2 standard. Is radiation a problem? Nothing has been proven conclusively.

How do you check the glare? Look at the monitor. Can you see yourself? If so, there's a glare.

To reduce your risk if you don't have a low-emission monitor, keep about an arm's distance away from the screen. (That means don't type with your nose pressed up against the screen.) Also, the greatest danger of emissions actually come from the sides and back of the monitor. Stay away from this area.

Where Are the Controls?

Most monitors have a set of controls somewhere on the monitor itself that let you control the brightness, contrast, and placement of the image on the screen. Check out these controls to be sure they are easy to reach.

The monitor may also come on a stand that should swivel so that you can adjust it. Try the swivel, too.

Choosing a Video Card

In most cases, you'll buy a card and monitor as a matched set—an arranged marriage, if you will. That's the easiest way. In this case, check the video card/monitor combination against the following information to make sure you are getting a good video card. That is, check out the memory that comes on the card as well as the bus type.

You can also buy the two items (monitor and video card) separately. Be careful, though. You have to match a lot of specs to be sure all the parts can get along. The video card has to be able to work with the type of bus you have (see Chapter 5 for more information on buses), and the video card has to work with the monitor. If you want to select the components separately, use this section to understand what features to look for in a video card.

Card Standards

Like monitors, cards also follow standards—the same standards that you read about a few pages ago. What type of standard do you want in a video card? SuperVGA.

VROOM with VRAM

To process the image, some video cards have built-in memory called video RAM or VRAM. Like anything else, the more memory the better. How much memory a card has affects the complexity of image it can display, the speed it can display, and the resolution and number of colors it can display. I'd recommend looking for a video card with at least 1MB of VRAM.

Special Seats on the Local Bus

Remember that the motherboard has some special seats on its bus for its most favored hardware friends. One of the friends that benefits the most from sitting in (plugging into) this special seat (the local bus) is the video card. Remember too, however, that to get on the bus, the card has to have the right ticket—in other words, it has to be the right type. You can use only PCI cards on PCI buses. For more information on buses, see Chapter 5.

A local bus video uses a special chip to speed up the communication between the microprocessor and the video card. Having a local bus video, then, is definitely a plus.

Video Accelerators

Another way to speed up the processing of images is to use a video accelerator card. This card, which replaces your current video card, takes some of the work off the microprocessor and does the work itself. Hence you get faster performance from the computer with a video accelerator.

For example, ATI Technologies has a 64-bit graphics accelerator board that sells for $600–$900. This accelerator would be a worthwhile investment for a graphics illustrator or someone using page layout software because these applications are graphics-intense.

Driver Files: Who's Driving?

To ensure that the monitor works with your software, you install a software program called a *driver*. The driver tells your programs how your hardware (the video card and monitor) works so that the programs can take advantage of the available features.

If you purchase a monitor and video card separately, you'll most likely get a disk with the software drivers. You can use this disk to install the right driver for the monitor. If you bought the monitor as part of a packaged PC and the PC is already set up, the right driver should be installed for you.

The Least You Need to Know

You'll be staring at the monitor every time you use your computer, so get one that will be easy on your eyes. This chapter also taught you about some other factors you should consider.

➤ A computer's display is created by the monitor and the video card working together.

➤ Monitors are measured diagonally, like TV sets. You want at least a 14-inch monitor.

➤ The resolution of a monitor is a measure of how detailed an image the monitor can display. The image quality is determined by the number of pixels that can be displayed, the dot pitch (how close the holes are that the electrons have to pass through), the refresh rate (how many times the screen is redrawn), and the convergence (how accurately the beams align).

➤ Different standards are used to define the features of a particular monitor. The most current standard is SuperVGA (SVGA). This monitor can display resolutions up to 1,024 ¥ 768.

➤ In addition to size, resolution, and standard, look for a video card that has at least 1MB of video RAM (VRAM) or DRAM. If you have a local bus motherboard, look for a corresponding local bus video card.

➤ Make sure that your monitor has easy-to-reach controls and some glare and radiation emissions protection.

Chapter 10

Keyboard and Mouse Antics

In This Chapter

➤ Keyboard layouts

➤ Picking a good keyboard

➤ The anatomy of a mouse

➤ Catching a good mouse

➤ Other input devices

How do you tell a PC what to do? Oh sure, you can try yelling, thought-transference, or physical coercion (lots of people do). But the most effective way is to use an *input device*.

The most common input device is the keyboard. You type away, and the computer does your bidding—well, most of the time. Nearly all computer systems sold today include a keyboard as part of the standard package.

In addition to the keyboard, you'll most likely get a mouse as part of the package. "Eeek! A mouse!" you may say. Don't fret. A mouse is an input device that makes graphical programs (such as Microsoft Windows and Windows programs) easier to use.

In the last chapter, you read about how to make your eyes happy. Here you learn how to make your fingers and hands happy by choosing a good keyboard and mouse.

How One Keyboard Is Different from Another

Most keyboards look about the same and have about the same number of keys. The most popular keyboard is the 101-key keyboard, which is available in two versions: the standard keyboard and the enhanced keyboard.

Standard —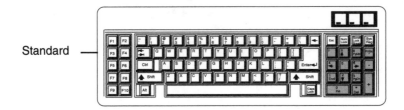

Enhanced —

The most common keyboard is the 101-key keyboard.

 The standard layout of the keys is called QWERTY (for the first five letter keys on the top row). That's the keyboard you learned with when (if) you learned how to type. Other keyboards have been developed that use a different layout, called Dvorak. This keyboard layout is intended to make typing faster by putting the most-used keys in the home row.

What About Those Other Keys?

If you take the time to count, you will find that there are 26 letter keys, 10 number keys, some "movement" keys (Enter, Tab, Backspace), and punctuation keys that you are probably familiar with from a typewriter. What makes up the other keys? Read the following table.

Keys	Description
Function keys	Function keys are labeled F1 through F12 and perform different functions depending on the program. For instance, pressing F1 in some programs displays help information.
Numeric keypad	On the right side of the keyboard, you'll find a separate bank of keys with both numbers, letters, and names, indicating the split personality of the keypad. You can use these keys to move around, or you can press the Num Lock key and use the keypad to enter numbers.
Movement keys	In addition to the movement keys on the numeric keypad, you may have a separate section of movement keys with arrows or names (such as Home).
Modifier keys	To type a capital letter, you press Shift and type the letter, just like on a typewriter. If you want to type all caps, you can use the Caps Lock key. The keyboard also has an Alt key and Ctrl key; these keys are used in different combinations with other keys to access shortcuts in some programs.
Esc	This is my favorite key. Although some programs use the Esc differently, most use this key as a "back-up" key. If you open a menu by mistake, press Esc to back up and close it. If you are hung (the system won't respond), press Esc to see if you can get out of the problem.

To make the keyboard as flexible as possible, some keyboard makers enable you to change the function of what keys do. For example, you can tell the keyboard to enter 7 every time you press 5. Changing the functions of the keys is called *remapping*. Be careful! It's easy to remap keys when you don't mean to. If you accidentally remap or program a key, check your computer's documentation to find out how to clear it. On a Gateway 2000 computer, for example, you can clear all the remapping by pressing the following keys simultaneously: Ctrl+Alt+Suspend Macro. Not exactly intuitive, is it?

Where, Oh Where Are the Function Keys?

The difference between the standard keyboard and the enhanced keyboard is the layout of the function keys. On a standard keyboard, the function keys appear along the side of the keyboard. On an enhanced keyboard, they are placed along the top. Most newer keyboards put the function keys in both spots (top and left) and have more than 101 keys, although they are still called 101-key keyboards! (101 is a popular number. Think of *101 Dalmatians*. How can you not like 101?) This keyboard also has a separate section of cursor movement keys, in addition to the numeric keypad.

A Hands-Friendly Keyboard

When you do the same thing over and over with your wrists and fingers, you can develop *repetitive stress injuries* such as carpal tunnel syndrome. To prevent this problem, you should keep your hands in the proper position when you type. Position the keyboard so that when you type, your fingers are even with your wrists—not crooked way up or way down. Your hands should be parallel to the floor.

To help keep your hands in the proper position and to provide support for your wrists, Microsoft has developed a new keyboard. This keyboard uses the same keyboard layout, but the keyboard is split into two sections, each angled and rotated so your palms turn inward when you type. The keyboard also includes a palm rest. If you type a lot, you may want to consider this type of keyboard, which costs around $99.

The new natural keyboard protects your wrists from injury.

Other Cool Keyboard Variations

Interested in other keyboards? Here are some of the latest products to hit the market:

➤ You can buy a keyboard (called the KidBoard) for kids that's done in fun primary colors. The keys have both letters and icons and are easier on little fingers. The keyboard is also an effective tool for teaching a child how to type. The cost is around $99.

➤ The Maxi Sound keyboard ($99) combines the keyboard, stereo speakers, a microphone, and volume control into one musical keyboard.

➤ Cramped for space? You can purchase a foldable keyboard: a full-size 101-key keyboard that folds in the middle for that New York studio apartment.

Selecting a Keyboard

If all keyboards have about the same keys, what's the big deal? Try typing on one. On some the keys clackety-clack so loudly you're sure Henny Penny is stuck inside the keyboard. Other keyboards squish when you press the keys, like typing under water. Test the keyboard to be sure you get a layout and a "feel" that you like.

The Anatomy of a Mouse

Why is a mouse called a mouse? The original design of this device did look like a mouse, and the term stuck. (Now the mouse looks more like a bar of Dove soap.) What's inside the mouse? What makes it work? This section explains the differences in mice.

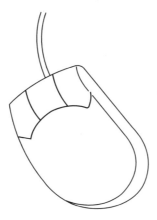

The basic mouse design.

Why a Mouse?

The purpose of having a graphical interface, such as Microsoft Windows, is to make the computer easier to use. You just point at what you want. However, it's pretty hard to point with a keyboard—which is why you have a mouse.

Add a mouse pad to your shopping list. A mouse pad is a thick piece of wet-suit like material that sits on your desktop. Moving your mouse around on the mouse pad makes it easier to slide the mouse around and protects the mechanical guts of the mouse from scratches.

The mouse sits on your desktop and displays a pointer on-screen. When you slide the mouse on the desktop, the on-screen pointer moves accordingly, making it easy to point at what you want. To select something on the screen, you use the mouse button. For example, you can click on a command to select it. (When you press and release the mouse button once, it's called clicking. Press and release the button twice quickly, and you're double-clicking.)

Older DOS programs don't require a mouse, and in some, you can't even use one. All Windows programs operate best if you have a mouse. When Windows became the standard operating environment, a mouse became standard computer equipment.

How a Mouse Works

On the underbelly of the mouse is a hole that displays a small part of a ball that's inside the mouse. As you move the mouse on the desktop, this ball rolls and in turn rotates encoders inside the mouse to create a signal. The signal is sent over the cable to the PC. The PC then converts the signal into a movement—direction, speed, and distance.

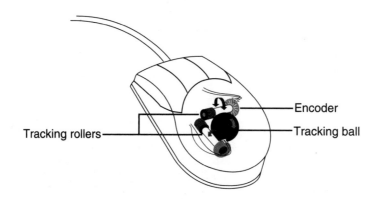

Tracking rollers

Encoder

Tracking ball

The guts of a mouse.

Most mice have at least two buttons; some have three. When you press the mouse button, the mouse sends a signal to the PC.

The mouse can be connected to the PC in several different ways, depending on the model. A serial mouse connects into one of the serial ports at the back of your computer. (Chapter 11 discusses ports in more detail.) With a bus mouse, there's a special expansion card inside the PC that the mouse plugs into. And with a PS/2 style mouse, there's a little round port in the back of your computer, like the one where your keyboard plugs in, designed especially for the mouse to plug into.

Selecting a Mouse

Most computers come with a mouse. If you don't like the mouse, you can always get a new one, but why not start out with one that you do like? Use the following list to compare the mice in the systems you are considering:

➤ Bus, serial, or PS/2 mouse? If your computer has a PS/2 style mouse port, PS/2 is the way to go. If not, and you have a free serial port, consider a serial mouse. They're slightly cheaper. If serial ports are scarce, consider a bus mouse.

➤ How many buttons? As mentioned, some mice have more than two buttons. However, most software programs are designed to work predominantly with the left button and sometimes with the right. Very few make use of the third mouse button.

➤ Who made the mouse? Different companies manufacture mice. Make sure you get a mouse that's Microsoft-compatible because nearly all programs support the Microsoft standard.

➤ Which one do you like better? Different mice feel different. One may feel more comfortable in your hand, or one may move more smoothly. The best way to pick a mouse is to try it out.

Interested in a designer mouse? The MouseMan Sensa was developed by Italian designers. These mice have a different contour and texture. You can buy Black Chess, Blue Leopard, or other styles, depending on which one suits your fancy. What will you pay for a designer mouse? Around $75.

Other Input Devices

Cramped for space? Love to play games? If so, you may want to consider two alternative input devices: the trackball or the joystick.

Trackball: An Upside-Down Mouse

If you look at a trackball, it looks like an upside-down mouse: the roller ball is right on top. To move the mouse, you roll the ball with your fingers. Some keyboards come with a trackball, which you can use if you prefer the feel of the trackball or if you are short on space. Many portable computers use a trackball (see Chapter 13).

Joysticks and Flight Yokes: Games Galore

Many games are easier to operate with an arcade-like piece of equipment called a joystick. (No comment on the etymological background of this term.) You use the upright stick and the buttons to kick, punch, duck, bomb, chop, dice, mince, and puree. You can play some games much more easily with a joystick than you can with any other type device.

One of the most popular games of all time is Microsoft Flight Simulator, which lets you fly different types of planes. There are other flight simulators on the market, as well as other input devices called flight yokes, which are designed specifically for this style of game.

Pens, Tablets, and Upright Mice

If you are an artist or you just like to be different, you may consider a different type of input device. An optical mouse works by bouncing a light beam off a reflective pad with a grid pattern. What's cool about this? It's a very accurate input device for special interest markets such as CAD.

The optical mouse isn't the breed for you? Then consider a mouse pen, which is just what its name implies: a mouse that looks like a pen. To roll the mouse, you "write" with the pen. The mouse buttons are along the front.

Scanners and voice recognition devices, which are also input devices, are covered in Chapter 17.

Don't like the idea of a mouse at all? Then consider a digitizing tablet, which is also suited for artists or illustrators. The grid has sensors on which you draw or write with a special stylus (a fancy name for a pen-type thingy).

And finally, there's the light pen. Just touch the pen on the screen to select the commands you want.

The Least You Need to Know

To communicate with the computer, you can use the keyboard or the mouse, both of which are essential input devices.

➤ The most widely available keyboard has 101 or more keys, including letters, numbers, punctuation marks, modifier keys, movement keys, and function keys.

➤ To select a keyboard, try it out. Different keyboards have different feels and sounds. Pick one that you like.

➤ To use graphical programs, such as Microsoft Windows, you need a mouse. The mouse enables you to point and select items on-screen.

➤ Most mice have two buttons, although you may find some that have only one button and some that have three.

➤ There are three types of mice: serial, bus, and PS/2. Serial mice connect to the serial port at the back of the computer; bus mice connect to an expansion card inside the system unit; and PS/2 mice connect directly to a PS/2 port in some computers.

➤ Test various mice and pick the one that feels most comfortable in your hand and moves most smoothly.

➤ Serious game players may want to consider other input devices, such as a joystick or flight yoke. Also, if you are cramped for desk space, you can use a trackball.

Chapter 11

Slots, Plugs, and Bays: The System Unit

In This Chapter

➤ What are all those plugs for on the back of the PC?

➤ Two types of ports for two kinds of equipment

➤ Extra slots for adding the latest and greatest to your PC

➤ Extra drive bays for sliding in new drives

➤ The power supply

➤ The case style

It's not enough to buy a PC with the minimum specs we've talked about so far. You also have to look into your crystal ball and plan for the future. What does the future hold for you? Watching TV on the PC? A tape backup unit? Easy money, fast cars?

When you're picking out a PC, take a look at the system unit (that boxy, rectangular thing). Of course it's able to handle all the components that come with it, but will it be able to handle the extras you want to add later?

Most PCs are designed to be somewhat expandable, though some more so than others. You can add fun stuff inside the PC (like a sound card) or connect new stuff to the back (like a modem or a printer). When you buy a PC, make sure you have room to expand. After all, you have to keep up with the Joneses. This chapter explains how to size up the system unit for future additions.

Plugs Galore: The Back of the System Unit

If you look at the back of the system unit, you'll notice all kinds of sockets to stick plugs into. There are power sockets, special ports for particular items (such as the keyboard), serial ports, and parallel ports.

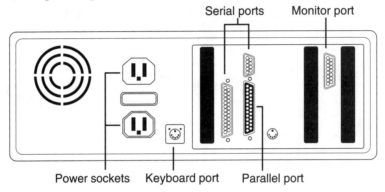

The back of the system unit.

Power Socket

Inside the PC, you have a power supply (covered later in this chapter). The power supply doesn't generate its own power; it gets its power from a wall outlet. You plug a power cord into the socket on the back of the PC, and then you plug this cord into an outlet. Every PC will have this type of socket. It's not really a port, but it shows up in the drawing, so I thought I'd explain it.

Keyboard and Monitor Ports

On the back of the system unit, you also have two special ports used to hook up your printer and your monitor. As you can probably deduce, the keyboard has a cable that hooks up to the back of the PC via the keyboard port.

You can't just jam in the keyboard connector any old way. If you look at the port and the connector, you'll notice that there's a certain alignment of dots or holes. You have to get the dots lined up to make the connection.

Also, you'll find a special port for hooking up your monitor. The monitor most likely plugs into a video card, which has a 15-hole port sneaking out the back of the PC.

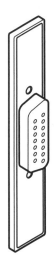

The monitor port usually has 15 holes.

Sometimes PC vendors are neighborly and label the ports; sometimes they are evil and let you guess which is which. You can usually tell by the size. For example, you probably wouldn't plug the little circular keyboard port into the trapezoid-looking monitor port, unless you didn't pass "Shapes" in preschool.

Ports of Call

What if you had only one outlet in your kitchen? What would you plug in? The refrigerator? The microwave? The toaster? Your little TV? Your curling iron? It'd be hard, wouldn't it? That's why you have lots of ports in your computer (hopefully).

A port is different from a power outlet because the port isn't supplying power (at least not directly). The port enables you to hook up extra components, such as a mouse or a modem, to the computer. The device can then communicate with the processor (say hello and all that).

On older computers, the monitor port may only have 9 holes.

Most PCs come with two types of ports (besides the one for the monitor): serial and parallel. These ports differ in look, in how they transmit data, and in what you can connect to them.

Serial Ports

If you look at a serial port, you'll notice that it's a group of pins that stick out. Hence, serial ports are male connectors (no comment). One type of serial port has nine pins; the other type has 25 pins. Most computers have one of each size.

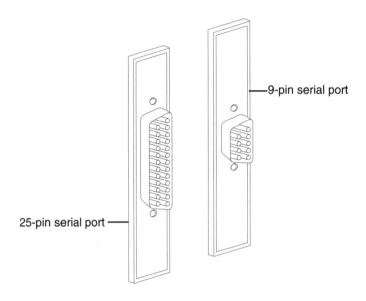

Serial ports come in 9- and 25-pin varieties.

You use serial ports to hook up serial devices. What are serial devices? Some mice, scanners, modems, and other equipment. (There are also some serial printers, although most printers are parallel devices.) Usually, you'll have two serial ports; to distinguish one from the other they are named COM1 and COM2.

When buying a PC, you want at least two serial ports. You'll also need to be serial-port aware when you add something new to the PC. How does it hook up? Does it use a serial port? Do you have an extra one?

Serial ports have 9 or 25 pins sticking out of them. **Parallel ports** have 25 holes for pins to be stuck into. Most modems and mice are serial devices, and most printers are parallel. Any computer you purchase should have at least one parallel port and two serial ports.

When you buy a PC, you won't care which is COM1 and which is COM2 or even what is plugged into each port. When you go to add something to the PC, however, you'll need to know the entire anatomy of the PC. What is connected to COM1? What is connected to COM2? What blood type is the PC?

Again, sometimes the PC manufacturer labels these, making them easy to identify. If not, you can run special utility programs that enable you to identify the COM ports and what's connected. (If you're interested in doing a system unit survey, see Chapter 22.)

Parallel Ports

Parallel ports are faster than serial ports. Therefore, they're often used for printers, tape backup units, and other devices that have to move a lot of data quickly. Parallel ports have 25 holes (making them female connectors—again, no comment). A computer should have at least one parallel port, named LPT1.

Parallel ports have 25 holes. They look like reverse serial ports.

Room to Grow: Expansion Slots

As technology advances, you'll find that you can do more and more with the PC. Right now you can have the PC answer your phone, capture and change video images, store your photo collection, and more. Each new feature requires a new piece of hardware, usually an electronic card that you plug into an open slot inside the system unit.

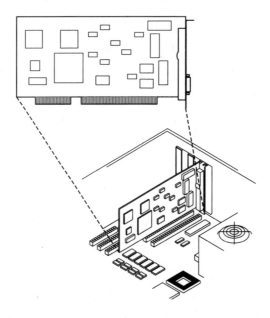

You can add new features to your PC by plugging an expansion card into an expansion slot.

The questions, then, are how many open slots do you have, how many are you using at the moment, and what type of slots are the vacant ones? This section explains all that and more.

Number of Slots

Depending on what equipment you get with your PC, you may already have some slots filled. For example, you may purchase a PC with a sound card and a fax/modem card. These two cards take up two of the expansion slots in the system unit. Because you're already starting with some extra equipment, you may not need that many more slots. Three or four extras might be sufficient for anything you'd want to add in the future. On the other hand, if you buy a PC with no extras (no sound card, no fax/modem card, and so on), you'll probably want more free slots—five or six.

Expansion cards that plug into expansion slots are connected to the system bus. On the other hand, some expansion cards plug into special slots on the local bus. If the card is on the local bus, the communication between the microprocessor and the board is faster. Buses are covered in Chapter 5.

How Long Is the Slot?

Remember all the acronyms and bit/bus bungo in the chapter on processors? Expansion slots and expansion cards are defined in a similar manner. First, expansion slots vary in the size or amount of data they can move. Second, expansion slots follow different standards, as covered in the next section.

> **Expansion card**
> There are a million and ten different names used to describe the expansion cards: adapters, cards, boards, controllers, or some combination of the terms (adapter card). They all mean the same thing: a flat piece of green board with electronic circuitry.

As for size, 8-bit cards move 8 bits (slowest), 16-bit cards move 16 bits (faster), and 32-bit cards move 32 bits (fastest). Although you have to match the card size to the slot size, you can put a smaller card in a bigger slot (such as an 8-bit card in a 16-bit slot). Because most expansion cards are 16-bit cards, you want most of your expansion slots to be 16-bit slots, plus a few 32-bit slots.

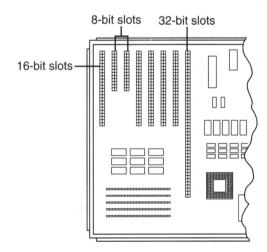

Expansion slots range in size from 8-bit to 32-bit.

Why is it good to get 16-bit or 32-bit expansion cards? Well, if you have a 32-bit processor communicating with an 8-bit card, there's obviously going to be a traffic jam. Imagine 32 lanes of a highway merging into 8. For the fastest performance, you want the largest size.

More Standards from the Acronym Committee

The expansion slot and card combinations follow the same bus standards you learned about in Chapter 5.

ISA	16-bit	Most common
EISA	32-bit	Not as common
MCA	32-bit	Found only in some IBM computers
VESA	32-bit	Used mostly for video cards
PCI	32-bit	Used mostly in Pentium-based computers

In addition to matching the size of the slot, you have to match card type A to slot type A. For example, you can put ISA cards only in ISA slots. Right now you'll do okay with mostly ISA type slots. You may also have a VESA bus for your video card or one or two PCI buses.

Drive Bays: Extra Shelves

You will, of course, want to have room for the extra drives you'll be adding later. (Trust me, at one point or another you'll want another drive of some sort.) Drives are housed in little shelves called drive bays.

How many extra drive bays should there be? It depends on what the system already has. Look for a total of five to six drive bays. If the PC you are buying has a CD-ROM, a hard drive, two floppy drives, and a tape back up unit, that's five drives, and there should be one extra. If the PC only has a hard drive and one floppy drive, it should have three or more empty drive bays.

Making Sure You Have Enough Power

Inside the system unit there's a big silver box with lots of colored wires running out of it. This is the power supply, and these wires connect to the other hardware components inside the PC and provide them with power. All computers come with a power supply, so you don't have to make sure the PC has one (unless you're buying it from the shark on the corner).

What you *do* want to check is that you have enough power to power all the equipment inside. You want to have ample wattage (200W or more) and enough connectors (at least four or five).

How the Power Supply Works

Why do you need a power supply if you are plugging the PC into a wall socket? Good question. And I've got a good answer. The power from a wall outlet is too rough and wild for the delicate innards of a PC. Therefore, the PC has a power supply that takes the rough AC power from the outlet and converts it to the more preferable DC power. To keep things cool, the power supply includes a fan that keeps the circuitry from overheating.

Unless you have a death wish, never, ever, ever open up the power supply. Even if the power is off, you could still send yourself skyrocketing through the ceiling by opening the power supply. If something goes wrong with your power supply, don't try to fix it, even if you fancy yourself an expert handyman. Just get a new one.

Keeping Power In Line

Lightning is tricky: not only does it strike trees, it can sneak into your house through the power lines. Because lightning can fry electronic data and components, and brown-outs (which are when the power level lessens) and uneven power surges can play havoc with your PC, you will most likely want some sort of protection from uneven power.

As a minimum, you'll want a power strip with a surge suppressor. This device is handy because it lets you plug all your equipment into one master strip, which you can flip on and off. More importantly, the device can provide protection against power surges. You can expect to pay $10 to $50 for a surge suppressor.

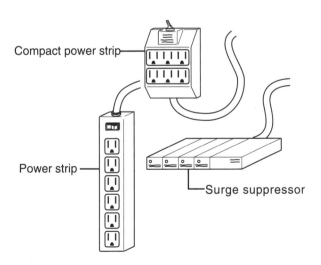

Compact power strip

Power strip

Surge suppressor

Power strips and surge suppressors come in a variety of shapes and sizes.

Some users, especially businesses, want to keep power flowing to the PC even during a blackout. To serve this purpose, you can purchase an uninterruptible power supply (UPS), which is essentially a big ol' battery. These cost anywhere from $100 to $2,500.

Selecting a System Case

Now that you know what the back and the inside of the system unit should look like, how about the outside? Which style is the one for you? What about the various buttons?

Case Styles

You can choose from these basic system case styles: tower, desktop, slimline, mini-desktop, and minitower. The tower model sits on the floor and can take up a lot of room on the floor, but it leaves you desk space. These models have the most room for expansion. You can get a minitower that is not as tall.

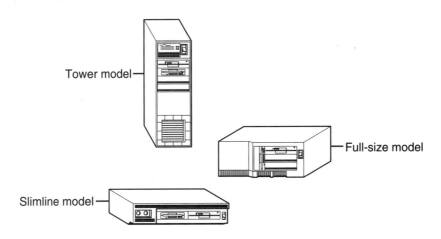

There are several case styles to choose from.

Not all power strips offer surge protection, so don't just buy any old one from the local five and dime. Get one that you know has surge protection.

If you don't want the bulk of the tower model and want the computer to sit on your desktop, consider the desktop style. You'll have enough room for expansion, as well as some room on the desk.

If you are short on desk space, you may want to opt for the sleek slimline case style or the minidesktop. Keep in mind that because the system unit is smaller, there may not be as much room inside—and there may be fewer drive bays or expansion slots.

Push the Buttons

In addition to selecting a model, take a look at the arrangement of buttons and drives. Are the drives easy to reach? My brother-in-law has a computer in which the drives are sideways; this drives me nuts because I'm never sure how to insert the disk.

Are the buttons easy to reach, but not too easy? The power switch is usually on the back or side, which is convenient enough. Some computers have the button on the front. Keep in mind that if you have little fingers around the house that like to press little buttons, this button location may not be ideal.

Footprint The size of the system case.

The PC is also likely to have a reset button, a lock, possibly a turbo button (for switching speeds), and indicator lights on the front of the PC.

The Least You Need to Know

To ensure that you have as much flexibility as possible to allow you to upgrade your PC, check out what you can connect to it via ports and what you can add inside the system unit.

➤ On the back of the PC, you have a connector for hooking up the power cord, a special port for the keyboard, and a special port for connecting the monitor.

➤ You should get a PC with at least two serial ports. The ports are named COM1 and COM2. You can hook up serial devices (some mice, scanners, some printers, modems, and so on) to the serial port.

➤ You should get a PC with at least one parallel port. The parallel port is called LPT1, and you usually use this port to connect a printer.

➤ Inside the PC you should have extra slots on the system bus for connecting expansion cards. The most common size and type card is the 16-bit ISA card. The wave of the future most likely will be 32-bit PCI cards.

➤ So that you can later add other drives (CD-ROM, tape drive, or extra hard drive, for example), you should have some extra drive bays inside the PC.

➤ You should look for a power supply with at least 200W of power.

➤ As for case style, you can select a tower model that sits on the floor, a desktop model that sits on the desk, or a slimline model that sits on the desk but isn't as big as the desktop model.

Chapter 12

Multimedia: CDs and Sound

In This Chapter

➤ What is multimedia?

➤ Should I get a multimedia PC?

➤ Picking a good CD-ROM drive

➤ Picking a good sound

➤ Building your CD collection

Want the coolest games? The best reference information? The best children's software? If so, you'll probably want to look into a multimedia PC.

Just what is multimedia? Multimedia is the combination of different types of media (print, audio, graphics, and animation) in one presentation. I'll be honest, though. I'm not sure whether multimedia is a noun, a verb, an adverb, or an adjective. Maybe it's all four! You can think of multimedia as the presentation: an encyclopedia entry about Charles Lindbergh, with a text entry, a video clip of his famous flight, a radio announcer describing the flight, and a picture of Mr. Lindbergh. You can also think of multimedia as the equipment you use to be able to view the encyclopedia entry. Or you can think of multimedia as the action of looking up the entry: doing multimedia. Multimedia is all of these things, and that's why everybody wants it.

When multimedia first was introduced, there wasn't a lot you could do with it. But now the software has caught up with the hardware, and you can do all kinds of cool things with multimedia. In fact, most PCs sold today are multimedia PCs.

Do you need a multimedia PC? What makes up a multimedia PC? How can you be sure you're getting a good multimedia PC? This chapter unravels these media mysteries.

What Can I Do with Multimedia?

Why would you want to do multimedia? There are many practical, educational, and fun reasons:

➤ **To aid in training** Multimedia presentations are often used in training because the sights and sounds make it more interesting than textbook learning. Also, in a multimedia presentation you can usually jump around from topic to topic. This flexibility not only keeps people interested, it enables them to put the information together in a manner that makes more sense.

➤ **To create training courses** If you develop products, you or your staff can put together a presentation to train others to use your product.

➤ **To look up information** You can find a lot of reference information on CD-ROM: encyclopedias, almanacs, dictionaries, atlases, books of quotations, histories, and literature collections are all available on disc.

➤ **To get software** Because you can store a lot of information on CD-ROM discs, they can be packed full of software or art. The CD-ROM versions of some popular application programs include bonuses not found in the diskette-based editions.

Disk/Disc No, it's not a typo: disk and disc are both correct spellings. In fact, they mean different things. A floppy or hard disk is D-I-S-K, but a CD-ROM is D-I-S-C (a carryover from music-type discs).

➤ **To teach your children** Lots of children's software is available on CD-ROM. For example, my son has Broderbund's Living Books, a program which reads the book aloud. But the book is more than just the story: the pages have "hot" spots. Click on the drawer in the bedroom, for instance, and slime oozes out. Click on a bird outside the bedroom window, and he sings a tune and does a tap dance. I like it as much as my son does!

➤ **To have some fun!** There are a lot of awesome games on CD-ROM. You can set up your own professional football team and play a season of games. Then on Super Bowl Sunday, you'll have no one to blame if your team doesn't win. You can race cars, fly planes, catch Carmen Sandiego, vaporize aliens, explore a mysterious island, and more.

What Is a Multimedia PC?

Does all that sound like fun? Are you ready to sign on the multimedia dotted line? Here's what you need to add to your growing list of equipment: a CD-ROM drive, a sound card, and speakers. These pieces and parts make up a multimedia PC (MPC for short).

Most multimedia programs include an enormous amount of information (and big, fat, disk-hogging files). Instead of clogging up an entire hard disk, the program is put on a CD-ROM disc that's just like the music CDs you buy. To "play" these multimedia CDs, you need a CD-ROM drive.

Most multimedia programs also incorporate sound as part of the thrill. To hear the sound decently on the PC, you need a sound card and some speakers.

Is it that simple? Of course not. Nothing worthwhile is ever that simple. There are standards for CD-ROM drives, sound cards to worry about, and minimum requirements to look for. But don't worry, you'll learn what you need to know in the following sections.

Just because a PC claims to be a multimedia PC and maybe even has an official MPC label doesn't mean it meets the current standards. Why? The standards continue to change as technology becomes more advanced. So you can't just see an ad for a multimedia PC and think, "Hey! Easy decision!" You've got to check out each component carefully.

Is a Special PC Required for Multimedia?

In addition to the CD-ROM drive and the sound card and speakers, you need a system powerful enough to do the magic. I recommend at least a 486DX, 8MB of RAM, 300+MB hard drive, and a SuperVGA monitor, regardless of whether you want to do multimedia. If you get a computer that matches these specs, you'll be able to do multimedia, as well as run most other common applications.

You may, however, see different recommendations, especially a lesser processor or less memory, in advertisements. You can try getting by with a less powerful machine, but you aren't going to be happy with its multimedia performance—or with its performance in general. Don't say I didn't warn you!

Do I Need Multimedia to Survive?

Do you absolutely, positively need a multimedia PC? Not right away. But looking into my crystal ball, I predict that these hardware components will be considered standard in coming years. And once they are standard, all the software companies will jump at the

111

chance to make their products bigger and better, and will utilize the features of a sound card and CD-ROM. The bottom line is, you can buy it now or buy it later, but I think you will be buying a multimedia PC someday.

 If CDs can store so much information, why don't we use the discs as a hard drive or as a better method than floppies for storing files? Because CD-ROM discs are read-only. You can only read information from the CD, not write to it. Also, the CD-ROM drive is much slower than a hard disk.

Many PCs sold today are advertised as multimedia PCs. You may be able to save money in the long run by buying this type of system initially (and saving yourself the cost and trouble of installing a multimedia upgrade kit later). Just make sure the computer meets the minimum specs you are looking for in a PC, and make sure the sound card and CD-ROM are up to standard (as covered in the next section).

If you want to wait and see if you'll really use the PC before you buy into multimedia, or if you're sure you don't need multimedia, it's easy enough to buy a PC without it. If you change your mind, you can add the equipment later, as described in the Chapter 24.

The Anatomy of a CD-ROM Drive

What's the most asked question about CD-ROM drives? "Can I play my music CDs?" The answer is yes. There are special programs (usually free with your CD-ROM drive or sound card) that enable you to turn your computer into an audio CD player so you can listen to music while you play games, type a letter, or whatever.

However, you will most often be using computer CDs, not audio CDs, in your CD-ROM drive. These CDs may include the complete works of Shakespeare, a game, an atlas of the United States, or any number of other things. The concept is the same. You use the CD-ROM drive to run the programs just as if the CD were a floppy disk.

So the CD-ROM Disc Is a Big Floppy?

The CD-ROM drive is similar to a floppy disk drive: you insert the disc in the drive and read information from the disc. A CD-ROM disc differs from a floppy disk in a few ways, though.

First, you can store an enormous amount of data on a CD-ROM disc (around 700MB, which may be more than you can fit on your entire hard disk). You will need this storage capacity because graphics and sound files can be huge.

Second, you can only read information *from*—not write information *to*—a CD-ROM disc. Hence, the name *ROM*, or read-only memory. You can copy individual files from the CD to your hard disk, and then make changes to the copy, but you cannot ever change the contents of the CD itself.

There are special devices that enable you to create your own computer CDs, but they're very expensive (definitely out of the home user's price range). And you can't just write to any CD. You have to buy special blanks (which are also rather expensive), and you can only write to a blank CD once.

To understand just how much information you can cram on a CD-ROM, think of this. You can store, say, 650MB on an average CD. At the most, you can store 1.44MB on a high-density floppy. Do the math. You'd need over 450 floppies to store the information you can store on one CD. And if you stacked them end to end, those 450 floppies would reach all the way to Myrtle Beach, SC. (Just dreaming!)

How Do CD-ROM Drives Work?

To use a CD-ROM disc, you put the disc in the drive. On some systems, you have to push a button and a little drawer pops out. You drop the disc (carefully!) into the drawer and close it. Presto! On other types of CDs, you insert the disc in a little caddy and plunk the caddy into the slot in the front of the drive.

So after that, how do these discs work their magic? If you remember, data is stored as bits that can be on or off. On a CD, a bit can be a pit (0 or off) or a land (1 or on). A laser bounces a light off of the pits and lands to read the data.

There are advantages and disadvantages to both insertion methods. With the drawer-type drive, you don't have a caddy to misplace, and it's quicker to insert and remove disks. With a caddy-type drive, the CD stays cleaner.

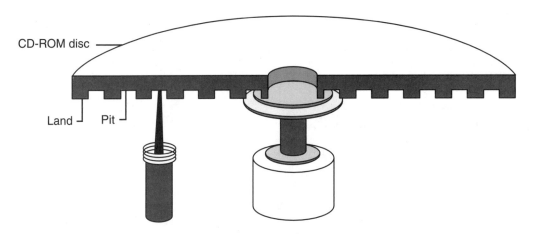

A CD-ROM drive works by reading bits of data stored as pits and lands.

The CD-ROM drive communicates with the processor through a controller just like a hard drive does. That means all those hard disk controller acronyms apply to CD-ROM drives. The most common type of controller is SCSI because they're faster. With a SCSI drive, you have to have a SCSI card.

Picking a Good CD-ROM Drive

You've probably figured out that the computer industry is competitive and has chronic "make it bigger, make it better" disease. What was a pretty decent CD-ROM drive last year is probably on the way out this year.

When purchasing a CD-ROM drive, be careful not to get an outdated model, either as part of a bundled system or separately. This section helps you understand the marketing hype.

What's the top-of-the-line CD-ROM drive? It's probably one of the newest quad speed CD players on the market with three cartridges that can each store 6 CDs. That means you can have 18 discs of information available. So, if you are playing Where in the World Is Carmen Sandiego? and can't remember what country uses the rupee as currency, you can switch from your Carmen CD to your encyclopedia CD and look it up (in short, you can cheat). This top-of-the-line player costs around $2,500.

Spin Time

You'll see advertisements that say single-spin (or speed), double-spin (which is sometimes abbreviated 2X), triple-spin (or 3X), or quad spin (4X). Sometimes the ads use the term "spin," sometimes they use "speed." The concept is the same: the double-speed drive is twice as fast as the single, and so on. That doesn't mean that your Hootie & the Blowfish CD will play twice as fast or that your Mega Race game will race twice as fast. It means the disk can get data twice as fast.

Which speed do you want? That's tricky. You definitely want double-spin or, if you can afford it, quad speed. Don't get a triple-spin disc. The performance increase over a double-spin isn't great enough to merit the extra cost.

However, you can't go by just the spin/speed factor because double-speed means the drive can operate twice as fast as the *normal* speed. But what's the normal speed? That makes a difference. Instead of relying on the spin/speed factor, check out the two times: access time and transfer time.

Find It, Get It: Access and Transfer Time

As with a hard disk, you can determine the performance of a CD-ROM drive by looking at the access and transfer times. The access time tells you how fast the drive can find the data you want. A good access time is in the range of 300 milliseconds. The transfer time tells you how fast the drive can transfer the information to the PC once it finds the information. A good transfer rate is in the 350+ kilobytes per second range.

Internal or External Model?

CD-ROM drives come in two styles. You can have it housed in one of your drive bays inside the system unit, or you can have an external drive that sits on your desktop and connects to the system unit with a cable. The external drive takes up disk space; the internal drive takes up a drive bay. You have to determine which you need more.

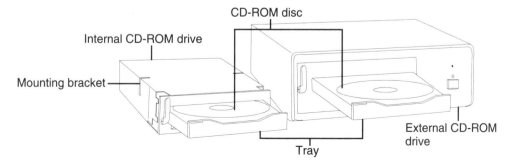

CD-ROM drives come in internal and external models.

115

If you're buying a PC that comes with a CD-ROM drive, it will probably be an internal one. If you buy it after you buy the PC, and you have a drive bay to spare, I suggest you go with the internal model. They're much more common and, therefore, cheaper. You can also find some great deals in which CD-ROM drives are bundled with sound cards, speakers, and CDs—and nearly all of these bundled deals feature internal drives.

On the other hand, if you need to share the drive with someone else, or if you don't have an open drive bay, an external CD-ROM drive may be for you. Keep in mind, though, that an external drive requires an interface card to run, so you have to have an extra expansion slot available. (Some internal CD-ROM drives require an interface card too; others can run off your sound card.)

Start Your CD Collection Early!

You can get just about anything you want on CDs now. You can read the *Playboy* interviews (sure!), learn anatomy from an animated Adam and Eve, look up information in an encyclopedia (the best-selling one is from Microsoft), play games, and on and on. Just browse through a software catalog or store to see what's available.

The cost of a CD can vary, depending on the complexity of the information. You may find games for around $30 and reference CDs that start at $100.

 In any system that's bundled with software, don't be swayed by all the *free* stuff you are getting. You are most likely paying—some way, somehow—for the "freebies." Also consider whether you will use the stuff. If you get $125 worth of free software that you'll never take out of the package, you aren't getting the deal you think you are.

The best way to start your collection is to get some CDs *free* when you buy your PC. Many of the bundled systems and some of the multimedia kits come with some CDs. This is a great way to compare two equal systems. Does one have better, more useful CDs? This is also a great way to start your collection.

Many programs come on a CD-ROM disc, which thrills the software manufacturers because they have just one disc to manufacture, and the manufacturing process is cheaper. For users, it's also easier to install and store one CD-ROM disc than it is to install and store a set of 32 or more floppies (which it seems some programs are swelling to). For most applications, you don't run the program from the disc (although you could) because it would be too slow. You install from the CD and run from the hard drive.

Sometimes you might see the same program available in both diskette and CD-ROM format, and the CD version will actually be cheaper even though it might contain more features! Why? Well, software manufacturers lose a lot of money every year to disk pirates (unscrupulous people who make copies of their software and sell them or give them away to their friends). The loss from these pirates forces the software companies to jack up their prices. However, because you can't copy a CD, the manufacturer doesn't make you pay the "pirate premium."

Jamming with Sound Cards

Unless you are satisfied with the beeps and chirps that you can make with your squawky PC speaker, you will probably want a sound card and speakers. Sound cards enable the PC to play digital sounds using better-quality speakers.

You need a sound card if you want to take advantage of multimedia programs such as books that talk, race cars that vroom, and guns that go bang. There are also some practical (boring!) purposes for sound. For example, you can have a training presentation where the engineer describes how a feature was created. For the most part, a sound card adds a level of realism to games and educational software.

In the future, though, sound will probably be extremely exciting and useful. With a microphone and a voice-activated program, you can tell your PC "Open this file and type this data." In fact, there are already some voice recognition programs available. (This topic is covered in Chapter 17.) Someday in the not-so-distant future, your PC may be able to tell you "Stop, you ninny! Don't format your hard disk!"

Selecting a Sound Card

Many PCs come with a sound card and speakers. If these items are included with the PC, make sure they are of acceptable quality—which you can do by reading this section. If you aren't happy with them, buy the PC without them and add the sound card and speakers separately. (See Chapter 24 for help installing sound cards.)

A sound card is an electronic card that you insert in an expansion slot inside your PC. Currently, the most common sound card is 16-bit. (Remember that expansion cards are measured by bits, as discussed in Chapter 11.) For better-quality sound, you can purchase a 32-bit card, which is top-of-the-line now and more expensive. (You also need a 32-bit expansion slot open in your computer for it.)

117

SoundBlaster is one of the most popular sound card manufacturers, so many software programs were written for SoundBlaster sound. (The software has to understand how to take advantage of the sound card features.) Although there are now many other manufacturers of sound cards, many of them advertise that their products are SoundBlaster compatible. This means that programs that work with a SoundBlaster card will also work with their card. You definitely want a SoundBlaster or SoundBlaster-compatible sound card.

Speakers

Sound cards are like stereo receivers: they don't have speakers built in, so you have to plug speakers into the sound card. If you purchase a PC that has a sound card, speakers probably come with it. If you purchase a sound card by itself, the speakers are probably sold separately. (Some multimedia kits include CD-ROM drive, sound card, and speakers all together, though.)

Speakers sometimes have magnets! Magnets are dangerous to a computer! High-quality speakers include magnets that create the sound you hear. Those designed to be used with a PC usually include shielding that protects the hardware from the magnets in the speaker. But be careful!

Even if there are speakers included with the sound system, they may be weenie ones. For true stereo-quality sound, you may want to invest in better-quality speakers. What's the price for high-quality speakers? Expect to pay around $350 to $400. The same features you look for in stereo speakers are important here. For instance, the more watts per channel, the better.

And, yes, you can connect your sound card to your stereo speakers. Connect a cable from the out jack on the stereo card to the in jack on your stereo. You'll probably need an adapter because the sound card and stereo use different size plugs.

Open Mike Night on the PC

In addition to the sound card and speakers, many sound cards include a microphone that you can plug into the sound card and use to record your own sounds. You can record

Want to compose songs with the PC? Chapter 17 covers some special musical equipment you can use in addition to your sound card to record and play sounds.

your own messages, such as your Arnold impression of "I'll be back," your dog barking, or your child saying his ABCs. With a microphone, you can also try out voice-recognition software, where you control your computer by issuing verbal commands.

The Least You Need to Know

The latest excitement in the PC world is multimedia. Multimedia applications combine several different media (sound, graphics, animation, video, text, and so on) into one presentation. If you want to use multimedia applications on your PC, you need a multimedia PC.

➤ A multimedia PC (MPC) includes a CD-ROM drive, a sound card, and speakers. The system should also be fairly powerful. I would recommend at least a 486DX, 8MB of RAM, SuperVGA monitor, and 300+MB hard disk.

➤ CD-ROM drives may be internal (housed inside the system unit) or external (sit on your desktop).

➤ CD-ROM drives differ in how fast they can find and retrieve information. You may see the speed advertised as double-spin or speed, triple-speed, or quad speed. Don't rely on the speed or spin spec. Instead, check out the transfer rate and access time.

➤ Sound cards are electronic expansion boards that you plug into your system unit. You can then hook up speakers and a microphone so that you can listen to and record sound. You want at least a 16-bit sound card that is SoundBlaster compatible. Many programs are designed to work with SoundBlaster cards.

➤ If you want true stereo sound, you may have to purchase speakers separately. Expect to pay $70–$150 for excellent quality speakers.

Chapter 13

On the Road Again: Portable PCs

> **In This Chapter**
>
> ➤ Are you a portable person?
>
> ➤ How portable computers differ
>
> ➤ Picking a portable
>
> ➤ The littlest of the bunch: special-purpose portables

Are you always on the go? Driving, flying, running, galloping? If you're never at your desk and always on the road, you may want to consider a portable computer. A portable computer is a computer you can carry around with you.

Although portable computers are smaller and more convenient, they are also more expensive. Why? Because they are the Ferraris of computing. This chapter explains how these computers differ and how to select a decent portable computer.

Are You a Portable Person?

Some first-time computer buyers think they should get a portable computer so they have the flexibility to take the computer with them if they need to. This is a mistake! You should only get a portable if you *really* need one.

A portable computer, for one thing, is more expensive than a comparable desktop PC. It's smaller, but there's more technology crammed into it, so it costs more. Therefore, you get more bang from your buck with a desktop model.

A portable computer also has to cram the keyboard and screen into a tiny little area. That means the keyboard isn't going to be as easy to use as a desktop model, and the screen isn't going to be as easy on your eyes as a regular monitor.

So, if a portable computer is more money, less power, and harder to use, why even consider one? The only reason is if you travel often. Your desktop model isn't going to be of much use if you are in New York on Monday, Philadelphia on Tuesday, Washington on Wednesday, and back in your office in Atlanta on Thursday. With a portable, you can take the computer with you and use it anywhere—in a hotel, airplane, home, office—you name it.

Portable computer
In this book, I'm using portable as a generic term to mean any PC that you can carry. As you learn later in this chapter, there are different types (and names) of portables, depending on the size. Just keep in mind that when you see portable, it means any class or style of a take-it-on-the-road PC. When I mean a specific type of portable, such as a laptop, I'll use that specific name.

You may also want to consider buying a portable as a *second* computer. You may already have a desktop and want a portable to take with you. Using cables, you can transfer information between the two whenever you need to.

The Anatomy of a Portable

Theoretically, all computers are portable. I mean, yeah, you could load your PC, monitor, and keyboard in your little red wagon and pull it along. You may look kind of silly going into a sales presentation, but hey, who cares!

Portable computers are designed to be easy to carry. In addition, they run on batteries if you don't have a power outlet available. This section explains some of the key differences among portables.

Small, Smaller, Smallest

The biggest difference among portables is the size. Computer designers have created smaller and smaller computers, and each time a new or smaller computer is designed, they come up with a new name. The following table explains the history and evolution of the portable PC (from big to little).

Name	Description
Luggable	The original portable computer resembled a desktop model, but the monitor and system unit were one component. You could lug the computer around in a huge case; hence the name.
Laptop	This type of portable weighs in around 6 to 9 pounds. They are usually bigger and thicker than a notebook, with a larger keyboard and screen.
Notebook	Think of your school notebooks: that's about the dimensions of a notebook computer (10" × 12"). These weigh as little as 4 to 6 pounds. You can fit a notebook computer inside your briefcase.
Subnotebook or handbook	Smaller than a notebook, these computers weigh 2 to 3 pounds. They usually don't have full-size keyboards, and the monitors are usually one-color.

There are other types of special-purpose portable computers, such as organizers, which are covered later in this chapter.

Portable Hardware

The portable PC, like the desktop model, is made up of the same parts: a microprocessor, memory, hard disk, floppy disk (most), monitor, keyboard, and pointing device (something that acts as a mouse). The portable usually includes some expansion room. Because the portable is small, though, you'll notice some differences between portable hardware and desktop hardware.

➤ The portable, like the desktop, is controlled by a processor. All the information about processors you read in Chapter 5 pertains to the processor in the portable. One difference is that sometimes you will see the suffix SL after the processor name. SL chips are often used in portable computers because they offer power-saving features: these chips can turn off power to components that aren't being used.

➤ The portable, like the desktop, uses memory to store programs and data that you are working on. That means everything you read about memory in Chapter 6 goes for portables as well.

➤ Believe it or not, most portable computers have a regular-capacity hard disk. You need a hard disk to store your programs and data that you are not working with. What you read in Chapter 7 on hard disks pertains to portable hard disks as well.

➤ Most portables include a floppy disk so that you can move data onto and off of the PC. The portable will most likely have a 3 1/2-inch high density (1.44MB) floppy drive. (You can also use a different method of transferring data; you can connect the portable to the desktop model with a cable and transfer data that way.)

➤ The monitor is connected to the system unit, usually on the inside of the lid. These monitors use a different kind of technology for displaying the image than the desktop models do. The section "Screen Displays" later in this chapter explains how to select a portable PC with a good monitor.

➤ Because the keyboard has to fit within a tiny space, the keys are smaller, and the keyboard doesn't have as many keys as the standard 101-key keyboard. The next section explains how to pick a keyboard that works for you.

➤ Because you may not have a desk on which to roll the mouse, portable computers use a different type of pointing device called a *trackball*. The trackball is basically an upside-down mouse. Picking a trackball that will keep you on track is explained in the next section.

➤ Like desktop computers, portables have ports to which you can hook up other equipment such as a modem or a printer. What you read about ports in Chapter 11 also applies here. Expansion slots are different, though. The next section demystifies the acronyms and technical specs for a portable's expansion slots.

➤ With a desktop computer, you plug the computer into a power outlet. A portable wouldn't be all that useful if you had to have a power outlet available. Instead, they are powered by batteries. The next section explains the differences in types of batteries.

Selecting a Portable

I'm guessing that if you got this far into the chapter, you're serious about purchasing a portable PC. Good for you. This section explains the key decisions you'll make when selecting a portable PC.

The Obsession with Weight

Do you ever read the personal ads? Do you notice that most of the advertisers want a *slim*, *fit*, or *trim* companion? Do you ever see one that says *fat*, *hefty*, or *obese*? I don't think so. Thin is in.

The same is true for portables. How skinny is skinny enough? Consider both the dimensions and the weight. You can review the available sizes in the advertisement: usually the dimensions are given as 9.75" × 5.9" × 1.6" (length, width, depth), and the weight is in pounds. Remember, six pounds may sound pretty good in an ad, but it may feel a lot heavier when you carry it around for an hour. Be careful!

First, it's much better to visit a computer store than to shop ads. You can visually compare the sizes of the computers, and you can pick up and carry the portables to compare the weights. Second, remember to balance size with usability. That tiny little subnotebook may be as light as a piece of paper, but try typing on its keyboard. Do you need fingers the size of an elf's? Third, find out the total weight. Four pounds doesn't sound like much, but in addition to the computer itself you'll be carrying the case, extra batteries, and other equipment (battery charger, disks, and so on). Be sure to find out how heavy the entire package is, not just the computer itself.

The Brains: Processor and Memory

As I said, portables are more expensive than desktop models. So to save money, you may want to scrimp on the features of the computer. For example, you may select a lesser processor and less memory. Again, caution, caution, caution!

You want to the portable to do more than just make you look hip. That means you want at least a 486 chip in your portable. If you have to cut somewhere, you may be able to compromise a little on the processor's speed. You also need memory. A lot of portables come with 4MB, but that's probably not enough. Get 8MB to be happy.

Drives, Drives, Drives

You want the biggest hard drive you can afford—at least a 200MB hard disk. Just because the computer is small doesn't mean the files are any smaller.

You'll probably also want a floppy disk drive (3 1/2-inch high density) so that you can copy files from the hard disk to the floppy. You can also use other methods of moving information, as covered later in this section.

When installing software on a portable, look for an installation procedure designed for portables. Because portables are becoming more prevalent, many software programs offer an installation option specifically for a portable computer. This installation copies only the minimum files you need, instead of every file possible. This procedure saves room on the hard disk.

125

Screen Displays

Not only is the screen on a portable smaller, it also uses a completely different method for displaying an on-screen image. Called a *liquid-crystal display*, or LCD, it consists of a light panel and a layer of liquid-crystal cells that can be electrically charged. These charged cells are filtered through one of three color filters, and the color is displayed on-screen.

The best test of the screen display is to try it out. Be sure to try it in different light settings. In the store, the screen may be easy to see, but what about outside? Think about where you will use the portable, and look at the screen in a similar setting.

In addition to your own evaluation, you can review the specs for the screen display. Here's how they vary:

What You'll See Advertised	Explanation
Color or monochrome	The display may be black and white or color. Color is more expensive, as you may have expected. Color displays also require more processing power.
Backlit or sidelit (reflective)	The screen can be lit from the back or side. Backlit displays are brighter and better-quality than sidelit ones.
Active matrix or passive matrix	Active has crisp, clean color and is preferable. Passive costs less, but does not offer the brightness or contrast that active matrix does.

When comparing screens, compare the size and the type of display (VGA, for example). Be sure that the screen tilts easily so you can view it from different angles.

Little Keyboards for Big Fingers

The keyboard is probably the biggest factor in determining how easy (or difficult) it is to use a portable. If you can't type on the keyboard comfortably, all the features in the world aren't going to make you like it.

Try typing on the keyboard. It takes some time to get used to the different layout if you're used to typing on a full-size keyboard. Still, you can probably feel the differences among different models. Also, listen to the keys. When you are flying overseas and want to use the portable at 2:00 a.m., you don't want your flight companions to hear clack-clack-clack (unless you want the complimentary peanuts crammed up your nose).

The portable will probably also have a trackball, which may clip onto the system (bad) or be integrated on the keyboard (better). Try out the trackball, too. They vary greatly in how easy they are to use. The best way to judge them is to try them out yourself.

Power Up with the Battery

As I mentioned, the portable runs on a battery. Find out what type of battery it uses, as well as the working time of the battery. Some portables also offer power-saving options, such as auto shutdown.

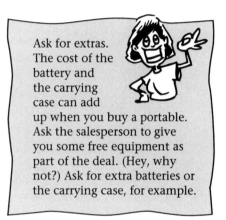

Ask for extras. The cost of the battery and the carrying case can add up when you buy a portable. Ask the salesperson to give you some free equipment as part of the deal. (Hey, why not?) Ask for extra batteries or the carrying case, for example.

There are two types of rechargeable batteries: nickel-cadmium (NiCad) and nickel-metal-hydride (NiMH). NiCad batteries are cheaper and use an older technology; NiMH are the newest standard and last longer. But don't expect miracles; even these batteries don't last long. Ask about the battery life (three hours working time is good), and ask how long it takes to recharge the batteries.

Room for Expansion?

When you want to add additional features to the portable, you do so by using a slot and a card called a PCMCIA (Personal Computer Memory Card International Association). Different cards are designed for different slots, as you see here:

Card/Slot Type	Used Mostly For
Type I	Adding memory
Type II	Modems
Type III	Hard drives

You want at least one, if not two, of each type of slot.

Dock It!

Some portables are designed to be both a portable and a desktop computer. You can take the portable part with you when you travel, and when you return you can plug the portable into a docking station (a desktop PC shell). Because the desktop PC has a regular size keyboard and monitor, you get the best of both worlds. If this sounds like what you need, pick a portable with a docking station.

127

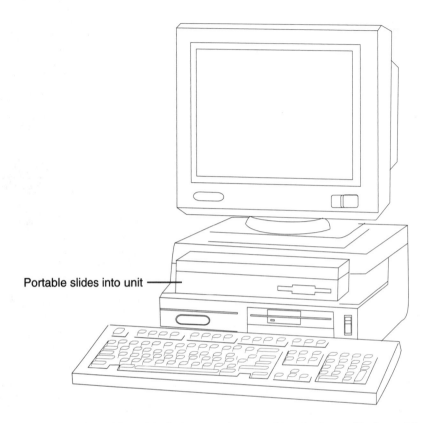

Portable slides into unit —

Portables with docking stations combine the best of both worlds.

Not Really PCs

Sometimes you don't need all the power of a PC. For example, you may only need a computer to do something simple, such as keep track of your schedule. Or you want to use the computer for a special purpose such as making notes or getting signatures. In cases like these, you might want to consider a different type of portable computer. Read on.

Purchasing a Palmtop

The next smallest in size after the subnotebook is the *palmtop*, which weighs about a pound. About the size of a checkbook, this type of computer usually includes a day planner, calculator, and other features. You can also buy software to run on the palmtop. On the downside, however, the keyboard is very cramped, and the processing power is limited.

128

Purchasing an Organizer

An *organizer*, a special type of palmtop, can fit in your pocket, is convenient, and has a long battery life. What can you do with an organizer? You can track appointments, do calculations, create to-do lists, and more. In addition to the basic features, you can usually purchase add-on cards for other features. These cards are about the size of a credit card and are purchased separately. For example, you can purchase a card that manages your stock portfolio.

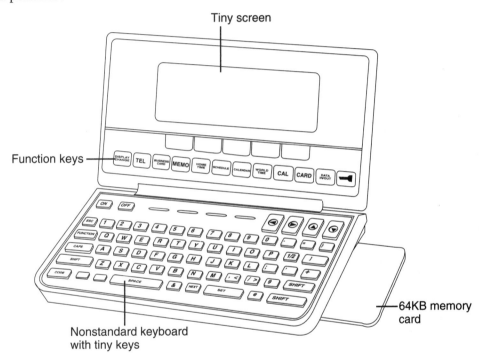

An organizer is part day-planner, part computer.

Purchasing a PDA

Still another type of palmtop is the *PDA* or personal digital assistant. Sounds impressive, doesn't it? "A meeting next Friday? Well, I'll have to check with my personal digital assistant," you can say. With this type of palmtop, you use a different technology called a *pen-based computer* to input data. You enter data using a touch screen and a pen or stylus.

You can take notes, make simple drawings, and schedule events on a calendar with this type of computer. You'll find that pen-based computers are used most for a specific purpose. For instance, the UPS man may use a pen-based computer to record your receipt signature for a package, or a policeman may use a pen-based computer to take notes at the scene of the crime.

The Least You Need to Know

If you travel often and want to have access to your computer, consider a portable computer. A portable computer is designed to be carried with you and operates on batteries so that you don't need an available power outlet.

➤ Buy a portable only if that type of computer is what you need. Portable computers are more expensive than their desktop counterparts; therefore, you'll get more power for your money with a desktop model. In addition, the keyboards of desktop models are easier to use, and the monitors are easier to see.

➤ As technology evolves, the portable becomes smaller and smaller and is given a new name. Subnotebook computers weigh about 2 to 3 pounds; notebook computers (probably the most popular portable now) weigh approximately 4 to 6 pounds. Laptops (once the most popular) weigh 6 to 9 pounds.

➤ The hardware on a portable computer and a desktop computer consists of the same components. You need a microprocessor, memory, hard disk drive, floppy disk drive, monitor, keyboard, and pointing device. However, the monitor, keyboard, and pointing device are different for portables.

➤ Portable monitors use a different display technology called liquid-crystal display or LCD. The best test of a portable monitor is your own eyes. As for specifications, backlit is preferable to sidelit, and active matrix is brighter than passive matrix.

➤ Try typing on the keyboard and using the trackball. Be sure they work for you.

➤ There are two types of batteries used to power the portable: nickel-cadmium (NiCad) and nickel-metal-hydride (NiMH). NiMH is the newest standard. Ask about the battery life (three hours is a good working time), and ask how long it takes to recharge the batteries.

Part 3
Extras

Goodies! Extras! More fun! And, of course, more money! In this part, you can read about all the super-dooper extras you can consider adding to your computer wish list. Some, such as a printer, are a must. Some, such as a fax/modem, are a maybe. And some, such as a TV card for watching TV right on your PC (Imagine!), are for the truly technical fast tracker (or the cool slacker).

THEY'RE JUST ABOUT RIPE...

Chapter 14

Picking a Printer

In This Chapter

➤ The different types of printers

➤ Understanding fonts

➤ Buying a dot-matrix printer

➤ Buying an inkjet printer

➤ Buying a laser printer

➤ Buying a color printer

You will most likely want to share all the cool things you create on the computer. What good is a budget if you can't print it out and give your spouse a good laugh? What good is a newsletter if you have to invite everyone over to read it on-screen? If you can't put your child's artwork on the refrigerator, how can anyone else appreciate his obvious talent?

To share your creations with others, you'll want to buy a printer with your computer system. There are several types of printers, each appropriate in different circumstances. This chapter helps you pick out the printer that's right for you.

Types of Printers

Here's how printers work: You attach the printer to the computer via a cable. The cable most often connects to your parallel (LPT1) port. When you issue the command to print, the computer sends the instructions over the cable to the printer, and—voilà—you have a printout.

Resolution The quality of a printed image; it's the same concept as screen resolution (see Chapter 9). The more detailed the image, the higher the resolution and the better the quality.

If all printers work the same, does that mean every printer's output looks the same? No. Does that mean they cost the same? No. Depending on the type of printer, the quality (*resolution*) of the printout will vary. And the higher the quality, the higher the price.

The three most common types of printers are *dot-matrix* printers, *inkjet* printers, and *laser* printers. You can also buy color versions of each type of printer. Dot-matrix are the cheapest, lowest-quality printer. Inkjets are middle range: okay price and okay quality. Laser printers provide the best quality and are the most expensive. The rest of this chapter explains the differences.

Buying a Dot-Matrix Printer

Bargain! You may not be able to get a computer dealer to come down on the price of a system, but you can ask for a break on the printer, especially if you buy the two together. Ask for a discount.

Before the advent of inkjet printers and before laser printers became affordable, most users had a dot-matrix printer. This type of printer works by firing a series of pins. When a pin is fired, it strikes the ribbon and places a dot on the page. The combinations of dots form characters and graphics. If you look closely at a printout from a dot-matrix printer, you can see these little dots.

The more pins the print head has, the better the printout quality. Originally, 9-pin was the most common; now most dot-matrix printers are 24-pins. Avoid 9-pin printers if you can possibly afford a 24-pin model. The difference in price is usually less than $100.

When Should You Buy a Dot-Matrix?

The advantages of dot-matrix printers are that they are cheap (starting at $150) and reliable, and the cost of the parts that need frequent replacement (ribbons and paper) is low. In addition, they are fast and work well for some special printing situations, such as when you need to print on a multipart form or when you need really wide printouts.

If you aren't too concerned with quality (you just want a cheap, reliable printer), you may be happy with a dot-matrix printer. This type of printer might also be sufficient for creating draft versions if you have access to a better printer for your final work.

If you want a better quality printout for only a little more money, consider the next in line: the inkjet printer.

Keep in mind that these printers don't print graphics well and have few built-in typefaces. (We'll talk about typefaces later in the chapter.) They can also be slow and noisy.

Comparison Shopping for Dot-Matrix Printers

So you want a dot-matrix printer. Here's what to look for when comparison shopping: resolution, speed, and paper handling.

The quality of the image (resolution) depends on the number of pins in the print head (9 or 24) and is measured in *dots per inch* (dpi). The higher the dpi, the better the quality. Average resolution for a 24-pin printer is 360×360. But don't just rely on the numbers; look at printouts from the printer. You can see for yourself which printouts look better.

```
Before you can run any program, you have to boot your computer.
Boot is a fancy term that means you have to turn on your computer
with the disk operating system files in place: the files have to
be on your computer's hard disk (if it has one) or on a floppy
disk that is in one of the floppy disk drives.
```
—24-pin output

```
    Before you can run any program, you have to boot your
computer. Boot is a fancy term that means you have to turn on
your computer with the disk operating system files in place:  the
files have to be on your computer's hard disk (if it has one) or
on a floppy disk that is in one of the floppy disk drives.
```
—9-pin output

24-pins give a better quality image than 9-pins.

In order to rush your latest, greatest work onward and upward, you'll want as fast a printer as you can get. For dot-matrix printers, speed is measured in how many *characters per second* (cps) the printer can print. Most dot-matrix printers can print in two speeds: draft and near-letter quality (NLQ). Draft speeds range from 240 cps to over 1,000 cps. NLQ speeds range from 48 to 130+. The faster the printer, the more expensive it is.

Paper Handling in a Dot-Matrix Printer

The final test of a dot-matrix printer is how you load paper. In the store, the paper is loaded, and the printer works easily. When you get home and try to load the paper yourself, you may be in for a surprise.

Some printers use a tractor feed. You hook up the paper to a little tractor with a little farmer. The farmer then pulls the paper through the printer. Okay, what really happens is the paper has little holes along the edges and feeds through the printer,

Don't just view a printout of text. Text is the easiest thing to print. Ask for a printout of a graphic image to see how well the printer does with graphics.

around the roller bar, and between the ribbon and roller bar. You have to weave and wiggle the paper through several bars, rollers, and pins. Get it wrong and your entire 1,000 page dissertation prints on one line. Bummer.

Some printers use a single-sheet feed: the printer carrier holds single sheets of papers and feeds them through the printer. Regardless of how the paper feeds into the printer, try loading the paper before you buy the printer. You'll be glad you did.

Dot-matrix printers also vary in how many columns they can print (how wide). You can purchase a wide-carriage printer that is great for really long or wide database reports (for example).

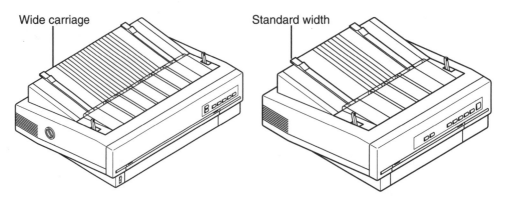

Wide-carriage dot-matrix printers are more versatile than standard width models.

Buying an Inkjet Printer

If you aren't satisfied with the quality of the dot-matrix printer but don't want to spend a lot of money, you may want to consider the middle-of-the-road printer: the inkjet. This type of printer provides better quality than a dot-matrix, but not as good quality as a laser printer. The printer is cheaper than a laser printer, but more expensive than a dot-matrix. It's definitely the middle guy.

Inkjet and You: A Happy Combination?

Inkjets, as I mentioned, are reasonably priced ($250 and up) and have reasonable quality. They are quiet and can print graphics. The drawbacks are the speed (slow) and the operating cost (high). You may even have to use special paper that won't smudge. But if you want a happy medium in price and quality, you may want to consider an inkjet printer.

Like that of a dot-matrix printer, an inkjet printer's printout is composed of tiny dots. However, instead of a pin striking a ribbon, the dots are sprayed on the page with a tiny nozzle and an ink-filled cartridge. Because the printer heats up the ink until it boils (or forms a bubble), this type of printer is also called a Bubblejet printer.

Comparing Inkjets

For any printer, you use the same basic criteria for comparing models: price, quality or resolution, and speed. And basically, the last two criteria determine the first (price).

The resolution of inkjet printers is measured in dots per inch (dpi) and is usually in the range of 300 to 360 dpi. The higher the dpi, the better the quality. 300 dpi is pretty good quality.

For an inkjet printer, speed is measured in how many pages per minute (ppm) the printer can print. The average speed is 2 ppm, which is approximately 30 seconds a page. (That's slow compared to 4 and up for laser printers.) When you are rushing to a sales meeting and printing your 40-page presentation at the last minute, you won't want to tick off 30 seconds for each page.

Don't forget to factor in the cost for supplies: ribbons for dot-matrix printers, ink for inkjet printers, and toner cartridges for laser printers. Plus paper. Dot-matrix printers are still the cheapest, around 1 cent per page. Actually, inkjets cost more per page to print than laser printers do. You can expect to pay 4.3 cents per page for an inkjet, compared to 3.5 cents per page for laser printers.

Buying a Laser Printer

Want the best-quality printer available? Then you want a laser printer. A laser printer offers the fastest printing and better quality than any other printer. Of course, speed and quality come with a price tag. You can expect to pay a minimum of $500 for a laser printer.

Like other printer types, you can compare the quality and speed of different models. You can also compare the amount of memory included and look into the printer language used, as described in the following sections.

Quality and Speed

As with other printers, the resolution of laser printers is measured in dots per inch (dpi). Resolution can range from 300 dpi up to 1,000 dpi. The higher the resolution, the more expensive the printer. If you're printing letters, reports, and personal documents, 300 dpi is okay; it's the current standard. However, 600 dpi is becoming more and more prevalent, meaning it will be the next standard. If you're doing desktop publishing work, you want a printer in the 600 dpi to 1,000 dpi range.

Speed is measured in how many pages per minute (ppm) the printer can print. The average speed ranges from 4 ppm to 8 ppm. The faster, the better.

Printers Have Memory Too

A laser printer creates an image of the entire page and prints it at once, which means it needs some thinking or visualizing room: memory. A laser printer also needs memory to store the fonts used on the page.

Like computer memory, printer memory is measured in megabytes (M or MB). The more memory, the better and faster the printer. You should look for a printer with at least 1MB. Also, look for a laser printer that enables you to add more memory, if needed.

A laser printer works a lot like a copy machine. Inside the printer is a drum that is covered with chemicals. When you print, a laser beam magnetizes the particles on the drum, creating the image of the page. These particles attract a fine powdered ink, called toner. As the paper is pulled through the printer, the pressure and heat of the printer presses the toner off the drum onto the page.

Other Printer Factors to Consider

No matter what kind of printer you go with, you're going to run into a few common issues. What printer language does the printer speak? How many colors does it print? What fonts does it come with? Let's take a look at some of these secondary, but important, issues.

Parlez-Vous Printer Language?

Printers "talk" in different languages—that is, they expect the input from the computer to come in varying ways. If the computer is sending data in one language, and the printer is expecting to hear it in another, you get a jumbled mess on your printout.

There are numerous printer languages. Most popular printers have their own native language but also speak the language of a few other printers. For instance, you might have a bargain-brand dot-matrix printer that not only speaks its own language, but also emulates (imitates) the language of a more popular printer, such as the Epson LQ-850.

Most software comes with driver files that enable the program to communicate with the 20 or 30 most popular printer languages. So it's important to get either a very popular brand and model of printer, or to make sure that the printer speaks one of the popular languages.

IBM Proprints and Epson LQ-850 are common dot-matrix languages. For laser printers, the popular standards are PostScript and PCL. PostScript printers have built-in scalable fonts and can print special PostScript graphics files that some software generates. PCL (printer control language) is the creation of Hewlett Packard (one of the most popular laser printer makers). All their laser printers use PCL, and so do most other bargain-brand laser printers. Don't buy a laser printer that does not speak either PostScript or PCL.

Color Printers

Until now, color printers were expensive (you can still expect to pay $5,000 for a color laser printer). However, in 1994, a whole slew of affordable color printers was introduced. The new color printers are inkjet printers and run approximately $400 or more. Each printer manufacturer has its own color model.

Consider the following when considering a color printer:

➤ Check out the regular inkjet features: resolution, speed, and price.

➤ Be sure the printer can print on plain paper, not just on special coated paper.

➤ Test the black-and-white printing. Your office mates will hate you if every document you turn out is in neon purple, orange, chartreuse, or lemon-lime. Remember that most text documents look best in black-and-white. You'll want great quality for black-and-white printouts.

➤ Compare the quality of the color. Do the colors look accurate (what you intended)? Are they smooth?

Color sounds cool, but do you really need it? Color is useful for printing presentations and artwork, but for your everyday documents, black and white is okay. You'll do best if you get what you need instead of what you think you want!

A Fountain of Fonts

All printers come with at least one built-in font, and some printers come with lots of them. Back in the early days of computing, you could only use fonts that were built into your printer, so the fonts that came in the printer were a big deal. Since then, things have changed, and there are several ways to use fonts that your printer never dreamed of.

A *font* is a set of characters in the same size and typeface. You may often hear the terms font and typeface used interchangeably, but they aren't the same. The typeface is the look of the font, such as Times New Roman. The font is that typeface in one size, such as Times New Roman 14-point type.

Printer makers are loose with the terms to make you think you're getting a lot more selection. For example, a printer may be advertised as having 12 typefaces, but if you look closely, that might turn out to be two typefaces in 6 sizes each.

To make more fonts available for use with printers, manufacturers have developed different ways to use and add fonts. First, some printers have a slot into which you can insert a cartridge with extra fonts. You buy a cartridge with the fonts you want, and plug it into the printer. Second, some software comes with downloadable fonts. For example, WordPerfect comes with its own set of fonts stored on disk that are sent to the printer through the printer cable (along with the data to be printed) whenever needed.

The latest and most popular font technology is TrueType, a type of downloadable font. TrueType fonts come with Microsoft Windows 3.1, and you can use them with any Windows-based program. Like other soft fonts, TrueType fonts are stored as files on disk. When you print with these fonts, the software program sends the instructions on creating the font to the printer. Windows 3.1 comes with several fonts, and you can buy more in a software store. Sometimes Windows programs come with additional TrueType fonts too, which you can use with any Windows program (not just the program they came with).

Here are some examples of the creative typefaces you can find:

In the beginning...

Call me Ishmael

My dearest darling:

APPROVED 8/5/92

Big Clearance Sale!

With typefaces, you can select the exact look you want.

The bottom line is, it's not that important how many built-in fonts your computer has, because you're probably going to use Windows and will have access to TrueType fonts. Even if you don't, most programs these days come with lots of fonts for use in that particular program.

The Least You Need to Know

You will most likely purchase a printer when you buy a computer system. There are three main types of printers. Depending on your needs, you can select the printer with the features you need.

➤ Dot-matrix are the cheapest, lowest-quality printers available. These printers start out at $150. If you aren't concerned with quality, need to print multi-part forms, or just want a cheap printer, consider a dot-matrix printer.

➤ Inkjet printers are the middle-of-the-road printers. They offer better quality than a dot-matrix at a reasonable price. They are not as expensive or as fast as laser printers.

➤ The laser printer offers the best quality and is the most expensive printer. You can expect to pay at least $500 for a laser printer.

➤ The quality of a printed image is called the resolution. Resolution is measured in dots per inch (dpi). 300 dpi is the current standard, but look for 600 dpi to be the standard soon.

➤ Before you decide which printer to buy, compare the speed of different printers. Dot-matrix printer speed is measured in characters per second (cps). Usually the printer can print in two speeds: draft and near-letter quality (NLQ). Inkjet and laser printer speed is measured in pages per minute (ppm).

➤ In 1994, color inkjet printers were introduced to the market. Before that, you had either poor-quality color or really expensive color printers. If you need to print presentations, you may want to look into an inkjet color printer.

➤ A font is a set of characters in one size and typeface. With Windows, you can take advantage of TrueType fonts, fonts that are actually files stored on your computer. The files tell the printer how to create the font.

Hooking Up to the World: A Modem/Fax Connection

Can you say "information superhighway?" Can you say "buzzword?" You can hardly open a magazine or turn on the TV without hearing some reference to the information superhighway or the (currently) most popular communication network, the Internet.

What's so cool about the Internet? How do you hitchhike, cruise, or just get on this information superhighway? How do you hook up to it so you aren't left standing on the sidewalk with the garbage? Read this chapter! I'll explain how you can telecommunicate using your computer and your phone.

Joining the Global Village: What Can You Do?

You probably understand the phone system—that is, you understand the concept. (Of course, you have no idea which phone carrier saves you the most money or what is the best way to make a collect call. Nobody does.) Most people have a phone. If you want to talk to somebody, you call them.

Network A series of computers linked with cables or wires. The computers hooked up to the network can share files and send messages. Usually one big powerful PC, called the server, manages all the network activities and contains all the shared files.

The same concept is true of telecommunicating using a computer. Your computer calls another computer, and they complain about their stupid owners. Actually, the two computers send data back and forth through the phone lines.

You can hook up to a single computer, as you would if you called your office computer from your home computer. You can hook up to an informal system, called a BBS. Usually a BBS is set up and maintained by a hobbyist for some common goal, such as collecting stamps or bringing back "My Favorite Martian." Or you can hook up to a bigger commercial network called an online service. Some popular online services include PRODIGY, CompuServe, and America Online.

Sending Electronic Mail

People use telecommunications to send messages (just like with the phone). Except now you type the messages. You can send a message to your co-worker down the hall ("Jane ate all the coffeecake again."). You can send your message to a computer across the country ("To the home office in Scranton PA: Jane ate all the coffeecake again."). Or you can send the message to strangers on a bulletin board system or an online system ("Hey, world: Jane ate all the coffeecake again."). The person or persons to whom you sent the message can then respond at their leisure ("I told you to hide the coffeecake."). These types of messages are called *e-mail*—electronic mail.

You can send messages specifically to one person, or, on a BBS or online service, you can post messages in a common area and meet other users online.

Sending and Receiving Files

In addition to sending messages, you can send and receive files over the telephone wires. For example, you can transmit your travel expenses or send the data needed for a report. The process of sending a file is called *uploading*. The process of receiving a file is called *downloading*.

When you hook up to a BBS or online service, you gain access to all the files stored on that BBS or service. For example, most online services are divided into sections. From the financial section, you can download today's stock prices. From the software section, you can download the latest shareware games.

You also have access to all the information and other services provided with a BBS or online system. For example, many online services offer shopping, travel arrangements, and more.

> **Shareware** Software that is not marketed commercially and is usually made available through online services and BBS systems. You can try out the software, and if you like it, you send a fee to the creator and register your copy. Some software is freeware—yes, free!

Sending and Receiving Faxes

If you have a special type of modem called a fax/modem, you can also use your PC to send and receive faxes. If you have this type of modem, you can send any document you create on the PC to any other type of fax machine (another computer with a fax/modem or a regular fax machine). However, with a computer fax, you cannot cut out today's cartoon and fax it to your mom at work.

You can receive faxes from any type of machine, a regular fax machine or a computer fax/modem. That means if your mom has a regular fax machine at work, she can send you a comic she cut from the paper. Your computer receives the fax and displays it on-screen or prints it. (Read more about buying a fax/modem later in this chapter.)

> Remember that with your computer's fax/modem, you can't fax just any picture or article you want to pass on to someone else. You can only fax PC document files.

Jump on the Internet

The Internet, the most popular communication "roadway," is kind of like an online service. You can do the same things (send messages, download files, chat with other online users), but it's different in a lot of ways.

The Internet isn't controlled by one company or person; there is not one central computer. Instead, the Internet is a network of networks, including networks for universities, businesses, libraries, government agencies, and more. Once you hook up to one network, you can navigate through to other networks.

The Internet was started in the 1970s as a way of keeping Defense Department networks up and running in the case of war. Other networks started tapping in and got

What do you call a person that is addicted to the computer and telecommunicating? A **mouse potato.**

connected, and now there are over 15,000 networks available on the Internet. Wow! Think of all the data you can collect and people you can meet. That's the cool thing.

The uncool thing is that it can be kind of difficult to get around one network, let alone 15,000. That's why you'll see many services for hooking up and many programs (for example, Mosaic) for getting around the Internet.

What You Need to Telecommunicate

Does all this sound like too much fun? If you're interested, here's what you need to telecommunicate: a modem, communications software, and a telephone line.

You Need a Modem...

Modem stands for MOdulator/DEModulator and is an electronic hardware component you use to hook your PC up to your phone line. The modem is necessary because phone lines and computers don't speak the same language. You can think of the modem as a translator.

Whereas the computer works with digital information, phone lines transmit information using analog signals (or sound waves). When you send a message, the modem on your computer translates the digital information to analog signals (modulates) and sends the analog information over the phone lines. The receiving modem then translates the analog signals back to digital information (demodulates)

You'll learn how to make an intelligent modem-buying decision later in this chapter.

...A Telephone Line...

To make the connection, your modem must be hooked up to a telephone line—just a regular phone line, nothing special. You can install and use a separate dedicated phone line just for the modem, or you can use an existing phone line. If you use an existing phone line, you'll have another person/thing contending for time on the phone line: the computer. If your phone is already tied up all the time, you might be better off considering a separate line.

...And Software

To manage the communication between the modem and the computer (make sure everything is going okay), you need a communications program. A communications program dials the phone, makes sure the data you sent gets there intact, and may include other features.

Sometimes a modem comes with communications software. You can also purchase communications software separately. One of the most popular communications programs is called ProComm Plus.

Selecting a Modem

If you're still reading, you must be interested in adding a modem to your system shopping list. There are a couple strategies for buying a modem.

First, you can look for a system that comes with a modem. Beware, though. Sometimes manufacturers throw in modems for free with poorly equipped computers they're trying to get rid of. If the PC comes with a modem, make sure it's up to your standards in all the other important areas. Don't let the free modem influence your decision.

Second, you can purchase the system and modem at the same time, but as separate components. This way you can select the exact modem and system you want, instead of having an arranged marriage. Ask about having the modem installed if it's an internal model.

Third, remember that you can always add a modem later. Adding a modem is covered in Chapter 26. The rest of this section explains what to look for when comparing modems.

What Makes One Modem Racier Than Another

The key difference in modems is speed: how quickly they can send and receive data. Speed is important because when you are exchanging shareware game files with Aunt Millie out in Nevada, you are racking up long distance charges. Also, many online services charge by the time you spend using the service. The faster the modem, the quicker you can get on and off, and the less expensive the call will be.

Modem speed is measured in bits per second (bps) and ranges from 2400 to 28,800. The current standard is 14,400, so that's your best bet (unless, of course, you want to spring for the top-of-the-line 28,800).

Keep in mind that your modem can only work as fast as the modem it's talking to. If you have a 14,400 bps modem and call a 2400 bps modem, you can only send information at the 2400 bps speed.

Internal or External?

Modems also differ in how they are connected to the PC. An external modem sits on your desk and hooks up to one of your serial ports. (See Chapter 11 for more information on ports.) External modems are easier to hook up, plus you get to see little flashing lights as you transmit data. For this, you pay more for an external modem.

Internal modems are expansion cards that you plug into an available slot inside your PC. These are harder to install, have no fancy lights, and are usually cheaper than their desktop counterparts.

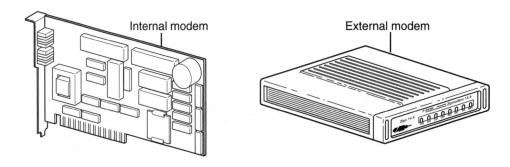

Internal modem   External modem

External and internal modems.

Standards, Compatibility, and Other Stuff

After making the two big choices (speed and internal/external), you can use some fine distinctions as a comparison. Here are some other factors you should consider:

➤ **Data compression**   Data compression makes the data you are sending smaller, so the transmission takes less time. Some modems offer data compression features. You may see data compression standards advertised as V.32 bis, V.42 bis, and MNP 5. MNP 5 is okay.

➤ **Compatibility**   The company that set the standard (called the AT command set) for modem communication was called Hayes. Because most modems and communication programs follow this standard, be sure to get a Hayes-compatible modem. (You may see this advertised as Hayes-compatible or as supporting the AT command set.)

➤ **Error correction**   Phone lines aren't perfect; you can have a scratchy connection or worse. To make sure the data is transmitted correctly, most modems and software follow protocols (standards) for checking the transmission. Advertisements will often give such CCITT standards as V.32 or V.42. Look for a modem with V.42.

➤ **Free software**   To get the modem to work, you have to have communications software. You can get software from many sources. Many modems come bundled with software, and many programs (such as Microsoft Works or Windows itself) include simple communication programs. Or you can purchase software designed specifically for communication.

Buying a Fax/Modem

Many modems sold today are both a modem and a fax machine (a fax/modem). You can use this type of modem to send and receive faxes.

When Is a Fax/Modem a Good Idea?

If you already have a fax machine, you may not need a fax/modem. Why have two pieces of equipment that do the same job? Plus, if you have to fax documents *not* created on the PC (for example, handwritten orders), you won't benefit from a fax/modem.

On the other hand, if you fax mostly letters or memos you type on the PC and you don't have a fax/modem, you'll probably want to consider this type of modem. Or if the modem and fax/modem cost the same, you might as well get the fax/modem. Fax/modems also offer these advantages over regular fax machines:

➤ You can automate your faxes; that is, you can send them when long distance rates are low.

➤ Fax/modemed documents look better. For example, when Joe carries his double-cheeseburger, large Coke, and his fax down the hall and then sends the Coke-stained, greasy fax through the regular fax machine, all the document's imperfections are transmitted. The document may look blurry and, in Joe's case, have huge grease splotches. With a fax/modem, Joe can get all the grease he wants on the keyboard or monitor; the document will still transmit clean and clear.

➤ Fax/modems are ideal for portable computers. You can fax from anywhere you are traveling.

How a Fax/Modem Works

A fax/modem works like a regular modem. You use the telephone line to call up another fax machine or computer and then transmit data. However, with a fax/modem, you can send only computer documents.

Basically, you create the document and then "print" to the fax machine. The fax software (yes, you need software for the fax too) translates the document into a picture and sends the picture over the phone lines. The receiving fax then prints the fax. If the receiving fax is a fax/modem, the receiver can choose to print the fax or just display it.

What's Different About a Fax/Modem?

The information you read in the modem section about data speed, error checking, and compression features all pertain to the component. Therefore, you should check out all of the same features when buying a fax/modem. Also, be sure the fax can both send and receive faxes. (Some older faxes could just send. What's the use?!) Finally, if the fax/modem comes bundled with software, check out the fax software that's included. If there isn't any included, you can purchase a fax software program. The most popular is WinFax Pro.

The Least You Need to Know

Phone lines are everywhere! You can use your computer, a modem, and a telephone line to use these phone lines to travel the world.

➤ With the proper equipment, you can send messages, send and receive files, and send and receive faxes. You can connect to a single computer, a BBS (informal network), or an online service.

➤ The Internet is the most popular communication "roadway" and is actually a network of networks, including networks for universities, businesses, libraries, government agencies, and more. Unlike an online service, the Internet is not run by one main person, company, or computer.

➤ To telecommunicate, you need a modem, communications software, and a telephone line. You can use a dedicated phone line or have a separate line installed.

➤ The most important difference among modems is the speed, which is measured in bits per second (bps). The current standard is 14,400 bps. Modems also offer different data compression and error checking features.

➤ Most modems sold today are actually a combination of modem and fax machine. You can use the fax/modem to send and receive faxes.

Chapter 16

More Drives!

In This Chapter

➤ What other kinds of computer drives are there?

➤ Backing up with a tape drive

➤ Buying a tape drive

➤ Storing huge files

You already know that you need a hard drive and a floppy drive. Is that all? For many users, yes. For other users, other drive types may pop onto the shopping list. This chapter covers some other drive types you may want to consider.

Drive Types to Know

Here's a quick rundown of all the different PC drive types:

➤ **Hard drives** You need a hard drive to store your programs and data; a hard drive is a must. Picking a hard drive is covered in Chapter 7. Adding a second hard drive is covered in Chapter 24.

➤ **Floppy drives** To get the programs and data onto and off of the hard drive, you need at least one floppy drive. Floppy drives are the topic of Chapter 8.

➤ **CD-ROM drive** To run multimedia presentations and software, you need a CD-ROM drive. More and more often, this type of drive is becoming a standard hardware component. Selecting a CD-ROM drive is covered in Chapter 12. Adding a CD-ROM drive is covered in Chapter 25.

➤ **Tape drive** To safeguard your data, you should make an extra copy of the data—a backup copy. Although you can backup to another hard drive or to floppy disks, if you have a lot to back up, you may want to consider a tape backup drive. This type of drive makes it easier and faster to back up data. Read more about tape backup drives later in this chapter.

➤ **Other drives** As technology advances, the program files and data files used in that technology get bigger and bigger and bigger. For example, a computer-generated illustration in four colors is probably too big to fit on a floppy disk. To make it easy to transport and store large files, you may consider a different type of drive, such as an optical drive, that can read and write data. These are covered later in this chapter.

Backing Up Quick with a Tape Drive

Suppose you keep your entire accounting system on a computer. You have all the related payroll, accounts receivable, accounts payable, tax files, and other accounting information easily managed on the system. Then the system crashes. What do you do when your accountant comes around?

Hopefully, you have a backup copy of all the data. Then you simply restore the backup copy and all is well. If you don't have a backup copy, well, I hope you kept good paper copies.

Because backups are so important (especially for businesses that need to update their backups daily), a different type of drive, called a tape backup, was developed to make backups easier.

 Tape drives aren't replacements for floppy or hard drives! The files are stored in sequence on the tape, and it takes the drive a long time to locate a particular file. Think of how long it takes you to locate a song on a cassette tape versus a compact disc!

Instead of backing up to floppy disks, you can back up to a magnetic tape. What are the advantages?

➤ The tape can hold hundreds to thousands of megabytes. You can fit the contents of a hard drive on one tape.

➤ The tapes are portable, so you can take the data with you. They aren't designed to make it easy to transfer files from one system to another, but they do make it easy to have one tape of your data for safekeeping at another location.

➤ Backing up with a tape backup drive is faster than backing up to floppies. And it's more convenient. You can schedule a backup during the night, when no one is using the computer.

Buying a Tape Drive

If you decide you want to buy a tape drive, you'll have some decisions to make. How much do you need to back up, and how fast? Do you want an internal or external drive? What type of tape drive do you need? The following sections will help you answer some of these questions.

Fill It Up! Data Capacity

If you look at advertisements for tape backup drives, you'll see a spec for the amount of data a single tape can store—for example, a 120MB or 250MB tape drive. The lower capacity drives are cheaper and are a good deal if you have less than their capacity's amount of data to back up. For instance, a person with a 100MB hard disk doesn't need a 250MB tape drive; a 120MB drive would do nicely.

If you have a lot of data to back up, however, consider the larger capacity drive. It will mean changing tapes less frequently during the backup.

Data Transfer Rate: How Fast Can It Go?

Tape backup ads also include the transfer rate (that is, how fast the drive can copy the data to the tape). This speed is measured in megabytes per minute; the higher the rating, the faster the drive. You'll find drives as slow as 2.2MB per minute and as fast as 9.5MB per minute. Cost will be your deciding factor. Again, you'll have to do some math to figure out how long your backup will take and decide how fast is fast enough.

Drive Types: Quarter-Inch or Helical?

In addition to comparing speed and size, you'll want to decide on the drive type. There are two types of drives: a quarter-inch tape drive and a helical scan tape drive.

The quarter-inch model uses a tape that is one-quarter inch wide (hence the name). DC2000 drives use a single head, and DC6000 drives use two heads. The advantage of the second head is that the tape can be formatted (prepared for use) as the data is backed up. The cartridges for these two types are different sizes, so you can't accidentally use the wrong type.

QIC (quarter-inch committee)   The industry standard you see associated with this type of drive. Usually, the format (or number of megabytes of uncompressed data you can back up) follows QIC, as in QIC-80.

Quarter-inch drives are rather inexpensive, starting at around $150. You can expect to pay around $15 to $20 for the tapes.

A helical scan drive uses a different method for storing information on the tape. These drives have greater capacity, are faster, and (you guessed it) are more expensive.

One type of drive, the 8mm tape drive, uses technology that was an offshoot of VCR technology. The other type of drive, 4mm DATA (digital audio tape), uses small tapes that measure 3" by 2" by 3/8". You can expect to pay $1,500 or more for a helical scan tape drive, and tapes run $25 to $40.

Other Drives for Handling Big Files

You may be considering another type of drive to store (and possibly transport) big files. You cannot write data to a CD-ROM, so you cannot use it for storage. They handle big files very well, but remember that a CD-ROM drive uses a laser to read data and that you can do only that—*read* data. However, there are other types of drives that enable you to store large files.

Bernoulli Drive

A Bernoulli drive is a combination of hard disk and floppy disk drive. It's a removable hard disk that plugs into a special disk drive and stores a lot more data than a floppy disk (90MB and 150MB are probably the most popular). Instead of storing the data sequentially (as with a tape), the data is stored and accessed randomly (as with a hard or floppy disk). That means you can use it to find and retrieve data. The disks are removable, so you can take the disk with you or pop in a new one when it's full. Expect to pay from $400 to $800 for this type of drive.

Similar in concept is the SyQuest drive, which is gaining in popularity.

Optical Drives

Just as the CD-ROM drive uses a laser to read data, an optical drive can use a laser to write data. This type of disk/drive combination can store a lot of data on a removable disk. The two most common types are floptical and magneto-optical drives.

Think of the floptical as a floppy optical (get the name?). Floptical drives cost approximately $500. The disks cost about $20 and can store approximately 20MB of data. These drives are also fast.

Magneto-optical (M-O) drives use a combination of laser and magnetic technology to store and access data. These types of drives are expensive: expect to pay $3,000 or more. But you can store a heap of information on the disks—1GB on one $50 to $250 disk.

ZIP Drives

The latest entry into the market is the ZIP drive by Iomega. Costing around $200, this type of drive can copy up to 100MB of information on a single floppy-style disk. Disks come in two sizes: 25MB ($9.95) and 100MB ($20).

Making a Choice

Deciding which type of drive is right for you depends on how much you want to spend and how much data you need to store. For the least amount of money, consider an Iomega or SyQuest drive. If you have a ton of data to store, consider a magnetic optical drive.

The Least You Need to Know

Most people will get by with a hard drive, a floppy drive, and probably a CD-ROM drive. In some special circumstances, you may want to consider another drive type.

➤ If you have a lot of data to back up, you may want to consider a tape backup unit. This type of drive backs up data sequentially to a tape, and this method enables you to store more data faster.

➤ Tape backup drives differ in the amount of data they can store on one tape as well as in how fast they can transfer the data (measured in megabytes per minute). You'll have to decide how big and how fast you want the drive to be.

➤ You can buy a quarter-inch backup tape drive or a helical scan tape backup drive. The latter is faster and can store more, but costs more money.

➤ A Bernoulli box is a combination hard disk and floppy disk drive. It stores data on a high capacity removable disk. You can access the data quickly (unlike data stored on a tape).

➤ Optical drives use a combination of laser and magnetic technology to store data. Floptical drives run around $500, and the disks for these drives cost around $20 for 20MB of storage. The magneto-optical (M-O) drives are expensive ($3,000 or more). You can store up to 1GB on these disks.

155

Chapter 17

Goodies
and Gadgets

In This Chapter

➤ Scanning pictures and words

➤ Becoming the next great rock star

➤ Watching TV on the PC on the QT

➤ Talking to your computer

There's so much new technology entering the market every day. And it keeps getting better and better. It's nearly impossible to keep up with it all!

It used to be a futuristic fantasy to have a computer that would recognize your spoken commands—it was even on "Star Trek." But now there are sound cards with voice-recognition features that recognize 40 or so commands that you speak into the microphone. Dictation systems that can be used to enter letters are on the horizon too, and that's just the beginning. There are dozens of exciting new ways to get pictures and words into your PC.

This chapter covers some of the cool, special-purpose things you can do with your PC. You may not want these devices right away, but you might find a use for them down the road a bit.

Scanning Pictures and Words

Sometimes you may wish there was a way to get something out *here* (outside the PC) into *there* (inside the PC). For example, you may want to include a family picture in your annual Christmas newsletter, or you may want a quick way to enter a typed document without retyping it.

You can do these things with a hardware component called a *scanner*. Scanners vary in price from a simple hand-held scanner that sells for $200 to a copier-style color scanner that sells for $1,000 or more. Depending on what you want to do, you can select a scanner to suit your fancy.

Reasons to Get a Scanner

First, decide whether you *need* a scanner or whether it would just be a fancy toy. (Of course, if you have money to burn, having a fancy toy isn't a bad thing.) Ask yourself these questions: What do I want to do with the scanner? How often do I need a scanner? What type of scanner do I want, and how much will I pay?

The following scenarios describe cases in which a scanner would be useful:

➤ You are an artist and need a way to convert drawn images to computer images.

➤ You are a desktop publisher and need a way to incorporate photographs into your publications.

➤ You have lots and lots of typed documents that are not on computer files. You need a way to enter them quickly *without* retyping.

➤ You need a way to incorporate other written information (such as a signature) into a computer document.

➤ You just want to have some fun.

If any of these sound like you, read on to find out just what you can do with a scanner.

How a Scanner Works

A scanner works much like a photocopier: both measure light reflected off a page to create an image. While a photocopier creates the image on another page, the scanner creates an electronic image stored on the computer.

Here's how scanners differ:

➤ **Size/style** You can purchase a *hand-held* scanner or a *flatbed* scanner. The hand-held scanner is like a big T-shaped mouse that you drag across the image. Flatbed

158

scanners are like photocopiers and work the same way; you place the image on the bed and scan it.

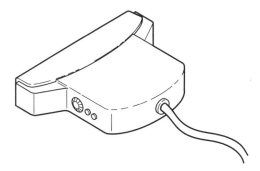

A hand-held scanner.

➤ **Resolution**   There's that term again. And again, it means the quality or crispness of the image. The image created by the scanner is actually a collection of dots. The more dots, the finer the image. As with printers, a scanner's resolution is measured in dpi or dots per inch (dpi). A good scanner should be capable of at least 300 dpi.

➤ **Colors**   You can purchase a color, gray-scale, or black-and-white scanner. Black-and-white scanners are the cheapest, but their capabilities are pretty limited. A gray-scale scanner can represent from 16 shades to 256 shades of gray. With a color scanner, the number of colors the scanner is able to recognize will be given as a bit number (8-bit, 16-bit, and so on) or a number of colors (256 colors).

If the quality of the scanned image is important to you (for instance, if you're going to be scanning important photos for your job), choose a flatbed scanner. If you just want to fool around with scanning, go with the inexpensive hand-held model.

Unfortunately, there are no easy answers for selecting a scanner. Look for what matches your needs. If you just need to trace line art, you can get by with an inexpensive hand-held black-and-white model. If you're doing four-color illustrations, you may need a more expensive color scanner with higher resolution. The next sections explain what to look for.

Buying a Scanner to Scan Pictures

A scanner is most often used to scan in pictures. You can scan in simple line drawings, full-color drawings, or photographs. The key here is the quality of the image that you need.

First, do you need color? If so, expect to pay from $500 to $2,500 for a good flatbed color scanner. Avoid the hand-held color scanners. If you're serious enough about scanning to need color, you're serious enough to get the better-quality flatbed model. Look for a scanner that provides 24-bit color.

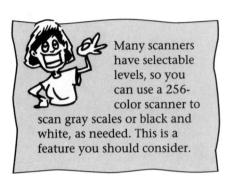

Many scanners have selectable levels, so you can use a 256-color scanner to scan gray scales or black and white, as needed. This is a feature you should consider.

If you don't need color, do you need gray-scale? In a gray-scale image, the colors are represented as shades of gray instead of actual colors. Most newspaper photographs, for example, are gray-scale images. Gray-scale scanners run from $200 to $2,000. If you don't need color or gray-scale, you can purchase a black-and-white scanner—the simplest, cheapest type of scanner. The minimum number of gray-scale levels you want is 256.

Second, what is the size and type of images you will scan? Imagine dragging a hand-held scanner over the image and photocopying the image. Which works better? Make your choice of scanner type accordingly. Also, keep in mind that your hand isn't as steady as you think. The quality of the image may not be as good with a hand-held scanner as with a flatbed scanner.

Third, do you need a high-quality image? Keep in mind that your output is going to be limited by your printer. If you have a 600 dpi scanner but only a 300 dpi printer, you'll only be able to print the image at 300 dpi.

Manipulating the Pictures

Most scanners provide software that enables you to save the file in several different formats. You can then plunk this file into another document, such as a word processing document. If you know exactly what program you want to use the picture in (for example, Word for Windows), check out what file formats that program accepts. Most scanning software enables you to save in a variety of formats, and most programs enable you to use a variety of formats, so you should be able to find a match.

If you want to manipulate the image (take the beer can out of Aunt Sunny's hand, for example), you need a program to do that. Adobe Photoshop is a popular program for manipulating scanned (and other) images.

Buying a Scanner to Scan Words

You can also use a scanner to scan in words and create a document from the words. In this case, you can get by with a simple scanner because you aren't concerned with the quality of the image.

The success of the scan (lack of mistakes) is determined by the software. To convert the image to text, you need optical character recognition (OCR) software. This software checks the scanned visual image against a table of characters and makes a pretty good guess at which letter is which. For typed documents in a plain font, the OCR software does a pretty good job. Handwritten documents, however, are too much of a challenge, although technology in this area has come a long way. (At one time, even typed text recognition was poor.)

There are a variety of OCR software programs available, ranging in price from $100 to $700.

> When selecting OCR software, look for one that points out the characters that it isn't sure about, instead of simply guessing. Also, make sure the software supports the scanner you are using.

Your Family Photo Album on the PC

Are all your photographs in a big shoe box under the bed? Do you wish you had a convenient way to keep these treasures safe and also to force others to look through your 1,000-picture montage of your trip to Dollywood? If so, you can purchase a special type of CD player (most are Photo CD compatible) and a scanner to scan in regular photographs. You can then play back these photographs on television using the CD drive. You probably guessed that Kodak is a leader in this new technology. They offer the Photo CD systems.

You can also use a digital camera to take digital pictures; the camera works the same. Shoot and snap. Instead of developing film, though, the camera translates the image into digital information that you can use on your computer.

> Right now there are a lot of competing technologies for photo CDs. Think of the competition between VHS and Betamax. Which format will win out hasn't really been determined. What that means to you is that you may be better off to wait a while to see which format becomes the leader before you purchase your photo equipment.

Watching TV on the PC

It used to be that the only way you could goof off on the PC was by playing games. Now with new TV/PC technology, you can actually watch TV right on your computer screen. So instead of working on that new budget, you can tune in to Oprah to see the show on cross-dressing alien Elvis impersonators. With a TV tuner board and a TV connection (from a broadcast antenna, cable TV, or VCR), you can watch TV in a small or full-size window on the PC screen.

The technology in this field is advancing quickly. At one time, the image from TV reception was poor and drained the system power. That's not true now. Soon you won't notice any difference between a TV show on the PC and one on the TV. Right now you can expect a PC video to output 30 frames per second, compared to 60 frames per second on broadcast TV (the more frames per second, the smoother the image).

 If you are shopping for a tuner board, make sure you buy one that lets you watch TV on the PC. There are also boards that go the other way: let you play PC images on the TV. Why would you want to do this? To create presentations or product demonstrations.

In addition to just watching TV, with some systems, you can capture, edit, and play back the video. You can have Beavis and Butt-head replace Dan Rather and Connie Chung on the nightly news. However, the more features that are included in the TV equipment, the more expensive the system.

If you are a TV nut, you can buy a PC that already has a TV tuner (many of the newer systems do) or you can buy a tuner board. The best way to pick a TV tuner board is to test it out at the store. The quality of the image, whether the TV window is resizable, and whether the image is smooth or jerky will vary from one board to another. Expect to pay $300 to $500 for the least expensive card and as much as $1,200 or more for the more powerful systems.

Sound and Music Accessories

If you have a sound card, you can play games. (What else matters after that?!) You can also do other useful things with the sound card. You can record voice messages with the microphone, you can use your PC as an answering machine, and you can even connect a keyboard and create your own music! Here's the lowdown on some of the coolest sound-related extras.

Answer the Phone!

Some newer systems come bundled with a telephone answering system. You can use the PC to answer the phone, to act as a speaker phone, and more. If you want to replace your current answering machine and use your PC, look for a system that incorporates this feature. If you want to add this feature, look for a sound card that also has answering machine capabilities.

Remember all the hype about the TV becoming a computer? Now it's starting to look the other way around. In the war between the TV and the PC, the PC is gaining more ground as the all-in-one machine for a family. Can your TV answer the phone? Can your TV record music?

Ordering Your PC Around

Like some of the other things we've discussed in this chapter, voice recognition software is quickly gaining ground. Right now you can purchase a $200 sound card with a speech recognizer that understands 40 or more commands. You can even create your own voice commands (such as Bold or Open) that work in Windows programs.

It's still hard to get the PC to recognize all the words in a vocabulary in order to do something as complex as entering text you dictate. But there are busy bees working right now, making advances in this area. Expect more powerful voice recognition applications in the future. For example, DragonDictate sells a $995 version of its dictation software that is pretty effective. Pretty soon you'll be saying, "Take a letter, PC."

Playing Music on the PC: You Are Beethoven!

Do you have any musical talent? Do you dream of jamming onstage with the Red Hot Chili Peppers? Do you think you could compose the next Grammy-award winning song? Even if you don't have any talent at all, you can use the PC to play and compose music.

When you are using the PC to create music, you will most often be working with MIDI (musical instrument digital interface) files. This type of file stores music data, such as which notes are playing when. It's basically a language that enables one piece of equipment to play back notes made by another.

What this means to you is that you can attach music synthesizers to your MIDI port (most sound cards have a MIDI port) and create beautiful music. You can purchase keyboards that let you play ragtime Jazz tunes (expect to pay $700 or more for a keyboard). If you have a lot of money, you can also add other musical equipment. Also, to manage all that music, you need a sequencer that enables you to edit the recorded sound. Think of the sequencer as a word processor for music.

If you are interested in playing music, you'll need to be extra careful when selecting your sound card. Some don't offer MIDI features, and some offer only mediocre MIDI features. Test out the sound card using a MIDI device to see whether the recording and playback are acceptable.

The Least You Need to Know

You haven't even begun to see all the things you can do with a PC. Every year brings new technology with new, sometimes practical, sometimes just cool products.

➤ You can buy a scanner to scan in words or pictures. Scanners vary in the type (hand-held or flatbed), in the resolution, and in the color (color, gray-scale, or black-and-white). To decide which type is appropriate for you, think about the type and quality of images that you need.

➤ With OCR (optical character recognition software), you can use a scanner and the software to scan in and convert hard copy documents to text documents. You'll still have to check the document because the software isn't always correct in its translation.

➤ With a TV tuner board and a TV connection, you can watch TV on your PC. You can buy a system that comes with this feature, or you can purchase a TV tuner board separately.

➤ Voice-recognition software is advancing quickly. Currently, you can buy a sound card with capabilities that enables you to use 40 or so commands. For example, you can program the commands to tell a Windows word processing program to make something bold or to open a file. Dictation systems are also on the market.

➤ If you have a sound card with a MIDI port, you can attach MIDI devices (such as a music keyboard) and record, edit, and play back music. You can attach more sophisticated components and use a program called a sequencer to create music.

Chapter 18

Accessorizing Your PC

In This Chapter

➤ Buying software

➤ Avoiding eye, wrist, and back strain

➤ Keeping the PC fed (disks, power supply, and so on)

➤ Consumables for the printer

➤ Other goodies

You're just about done with your shopping list. Is it as long as your arm? Well, make some more room because there are bound to be some little things you'll forget, such as disks, paper, and even a place to park your new PC.

This chapter covers some of the extras to consider purchasing while you're in the spending mood. All you budget-minded people, get out your calculators. The little stuff can add up.

Don't Forget the Software

Way, way back in Chapter 2, you took the first step toward buying a PC: you decided what you wanted to do with the PC. In essence, you decided then what types of software programs you're going to need. Having read from Chapter 2 to here, you now know the system you need for those programs (I hope!). So go back to step 1 and be sure you've included programs on the list. Without software, the PC is going to be as boring as a Congressional hearing.

You may get some software free with the system; that's great if you *need* the software. If you don't need it or won't use it, it's not as valuable to you as the salesperson says. You may also want to buy some software when you buy the hardware.

Picking Your Furniture

When you finally do make that final step and actually buy and bring home the PC, you may not have thought about where to put it. On the kitchen table? On your grandfather's antique desk? It's important to have the "right" furniture, furniture that enables you to comfortably use your PC.

Set It Down!

The first thing you need is a desk or some other flat surface for the PC. You can pick any flat surface you want, but consider the following things when deciding where to place and position your computer equipment:

➤ When you look at the monitor, it should be at eye level. You shouldn't have to crane your neck up or down to view the screen. If the monitor is too low, you can try setting it on the PC if you have a desktop model. Phone books work pretty well too, and some desks have a little shelf for the monitor.

Some computer desks provide little cubbyholes for everything. You can invest in one of these, but be sure your system fits. Your 15-inch monitor isn't going to fit in that 14-inch monitor cubby, no matter how hard you shove.

➤ When you type, your hands should be parallel to the floor. That means you shouldn't crimp your wrists way up or way down. Hold your fingers out straight. Your keyboard should fit right under your fingers. Why is this so important? Because you can develop RSI (repetitive stress injuries, such as carpal tunnel syndrome) if you strain your fingers or wrists.

➤ When all your hardware is on the desk, you'll also want some room for your stuff, unless you want to balance everything on your lap. You'll need some desktop room, as well as some drawers to cram all your other various supplies in.

166

Don't assume that every piece of furniture that's marketed as a computer desk is automatically a comfortable, roomy place to set your computer. Some of them are too high and will force your wrists up into an uncomfortable position as you type. Before you buy, make sure you sit at the desk with your body positioned exactly as it will be when you use the computer.

Don't forget to have space for the printer. You may have room for the printer on the desk, or you may need a separate printer stand. Keep in mind that the printer and PC are connected by a cable, which means you can't have the PC in the den and the printer on a table in the dining room, unless you have a really long cable.

You can't plan on having a long cable that connects a parallel printer to your computer. Parallel cables can't be longer than 15 feet because they lose their reliability. If you really must put the printer far away from the computer, you need a serial printer. Chapter 14 describes printers and their interfaces.

Have a Seat

The next important item is the chair. You'll have to find the perfect chair: one that isn't too soft or too hard, but just right. "Just right" means you can easily adjust the height and armrests so your eyes and fingers are in the proper positions. Also, look for one that is comfortable and provides some back support. Try sitting in the chairs at the office supply store—all of them. The clerks may give you dirty looks, but just ignore them.

Picking Out Disks

When you buy software, you'll have the disks it came on (unless it came on a CD, of course). You should also buy some blank disks so you can make copies of your files or take files with you. For example, if you transport data from your work PC to your home PC, you'll need some disks. You'll also need disks if you want to share your data with others (for example, if you wanted to send a disk version of your romantic/ thriller/how-to/self-help book to an editor). Some people make backup copies of their software disks too, in case anything should happen to the originals.

One of the first things to do is make an emergency boot disk. If something goes wrong with your computer, you can use the boot disk to start the PC and see if you can diagnose and fix the problem. Think of the boot disk as an emergency startup key. You can read more on boot disks in Chapter 23.

If you have more than one drive type (for instance, a 5 1/4" drive and a 3 1/2" drive), buy disks for the 3 1/2" drive. These disks tend to be more durable than their 5 1/4" counterparts.

Disks range in price from about $5 for a box of ten double-density disks to around $10 for a box of ten preformatted high-density disks. Be sure to get the disk type that matches your drive type. (See Chapter 8 for an explanation of floppy disk sizes.)

To keep your disks organized, you may also want to buy a disk holder. Disks multiply quickly. Instead of cramming them in drawers and cabinets and shoe boxes, buy a disk holder and cram them all in one convenient place. You can get a disk holder for $5 to $10.

Power Strip

As I mentioned in Chapter 11, you'll most likely want to purchase a power strip so that you can plug all the equipment into one place. You'll have to plug in the PC, the monitor, and the printer—minimum. If you have other external equipment (for example, a desk lamp or an external modem), you may need to plug these pieces in as well.

If you're really concerned about power surges, get an uninterruptible power supply, as covered in Chapter 11.

Don't just buy an ordinary power strip, get one with surge protection. Remember that your equipment and data are fragile. One lightning strike or surge of power through the power lines, and BOOM! There goes the hard disk. A surge suppressor can protect against this type of damage.

Printer Supplies You'll Need

To use your printer, you're going to need a few supplies, paper being the most obvious. Check this printing supply list:

➤ **A cable** To hook up the printer to the PC, you need a cable. Sometimes the printer comes with a cable, but you often have to purchase the cable separately. Ask your salesperson. Make sure you get the right kind (parallel or serial) with the right connectors for your equipment on each end.

➤ **Paper** To do any printing, you're going to need paper. Depending on the type, quality, and quantity of paper you use, the price is going to vary. I pay about $20 for a case (10 reams) of laser printer paper. It's cheaper in the long run to buy an entire case—and more convenient, too.

➤ **Printer stand** In addition to finding space for the computer, you will also have to find a place to put your printer. The printer must be close enough to the computer to connect it via a cable. You may be able to purchase a computer desk with an area designed specifically for the printer, or you can purchase a separate printer stand.

➤ **Ribbon, ink cartridges, or toner cartridges**   Depending on the type of printer you purchase, you will eventually need to replace the thing that makes the ink. On a dot-matrix printer, that's a ribbon (running from $4 to $20 depending on the ribbon type). Inkjet printers use print cartridges that cost from $12 to $25. If you have a laser printer, you use toner cartridges, which cost $50 or more. You won't need a new ribbon or cartridge right away, but you will soon enough. I just wanted to remind you!

➤ **Printer cover**   If you purchase a dot-matrix printer and it is loud (they can be), you can purchase a sound-deadening cover to stifle the noise. Regardless of which type of printer you have, if you are in a really dusty place, you might also want to purchase dust covers for your hardware.

Other Goodies to Covet

There's always *something* else to buy. Whether you really need these other items or whether they are of any use to you is your call. Here are some other things to consider.

Extras for the Monitor

If your monitor reflects a lot of glare, you can buy a cheap glare screen to put over the monitor (around $20). Or if you have money to blow, you can get a really expensive antiglare glass filter ($60).

But wait, that's not all you can get that falls into the category of monitor accessories. You can also buy a clip (for approximately $4) that clips onto the monitor and holds copy, making it easier to type from hard copy. However, for a modest $20, you can buy a plastic copy holder that sits on your desk and does the same thing.

A Pad for the Mouse

Of course, you don't want to scratch up your mouse's belly (the exposed roller ball under the mouse), so it's a good idea to use a mouse pad. A mouse pad is a thick piece of wetsuit-like material that keeps your mouse's tummy protected and makes it easy to slide the mouse around.

Ask your salesperson to throw in a mouse pad free with your computer (or just spend the $2 to get a cheap one). If you are really into designer accessories, you can purchase a mouse pad with a famous painting on it, such as the Mona Lisa or part of the Sistine Chapel. Expect to pay around $20 for a designer pad.

A Rest Stop for Your Wrists

To protect your wrists and prevent incorrect positioning and excess stress, you may want to invest in a $5 to $10 wrist pad. This pad, like a mouse pad, is a thick piece of material that sits in front of the keyboard. You rest your wrists on the pad to keeping from having to arch them up as you type.

Cleaning and Maintenance Supplies

If you plan to do any upgrading, you can buy a tool kit with all the cute little screw-drivers you need to open the system case and add something new (such as a new hard disk). These usually have some handy special-purpose tools too, such as a chip inserter. More on tool kits in Chapter 23.

You can also purchase a disk drive cleaner, a vacuum to vacuum out your system unit, pre-moistened towelettes to clean the monitor, and other cleaning supplies.

Books...Like This One!

No matter what you want to do with your PC, there is surely a book about it. Alpha Books, the makers of the fine volume you hold in your hands, publishes books especially for the new or casual computer user. Here are some titles you might enjoy:

The Complete Idiot's Guide to PCs, by Joe Kraynak

The Complete Idiot's Guide to Windows, by Paul McFedries

The Home Computer Companion, by Clayton Walnum and John Pivovarnick

The Complete Idiot's Guide to the Internet, by Peter Kent

There are lots more titles than those listed here! You can call 1-800-428-5331 and request a catalog for full details.

The Least You Need to Know

Don't rush out just yet to buy that PC. You need to make sure your list is complete. You can purchase extra supplies that run from the absolutely necessary to the frivolous.

➤ To make your PC do something productive, you need software. Don't forget to include your software programs on your shopping list.

➤ You'll need comfortable, functional furniture: a flat surface for the computer and the printer and a chair for you.

➤ You should select and arrange the furniture so that the monitor is eye level and the keyboard is positioned so that when you type, your hands are parallel to the floor.

➤ To make copies of your work or to take files with you from one place to another, you need some disks. Buy the disk type that matches your drive.

➤ Get a power strip that provides surge protection to protect yourself from electrical problems that could fry your PC and your data.

➤ To use your printer, you'll need a cable to connect the PC and the printer, as well as some paper. You may also consider a printer cover, a printer stand, and extra supplies.

Part 4
Making the Purchase

Your shopping list is complete, and you're ready to step out the door. But where are you headed? Where is the best place to shop? How do you decide which brand to buy? How do you deal with the salespeople?

This part covers taking that final plunge: going to the store, taking out your cash, and making the purchase.

Doing Your Homework

Do you fancy yourself as a private investigator, a PI? If so, you'll like this chapter. In this chapter, you do some snooping around—some footwork, if you will. Scope out the local news to get a sense of the systems you are hunting. Then stalk the prey in your local computer stores. And finally, interrogate anyone associated with the prey (which is the computer).

Why the investigation? To help you find out what's on the market and to find out what others think and recommend.

The Tower of Babel: Computer Magazines

Want to feel like a complete idiot? Open a computer magazine and try to make sense out of some of the articles. Here are a few headlines from a recent edition of a popular industry publication:

Novell Chooses OpenDoc: Company Plans Distributed Object Repository

PCI-IDE Controller, Host Adapter Announced

Does Santa Claus Have a World Wide Web Home Page?

Wow! You need a crib sheet just to understand the articles. Still, reviewing a few computer magazines can teach you the "flavor" of what's available. You can get an idea of the systems and software available, as well as the pricing. Plus, you can see what you do know (which by now may be more than you think) and what you don't know.

Here's a suggested plan for using a magazine:

1. Pick up a magazine that looks easy...well, easier than the others. Look for a magazine geared toward beginners, such as *PC Novice*. You may want to buy more than one.

2. Flip through the pages. What topics are covered? What seems to be the main thrust of the articles (read the summary blurbs)? If there are any articles of interest, flag them. Also, flag the system reviews. Most magazines review systems in each edition.

3. Flip through the pages and read the ads to get an idea of what systems are offered at what prices. You can also see what software is available. Tear out a few advertisements to use for the next section—the test!

4. Look at the reviews but don't read them in their entirety. Usually the review summarizes the strengths and weaknesses of the system.

Most reviews include some sort of lab test (such as how many seconds it takes to calculate the national budget using a spreadsheet or how long it took to spell check the Gettysburg Address). You don't need to bother with these petty distinctions. Instead, read the summaries.

5. Look for the editor's picks (seal of approval, best buy, or some other "Good Housekeeping" selection). In most reviews, the editor picks a favorite. That doesn't mean you have to pick the same system, but be sure to see who manufactures it. Who manufactures the most often-picked machines? This usually indicates which manufacturer creates a good dependable system.

6. Skim the help sections. Most magazines usually include one or several columns devoted to answering user questions. Glance around for hardware problems that relate to a particular system. For example, if you read 12 letters that tell of problems with DOA Computers, make a note not to buy that brand.

After you review the magazine, you can test yourself to see how many specs you can decode (see the next section "The Tower of Babel II: Computer Advertisements").

The Tower of Babel II: Computer Advertisements

When you are checking out the advertisements, tear out a few and then see if you can decode them. Here's a sample system advertisement:

XPS P75

➤ Pentium processor, 75MHz system

➤ Tower model

➤ 8MB RAM

➤ 340MB Hard Drive (13 ms)

➤ VS15 Monitor (15")

➤ 64-bit PCI 1MB RAM video card

➤ 256KB Cache

➤ 3.5" Diskette Drive

➤ Spacesaver keyboard

➤ Microsoft mouse

➤ MS-DOS 6.2 and Microsoft Windows 3.1

➤ $1,999

Place a check mark next to the lines of the advertisement that you know. How many do you understand? Good for you! Circle the ones that you don't understand. Use the following table as an answer sheet. Then, for those you don't understand, review the chapters of this book that cover that component.

Line Number	Explanation
Line 1	The product name for this computer system.
Line 2	The type and speed of the microprocessor. See Chapter 5 for more information on this topic.

continues

177

continued

Line Number	Explanation
Line 3	The style of the case. Case styles are covered in Chapter 11.
Line 4	The amount of memory. See Chapter 6 for more information on memory.
Line 5	The size (340MB) and speed (13 ms) of the hard drive. Sometimes you will also see the controller type (for example, IDE) included. Flip to Chapter 7 for the hard stuff on hard disks.
Lines 6 and 7	The type of monitor and size (15-inch) and video card (64-bit PCI card with 1MB of memory). For more on monitors, see Chapter 9.
Line 8	The size of the disk cache (256KB).
Line 9	The size of the disk drive (3 1/2"). Chapter 8 includes all you need to know about floppy disk drives.
Lines 10 and 11	The type of keyboard and mouse.
Line 12	The software included with the system.
Line 13	The price.

The advertisement may include other information, such as the number of expansion slots or drive bays. If the system includes additional equipment (a CD-ROM drive, a sound card, or a fax/modem), that component will also be listed, possibly with some "spec." For example, if the system includes a double-speed CD, you may see "2X CD-ROM" in the advertisement.

As you read computer magazines, tear out advertisements of systems that interest you. Then you'll have something with which to compare when you decide which brand and model to purchase.

Snooping Around Computer Stores

Don't stop at reading magazines. You should also stop by the computer stores in your area. As you will read in the next chapter, you can buy a computer from many different places now: an electronics store, a wholesale club, or a department store (for starters). To do your snooping, pick a computer superstore if there is one nearby or a computer dealer. You'll find the most knowledgeable salespeople at these stores. Well…you *should* anyway.

Quizzing the Salesperson

There's no tried-and-true test for finding a good salesperson. You may find that the teenager at Best Buy knows more than the older guy at the computer superstore. Plus, since you may be a beginning computer user, you may think you can't even judge who knows what. But you can.

Ask the salesperson a lot of questions. If the person explains concepts in terms you can understand, he probably knows about computers. If that person can't explain the concepts, or he sticks to a repetition of the specs, he doesn't understand it himself. ("It's a 66MHz," he says. "What is that?" you ask. "Well, it's a 66MHz.")

If you do find a good salesperson, ask what he recommends. Here are some questions to consider:

> Don't tell the salesperson how much money you want to spend (although that's probably one of the first questions the salesperson will ask). Price is certainly a consideration, but you don't want to make a purchase based solely on price. You want a computer that will meet your needs.

➤ What system would you recommend? Why?

➤ Do I need _____ component (fill in the blank)? What will it do for me?

➤ Which are your most reliable systems?

➤ Which systems have you had the most returns or repairs with?

➤ Do you have a computer? What kind?

➤ Which is your best-selling computer?

Getting Product Sheets

While you are visiting stores, pick up the "spec" sheets. Many stores put a one-page summary of the system next to the system. You can pick these up and take them home to compare. You can look through them to see if any of the systems match what you need, and you can compare systems and prices from store to store.

Test Drives!

Another good reason to visit a store is to try out different systems. When you try to narrow down exactly which system you want, you're going to be faced with lots of contenders (the next chapter covers how to select one model and brand). Sometimes the decision is going to boil down to one that you just plain liked better. (I saw an all black system that I really liked because of its sleekness!)

Try out the keyboard to see if you like one model better than another. Test the monitors; there's no better test of the monitors than your own eyes. Try the mouse. See which system case style you like. You don't have to buy the computer from the store in which you test it, but you can at least get a sense of what you like.

Dear Ann Landers: Which System Do You Recommend?

Another source of research and opinions are the people you know. Even though Uncle Charlie may be a grumpy old guy who cheats at cards, he may know something about computers since he uses one in his business. (On the other hand, he may not.) Still, you can ask anyone: co-workers, friends, family, people on the street. You don't have to take the advice you get, but you'll at least get a sense of what other people are using.

Ask these questions:

➤ What kind of system do you have?

➤ What do you like about it? What do you dislike?

➤ Have you had any problems? If you had a problem, did you get it fixed? How much trouble was it to get the computer fixed?

➤ Where did you buy the computer? Did you shop around? Why did you buy there?

➤ What type of system would you recommend?

Another source of help is your local computer society. At these high teas, computer geeks with pocket protectors debate VESA buses versus PCI buses, discuss the advantages of Oxydol over Purex, and then play chess. Just kidding. Although the concept sounds geeky, most computer societies are made up of people just like you. You can meet other users and ask for their recommendations. Check with your local library or the phone book for information about computer associations in your area.

 In addition to test driving the hardware components, you can try out different software programs to decide which ones you like. Take this opportunity to compare two similar programs: for example, see whether you like Word for Windows or WordPerfect for Windows better.

Ask other people that work in your field. For instance, if you are in the legal field, you may want to ask other law offices what type of system they have and what type of software they use. Doing so will give you an idea of the type of system and software common for your particular line of work.

The Least You Need to Know

When you buy a car, you don't go to the first car place and make a purchase. No, you do some research. You read *Consumer Reports*. You visit some stores. You quiz some salespeople. You should do the same when buying a PC.

➤ Start your research by buying a couple of computer magazines.

➤ Don't get overwhelmed with all of the magazine's details. Instead, skim the magazine. Which systems get the buyer's seal of approval? Which systems appear a lot in the help columns? What systems are advertised?

➤ Look through an advertisement and make sure you can decode all the specs listed. If you see something you don't understand, ask the salesperson or look it up in this book.

➤ Visit some computer stores and try out different systems and software. You can also ask the salesperson what he or she recommends.

➤ Ask others for their recommendations. Knock on some doors and get the dirt from anyone who has a computer. Doing so will give you a good idea of what people like about a particular system and what they don't like. You just *might* get some useful advice.

Taking the Plunge!

This is the moment of reckoning, the final step in buying a computer: actually making the purchase. By now, you should know exactly what you need. So you simply need to find a PC to match your wish list.

Where can you find your dream PC? Lots of places. How many PCs match your dream PC? Probably lots. Unfortunately, the work isn't quite done yet. You need to decide where to shop, and you need to decide which brand and model you want to purchase. Both of these topics are covered here.

Picking the Place to Shop

It used to be that you could buy a computer from only a few places, and there were only a few models. Not so any more. It almost seems like you could pick up a PC along with a bag of Doritos and a 12-pack at the Seven-Eleven. *Everyone* is selling PCs.

Pick the place you feel most comfortable with. If you pay a little more by shopping at a store you like, with that price comes the advantage of feeling secure with the store and its salespeople.

What's the best place to shop? It depends on what you want. Do you want the lowest prices? The best support? The most knowledgeable salespeople? The widest selection? Each place that sells PCs offers some combination of these things.

Here's a quick list of the main places you can buy a PC: computer dealers, computer superstores, electronics stores, department/office supply/discount stores, mail-order vendors, and local box makers. The rest of this section explains the advantages and disadvantages of each.

Dealing with Dealers

Before computers became so popular, they were mainly sold by dealers and through the mail. Therefore, if you shop a computer dealer today, you can expect the dealer to be fairly knowledgeable about PCs and to stock a few brands. However, this type of store seldom offers the lowest price, and because of their high overhead, most computer dealers have been hurt by the onslaught of computer superstores and the mainstream department stores that are beginning to stock computers.

The following list summarizes the pros and cons of shopping at a computer dealer's:

Pros	Cons
Knowledgeable salespeople	You sometimes pay a premium for the service; computers may be more expensive.
You can try out different software and hardware to see what you like.	The selection may be limited.
The store may offer a variety of services, including setup and training.	

Recommendation: This is the best place to shop if you want the most hand-holding and don't mind paying for it.

Computer SuperStores

When computers became mainstream, a new type of store was introduced: the computer superstore. In this big computer warehouse store, you can find aisles and aisles of computer equipment and software. Geek heaven! Some popular superstores include CompUSA, ElekTek, and Computer City.

Here's a summary of the pros and cons of shopping a computer superstore:

Pros	Cons
This type of store offers a great selection.	The "good" models are mixed in with the "bad." You have to be careful in your selection.
Knowledgeable salespeople	Depending on where you live, your city may not have a computer superstore.
Good, competitive pricing	
You can purchase all your equipment at one place.	
Most stores offer a variety of services, including setup, training, and upgrades.	

Recommendation: One of the best places to shop for computer systems and accessories—if there is one in your area.

Electronics Stores

An electronics store stocks all kinds of products: washers, dryers, stereos, TVs, and computers. These types of stores range in size from small-to-medium stores to giant electronic warehouse stores. I personally like shopping at these stores, especially for software. I also like gadgets, so I like to browse through the other products: CDs, videotapes, cameras, and so on. Plus I can talk my husband and son into going with me.

You can buy a bundled system if you want, but be careful. Many of these stores run ads in the Sunday paper, and they're usually for complete computer systems. Be sure the bundle is powerful enough for your needs. Often these general-purpose PCs don't have enough memory or a big enough hard disk.

Here's a list of pros and cons for shopping in an electronics store:

Pros	Cons
Competitive pricing	May not have as wide a selection.
You may feel more comfortable in a general-purpose store. (You can always go to an area, such as the music CD section, if you start feeling like an idiot in the PC section.)	Salespeople may not know a lot about computers.

Recommendation: Check out the services (upgrading, training, setup) offered. If the store offers these services and you find a system you like that is competitively priced, there's no problem with buying from an electronics store.

Department, Discount, and Office Supply Stores

There are several other types of stores that stock computers. You may find them at your local department store, at an office supply store, or at a discount store (such as SAMS). Here are the pros and cons for this type of shopping:

Pros	Cons
The store may be convenient.	Most of these stores will have a limited selection of computer systems. Usually, the system will be sold as a bundle: system unit, monitor, printer, software, add-ons. There's no chance to customize.
Okay prices	You aren't guaranteed that what is stocked is a quality product. Sometimes the product is included in the store because it is inexpensive.
	Salespeople are most likely not knowledgeable about PCs.
	Don't expect to find after-sale support, such as setup, training, and service.

Recommendation: Probably not the best place for a beginner to shop.

Mail-Order Vendors

A lot of PCs are sold through the mail, and many popular PC manufacturers (Dell, for example) started out as mail order companies. One top-rated mail-order company is Gateway.

Here are the pros and cons of shopping through the mail:

Pros	Cons
Great pricing	You may have to pay up to $100 extra for shipping and handling.
Widest selection of models	You have to know what you want; don't expect the salesperson to tell you.
You can customize the system, picking exactly the components you want.	You can't try out the system before you buy.
Most mail-order vendors will preconfigure your system (install the operating system, drivers, and software).	You may feel insecure not being able to cart the PC back to the store for repairs or returns.
Because you are buying the computer sight-unseen, most mail-order vendors have a liberal return policy.	You may end up paying the shipping costs to return the computer if you decide you don't like it.

Recommendation: If you are confident about what you want, you can get a great bargain through the mail. To find mail-order vendors, look through computer magazines. Before you buy, however, do some checking to make sure the company has been in business for awhile.

If you purchase a computer through the mail, use a credit card to pay for the system. If for any reason you don't receive the computer or have problems with the company, the credit card company can help mediate the dispute.

Local Box Makers

Anyone can put together a PC: you just collect the different components and shove them in a box. Well, it may not be that easy, but there are makers other than the big boys who market PCs nationally. Consider these pros and cons of shopping a local box maker, as these local vendors are sometimes called.

Pros	Cons
You can customize your system.	You have to know what you want.
Usually the prices are low because the company does little advertising and has few other overhead costs.	You have to do your homework. Be sure you get quality components in the PC, and check out the company's reputation.
The company usually offers decent support and service.	

Recommendation: This type of place is probably more geared toward advanced users who know exactly what they want. To find this type of vendor, check your Yellow Pages. If you do shop here, you should be confident of what you want and confident of the company's history and commitment.

Picking the System

As you've read this book, you've been building a shopping list of what you need and want. (The tearout card includes a place to record your decisions.) That's the best way to select a system: know what you want to do and build your list around those needs.

When you are shopping, you may be tempted to buy a one-for-all system that is advertised. This type of system may include a printer, software, and extra equipment (such as a modem, CD-ROM drive, sound card, telephone answering machine, and espresso maker). There's nothing wrong with buying a bundle *as long as you do these things*:

➤ Check out the system's power. Most systems included in a bundle are low-end machines; they may have a medium-size hard disk, less memory, or a slower processor, for example. Be sure you get a computer powerful enough for your needs.

➤ Check out the company's reputation and the warranty and service agreements. Although most bundles are from reputable manufacturers, you still need to do your research. Also, check out the warranty, as covered in the next section.

➤ Be sure you need the extra equipment. If you *need* this equipment, the bundle might be a good choice. If you don't need the equipment, you should consider whether you can spend the same amount and get a more high-powered system.

➤ If you need the extra equipment, be sure it is the type and quality you need. For example, some bundles include a dot-matrix printer. If you need a laser printer, that dot-matrix printer is not really an added value.

➤ Be sure you like and will use the software included. When you read the ad, you may think you are getting the software free. But hidden somewhere is the price of that software. If you like the software, it's of some value. If you won't use the software, where is the value?

When you are shopping for a system, get the deal in writing. You want to have a list of exactly the components you expect. Then if you get a PC with a different speed processor or with less memory, you can go back to your written deal and contest the system.

Service Please!

You are going to find that there are a lot of PCs that match your wish list, and they all may be priced similarly. How can you narrow down your choices even farther?

One of the main factors is service. You want a reliable PC that works when you open the box and won't break down. In addition, make sure that when it does break down, it is backed by a warranty, and that when the warranty expires, you can still get parts and service. You can compare the reputation, service, support, and warranties among the PC makers to help you make a decision.

Is It Easy to Set Up?

I just read an article in *Time* magazine about the huge sales of PCs for 1994, and it predicts huge returns for 1995. Why? Because when buyers get the "easy-to-use" PC home and try to set it up, they have problems. PCs still have a long way to go to be as easy to use as the ads claim.

Ideally, you want a PC that is already set up; you simply open the box, connect the different pieces, and turn it on. Most PCs come this way, but you will want to ask. Is the hard disk formatted? Is the software installed? Are the device drivers (software that control hardware components such as the mouse, printer, and CD-ROM drive) installed and set up?

How Long Is the Warranty?

You will also want to look into the warranty. The minimum warranty you should accept is two years, but three is better. More and more companies are offering three-year warranties.

In addition to the length of the warranty, ask who's backing the warranty: the vendor or the manufacturer. Both should back it.

Hello? Technical Support?

Find out who to call if you have a problem. Is technical support free or do you pay a fee? If you pay a fee, how much is it?

Check out the hours for technical support. The free support isn't going to be of much help if the hours are 4:00 am to 4:45 am every other Monday. Also, try calling the technical support number. That 24-hour free technical support also isn't going to be of any help at all if the line is always busy. And you aren't going to be happy if you do get through and get a nimrod who can't help you, who promises to call you back and doesn't, or who tries to sell you something.

What If You Need Repairs?

Find out, if you do have problems, how they are handled. If the PC doesn't work, where do you take it? Back to the store? Do they fix it there, or do they ship it back to the maker? Or do you ship it back? If so, who pays for shipping?

Look for a vendor that provides a year of on-site service; that is, they come to you.

Ask about broken parts. If a part breaks, will it be repaired or replaced? It's better to have the part replaced. Who's to say the fixed broken part won't break again? Plus, you can get a replacement faster.

Can I Take It Back?

You'll also want to check out the return policy. If you get the PC home, can't get it to work, and just want to give up, can you take it back? What's the money-back guarantee? Can you get a full credit? Some companies charge a restocking fee for the return. You should have a 30-day money-back guarantee and no restocking fee.

Hello? Hello? Anyone?

If the company offers impeccable warranties and service options but goes out of business, well, you are out of luck. Therefore, in addition to making sure you are comfortable with what is offered, make sure the company is going to be around to honor the agreement. Find out how long the company has been in business. Check the Better Business Bureau for complaints. Read reviews of systems made by this manufacturer and see how the company is rated in general.

> To check out the reliability of a system, call some computer repair centers. Ask what their experience has been with a particular brand. Do they see a lot of problems with that type of machine? Have they heard of any problems?

Picking a Brand

All this research and reading and decoding of specs boils down to the last decision: which brand? The list of brands may seem endless: Acer, Compaq, Dell, Gateway, IBM, Packard Bell, Zeos, and so on, and so on. Each one may offer a competitively priced system with just the components you need and with similar service. How do you pick one?

This section covers some strategies.

Buy Based on Reputation

You want the most *reliable* PC, and one of the predictors of reliability is the company. You can research the top-rated PC makers and select a brand this way. For example, *PC World*'s November 1994 issue rated 40 or so manufacturers based on research and feedback from 96,000 readers. You can read this review summary or other similar studies to determine the brand you want.

When you shop based on reputation, keep a few cautions in mind:

➤ Reliability may come with a price. For example, you can expect to pay more for a PC from the top-rated companies (Compaq or IBM, for example). Be sure you are comfortable with that premium.

➤ Be sure you aren't paying extra for hot air. Because they advertise heavily, major companies usually have more overhead than smaller companies. Are you paying for the ads or something more tangible? Does the company really make better PCs, or does the company just make you *think* it makes better PCs? Also, how much better are the PCs? Is the difference in price worth it?

Buy Based on Price

If you are considering two equal computer systems and one is cheaper than the other, you may want to purchase based on the price of the systems. Buying on price is an acceptable strategy as long as you are sure the two systems are comparable. Do they offer similar components and power? Are both manufacturers reputable (been in business)? Are the warranties and service agreements similar?

Buy What You Know

If you already have a PC and are buying a new one, or if you use a computer at your office and are happy with it, you may want to purchase the same type of system for your new computer. You will most likely know what you like and dislike about the system.

Buy Based on Recommendations

When you do your research, quiz anyone you know who has even touched a PC. This research may net you some results. For example, you may have heard from your neighbor that her Cheap-O PC has been back to the manufacturer 15 times since she purchased it. In that case, you know what you *don't* want. You may have a lot of stay-aways on your list. You may also have some positives: users that love and haven't had problems with their PCs. You may want to consider picking a brand based on these recommendations.

Buy Based on the Extras

As mentioned earlier, you can compare the warranty and service to come up with a winner in the brand race. You can also compare the "extras" offered. Does one system come with software? Do you like the software better? Does one system have extra equipment?

Buy Based on Look and Feel

Why does one person buy a Ford pickup truck and another person buy a Chevy? Sometimes it boils down to something intangible: the look and feel of the truck.

The same may be true of the PC. You may find a system that you just *like*. Perhaps you like the color or the feel or the keyboard or the shape of the monitor or something else. All in all, you'll do well to purchase a computer that you feel comfortable with.

The Least You Need to Know

Once you know which system you need, you simply need to go out and buy it.

➤ Probably the best place for beginners to shop is a computer superstore. These offer a good selection, good services, and good prices.

➤ If you decide to purchase a bundled system, be sure the system includes the power you need. Sometimes the system will have less memory or a slower processor than you really need.

➤ Don't be duped into thinking you are getting all the extra equipment free. You are paying for everything. Check out each component included in the deal to be sure you need it, and if you do need it, make sure that the piece is of an acceptable quality.

➤ One way to compare similar systems is to compare the warranties and service. You want at least a two year warranty backed by the vendor and manufacturer and free technical support. On-site service is preferable. If you do have to return the system to the manufacturer, the manufacturer should pay for shipping.

➤ Check out the reputation of the manufacturers. How are systems from the manufacturer reviewed? Mostly positively? How long has the company been in business?

Part 5
Upgrading

Some of the coolest things about a PC are also some of the most frustrating. For example, PCs continue to get more and more powerful. That's cool because you can do more faster. However, it's not so great when you consider that today's standard is tomorrow's garbage. To keep your PC up to date, you can make some performance upgrades, as explained in this part.

The other neat thing about PCs is that they are so flexible. There's always some new component you can add, and new technology is introduced daily. For example, you can now buy a PC that enables you to watch TV right on the PC screen. As you become more and more used to your PC, you'll want to add more and more features. There's always something new on the horizon—something you'll have to have. This part also covers some of the feature upgrades you may want to consider.

Chapter 21

The Who, What, and When of Upgrading

Why Upgrade?

Is your PC perfect? Not too slow? Not too hot? Not too big? Does just what you want it to (well, most of the time)? In that case, you may not need to make any changes. However, if your PC is too slow, or if you want to do something new with the PC, you may want to consider some upgrades.

If you give the command to open a file and during the load time you can get a Danish, brew a pot of coffee, put in a load of laundry, and complete a triathlon, you may want to consider some performance upgrades. You might also consider upgrading if you want to do something new. For example, if you want to be able to send e-mail via the Internet and you don't already have a modem, you can add one. You may also need to add new hardware when you buy new software.

What Can You Upgrade?

What can you upgrade? Technically, just about everything. Consider the following list:

➤ **Upgrade your processor.** In some cases, you can increase the speed of your processor by buying a new processor. For example, if you have a 486DX 33MHz, you can buy a 486DX2 to double the speed. You should also be able to upgrade from one class of processor to another. For example, you should be able to upgrade from a 486 to a Pentium; however, the necessary chips haven't quite made it to market yet. Upgrading a processor is tricky; this topic is covered in Chapter 28.

 When buying new software, always read the list of system requirements carefully. If your system does not match the requirements, you will have to add or upgrade the components in order to use the software. For example, if you want to use Broderbund's Living Books series (cool kids' books), you need a CD-ROM drive and a sound card.

➤ **Add more memory.** As programs become more complex, they require more memory or working room. Also, if you run more than one program at a time, you'll need a lot of memory. At the minimum, you need 8MB of memory, but expect that bar to raise as new technology is introduced (particularly the next version of Windows). Adding more memory is the topic of Chapter 25.

➤ **Add another hard drive.** If you're running out of disk space because you keep every document you've ever typed (including one your cat typed, which you are thinking of marketing as "Molly the Cat Tells All"), you may want to add a second hard drive. On the other hand, you might want to simply replace the hard drive you have if it is too slow. The details of adding another drive are covered in Chapter 23. You can also add another floppy drive or replace a floppy drive, if needed; however, that topic is not covered in this book.

➤ **Add a CD-ROM drive and sound card.** All the cool games and great educational software comes on a CD-ROM and requires a sound card (or so it seems). If you didn't purchase these components when you bought your PC, you can add them now. Adding these multimedia elements is covered in Chapter 24.

➤ **Add a fax/modem.** With all the information superhighway hype, you may feel like you are standing on the curb. Get in the fast lane and add a modem if you want to take advantage of online services or the Internet, or if you just want to be able to send a fax. Chapter 26 explains how to add a fax/modem.

➤ **Get a new monitor or video card, or speed up your video.** If you don't like your monitor, you can get a new one with a new card (remember, your card determines the quality of the image). If you have a good monitor but a crappy video card, you can just get a new card. You can also buy a video accelerator to increase the performance of your monitor; however, that topic is not covered in this book.

➤ **Get a new keyboard or printer.** If you don't like the feel of your keyboard, buy a new one. You can also buy a new printer. These are easy upgrades. Just buy the keyboard and plug it in, or buy the printer and connect it.

➤ **Get a new mouse or a joystick.** You can also buy a new mouse, such as one of the recently introduced designer Sensa mice. Attaching a mouse is not covered in this book, but it's a pretty easy upgrade. You just connect the mouse and then run the mouse software. Most joysticks are also easy to attach if you have a sound card with a game port. Just plug in the joystick to the game port.

When you upgrade, upgrade only one thing at a time. If you do several things at once and then can't get the system to work, you'll have a heck of a time figuring out where the problem is. Instead, install one component and test it to make sure it works before you install another.

What Should You Upgrade?

Just because you *can* upgrade doesn't mean you should. Upgrading can get expensive, and deciding whether it's worth it requires some planning.

Cha-Ching! How Much Does the Upgrade Cost?

The first thing you should do when considering whether to make an upgrade is to consider the total cost of upgrading and compare this with the price of getting a whole new system. The trick here is to think of all the costs you may incur.

Here's an example. Suppose you want to add a CD-ROM drive and sound card so that you can do multimedia on the PC. Expect a multimedia kit to run $300 to $500, obviously less than you would spend to purchase a new system.

But to really do multimedia, you need 8MB of RAM, and you only have 4MB. Add another $200 to your upgrade budget for the memory. In addition, you have a 386 processor that you should upgrade to a 486. Cha-ching! Add another $250 item to your budget. You're now in the $1,000 range. The cost may not be as great as a new PC, but consider the power you get for your money.

A Customized Chevette

When you start upgrading, you can easily make change after change so that what you end up with is the equivalent of a Chevette with chrome wheels, a killer CD sound system, a racing engine, and a custom paint job. All that on a Chevette? Don't fall into the same trap with your PC!

Upgrading Tips

Here's what you have to remember. First, be sure you understand the total cost of upgrading. Will you really only have to change one component? Or will changing one component start the domino effect so that you have to upgrade everything? Second, be sure the total cost is worth it compared to buying a new system. You may have to pay more for a new system, but at least you will be getting a newer, more powerful system for the price. Third, understand what you hope to gain from the upgrade. Adding a new feature is pretty simple to rationalize:

➤ You don't have a modem.

➤ You want to connect to online services.

➤ Ergo, you need a modem.

Utility software
Software that improves the performance of your system. You can buy packages dedicated to one purpose, such as compressing your hard disk, or you can buy packages, such as the Norton Utilities, that are actually a collection of tools or programs.

Performance upgrades are a little more speculative. Sure, it's easy to say that you want a faster computer, but what will really make it faster. More memory? A faster hard drive? A faster processor? Speed is determined by a lot of factors and is relative to what you do with the computer.

Your best bet to answer this question is to visit a computer store with an upgrade center and ask for some expert advice. Tell the upgrade person what type of system you have and what you find too slow. Doing so will help you pinpoint the bottleneck. For example, does it take a long time to load files? If so, your hard disk may be slow. Or does it take a long time to switch from one application to another in Windows? If so, you may want to add more memory or consider a graphics accelerator.

Alternatives to Upgrading

In addition to adding new hardware, you can also use software to increase the performance of your system. Software is usually cheaper and can give you a decent performance boost.

Suck It In: Disk Compression

If you need more space (and don't we all), you can consider squeezing more room out of your current hard disk by using a disk compression program. This type of program can double the amount of disk space you have by organizing files more efficiently and by shrinking them. The most popular disk compression program is called Stacker and runs approximately $100. You can also use DBLSPACE or DRVSPACE, the disk compression programs that are included with DOS version 6.x.

Organize Better: Disk Defraggers

To understand how a disk defragmenter works, you have to understand a little about how files are stored on disk. Think about a huge wall of mail boxes and a little mail clerk. The mail clerk can only fit so much mail in one box. If there's too much to fit, the mail clerk has to use another box until all the mail is crammed in some little box.

That's how files are stored, only the mail boxes are called clusters and the mail clerk is DOS. When you save a file, DOS crams as much as will fit into the first cluster. If the file is too big to fit in one cluster, DOS goes to the next cluster and crams more of the file in, and so on until the file is stored. (The file allocation table—FAT—keeps track of which clusters are used.)

When you first start using a new disk, it's clean and empty for the most part. DOS can move from one cluster to the next and keep all the files in a neat little section. However, when you start filling up the disk and deleting files, the empty clusters are scattered, as are the new files you store on the disk. DOS may store part 1 of a file in cluster 10, part 2 in cluster 23, and part 3 in cluster 69. Imagine all the hustling around DOS has to do to pull together a file. When files are scattered all over, the disk is *fragmented*. You can fix it by defragmenting it or optimizing it.

When you run a defragmenter program, the files on the hard disk are reorganized so that all the files are put back in a row. It's much easier to locate and load a file when the file clusters are stored together, which means the hard disk works faster.

The most popular collection of utility programs is Norton Utilities, which includes a disk defragmentation program. DOS version 6.x also has a defragmentation program called DEFRAG.

Think Better: Memory Managers

Another type of program you can use to enhance your system performance is a memory manager. Memory is finicky, and different programs use different types of memory. More technical details!

The first 640KB of memory is called conventional memory. Some programs can use only this type of memory. Also, device drivers (that control your hardware) and other programs are often loaded (take up space) in this key 640KB.

The next chunk of memory (384KB) is called upper memory. Without some special software, this memory is not usable by most programs. DOS hogs this memory for itself.

To get DOS to use more memory beyond the first 1MB, you have to trick it. The memory beyond 1MB is called extended memory and is made available by using a software program called a device driver.

Before extended memory became *the* way, another type of memory called expanded memory was introduced to the market. You bought special expansion memory boards that included the extra memory. You can also configure your extended memory as expanded memory.

Too much to keep track of? That's where a memory manager comes in. You can run a simple program and let it do the dirty work of figuring out which memory you have and how that memory is allocated. DOS 6 comes with a memory manager, called MEMMAKER. You can also purchase other memory optimizer programs, such as QEMM.

The Least You Need to Know

If you want to add a new feature or increase your system performance, you can consider upgrading your current computer.

➤ You can upgrade a PC by adding new features, such as a sound card, CD-ROM, or fax/modem. You can also replace or add to existing hardware, such as adding more memory or a second hard disk.

➤ When deciding whether to upgrade, consider the total cost. Sometimes changing one component will mean changing others, and the cost can add up. Compare the total upgrade cost to the cost for a new system. In some cases, you may want to go with the new system.

➤ In addition to hardware upgrades, consider some software solutions to performance problems. You can buy a disk compression program that will give you more room on your hard disk, a disk defragmentation program that will improve the performance of your hard disk, or a memory manager that will optimize your memory.

ON YER MARK...

Chapter 22

What You Need to Know Before You Upgrade

In This Chapter

➤ What to expect when upgrading

➤ The anatomy of your system

➤ Important files

➤ Backing up

➤ Making an emergency disk

When it comes right down to it, I am not very technically inclined. It took me several hours to hook up a VCR when I was in grad school. When I finally accomplished it, I won a bet with my roommate and she had to tell me every day for a week that I was a technical genius. Although the experience really boosted my ego, I still know that I'm no technical genius. But I can and did make some upgrades to my computer, and so can you.

Upgrading sounds like something only a computer geek with Coke-bottle-bottom glasses and a little pocket protector can do. But it's not. Upgrading your system isn't all that difficult. All you need is a little mechanical skill (to unscrew the screws and so on) and some technical know-how. This chapter prepares you for the adventure ahead.

What to Expect When Upgrading

Do you need to know all about audio file formats to install a sound card? Do you need to understand hard drive interleave factors to install a hard drive? Nope. You just need to know how to work a screwdriver, follow some steps, and run some software. Here's the general procedure for most upgrades.

Step 1: Know Your System

In order to introduce a new card to the other players in your system, you need to know what type of equipment you have and what's located where. Read the section "The Anatomy of Your System" later in this chapter for a short anatomy lesson. The next chapter discusses exploring the guts of your computer too.

Step 2: Take It Apart

Most of the upgrades you make involve surgery: you have to take apart your system. The steps for this type of surgery are in the next chapter. All you really need is the ability to unscrew some screws.

Step 3: Plug It In

Once the system case is off, you can see all the electronic wizardry that makes a computer capable of magic. This is also where you plug in the new component. If you are adding a new drive, you slide the drive into one of your available drive bays. If you are adding a new expansion card, you plug it into one of the available expansion slots. If you are adding memory, you plug it into one of the available memory slots. You can also pop out your current processor and pop in a new one. All you have to know is where to plug it in, which isn't too hard if you follow directions.

Step 4: Set It Up

Most new equipment comes with software that helps you get the equipment set up. Luckily, most of the software is easy to use. You type a command and maybe answer a few questions, and the software handles all the technical aspects (such as setting IRQ settings and DMA channels and calculating the distance from Jupiter to this particular PC). You don't have to wade into the gobbledy-gook of the arcane technical commands to set up the component manually.

Sound easy enough? Great. The rest of this chapter prepares you for the upgrade process.

The Anatomy of Your System

Before you tear up your PC, you should have a good idea of what you have. First of all, if you know this stuff, you can use it to impress other geeks at Christmas dinner parties. "I have a 486DX 50MHz Gateway with a 340MB hard drive and 8MB of RAM." Here's a pronunciation guide for those who want to try this:

"I have a four-eighty-six D-X fifty megahertz Gateway with a three-forty meg hard drive and eight meg of RAM."

You can also use this information when asking for advice on upgrading.

Whatcha Got: Your Current System

You should know the following information about your current system:

Equipment	Examples	Record Your Info Here
Type of microprocessor	486DX, 386SX, 486SX, 486DX2	_____
Speed of microprocessor	33MHz	_____
Amount of memory	8MB	_____
Size of hard drive and controller type	340MB IDE	_____
Size of floppy drives	3 1/2" 1.44MB floppy drive	_____
Number of parallel ports	1	_____
What's hooked up to the parallel port	Printer	_____
Number of serial ports	2	_____
What's hooked up to the serial ports	Modem (COM1) Mouse (COM2)	_____

continues

continued

Equipment	Examples	Record Your Info Here
Type of monitor	SuperVGA	_____
Number, size, and type of available expansion slots	6 16-bit ISA slots	_____

Ways to Cheat

If you don't know the preceding information off the top of your head, don't worry. That's not uncommon. You can find out the information without begging some geek to help you. Use the following cheat list:

➤ Look at your original invoice from when you purchased the PC. This invoice should list each component. If you can't find the invoice, look through your documentation; sometimes this lists the equipment you have.

➤ Look at the outside of your system. Sometimes the type of processor and speed are apparent from the model name. For example a 4SX-33V probably means you have a 486SX 33MHz microprocessor.

➤ To find out how much memory you have, watch your system when you turn it on. The computer will do a power-on self-test (POST) that will check your RAM. You'll see 256KB, 512KB, and so on flip by on-screen as the computer goes through the memory. The last number shown is the amount of memory you have. You have to be quick to catch this!

➤ You can use DOS commands to find out how much memory you have (use the MEM command) and the size of your hard disk (use CHKDSK). You can also use the MSD command to find out various information about your system. Most utility programs, such as Norton Utilities, have a system information command that can give you information about your system.

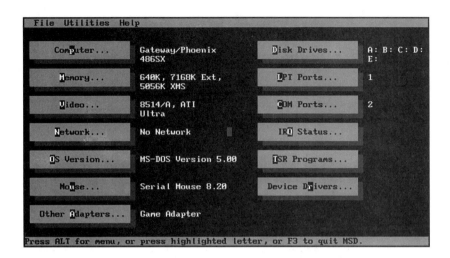

Use the DOS command MSD to find out information about your system.

➤ Run your setup command, as covered in the next section.

See MOS Run

CMOS (pronounced "see moss") stands for complementary metal-oxide semiconductor. Impressive, huh? The CMOS chip keeps track of configuration information about your PC, such as the type of monitor, floppy disks, and so on.

You can use your PC's setup command to display these key factors to complete your system inventory. You should also record the information so that if anything goes wrong, you know what the original CMOS settings were.

How you run the setup program depends on your system; check your documentation. With some computers, you can run it anytime from the DOS prompt by pressing some combination of keys (on my computer it's Ctrl+Alt+Esc). On others, you have to watch for a message at startup, such as **Press F2 for Setup**, and then do what it says. When the system information appears on-screen, copy it down on a piece of paper or press **Shift+Print Screen** to print it.

It is especially important that you write down the hard disk information. You can figure out most of the other stuff later.

207

Checking Out Important Files

When you run the software to install new hardware, it's going to change certain key files on your system. Those changes are fine if (and this is a big if) they don't screw up what you already have set up. This section explains the key files. The next section explains how to make an extra copy of these files.

CONFIG.SYS

When you start a computer, it gives itself a wake-up call, shakes itself, and makes sure all its limbs (components) are still there. The computer then looks for and runs some key files. The first file is CONFIG.SYS.

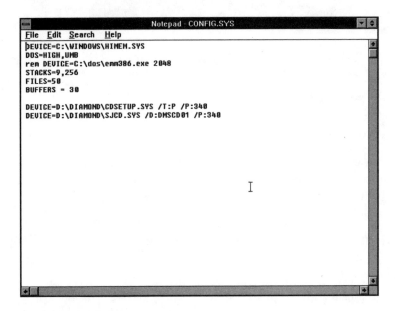

A sample CONFIG.SYS file.

In this file, you find commands that set up your system: mouse, modem, sound card, memory, and so on. Many times when you add a new piece of hardware, the software program used to set up the hardware will insert some new commands in this file.

AUTOEXEC.BAT

This file (pronounced "AUTOEXEC-dot-BAT") contains commands that are run each time you turn on the computer. You'll also find commands that set up the system, for example, telling DOS where to find your programs and other key system information.

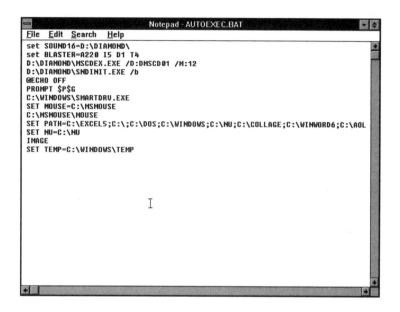

```
                    Notepad - AUTOEXEC.BAT
File  Edit  Search  Help
set SOUND16=D:\DIAMOND\
set BLASTER=A220 I5 D1 T4
D:\DIAMOND\MSCDEX.EXE /D:DMSCD01 /M:12
D:\DIAMOND\SNDINIT.EXE /b
@ECHO OFF
PROMPT $P$G
C:\WINDOWS\SMARTDRV.EXE
SET MOUSE=C:\MSMOUSE
C:\MSMOUSE\MOUSE
SET PATH=C:\EXCEL5;C:\;C:\DOS;C:\WINDOWS;C:\NU;C:\COLLAGE;C:\WINWORD6;C:\AOL
SET NU=C:\NU
IMAGE
SET TEMP=C:\WINDOWS\TEMP
```

A sample AUTOEXEC.BAT file.

You don't have to worry about memorizing what each command does. But you should be aware that you have this file and understand that its contents are important.

WIN.INI and SYSTEM.INI

You can think of these two files as AUTOEXEC.BAT and CONFIG.SYS files for Windows. SYSTEM.INI is kind of like a CONFIG.SYS file: it tells Windows techie stuff, such as what drivers it needs to operate. WIN.INI keeps track of the housekeeping, such as what colors you prefer and what fonts you've installed.

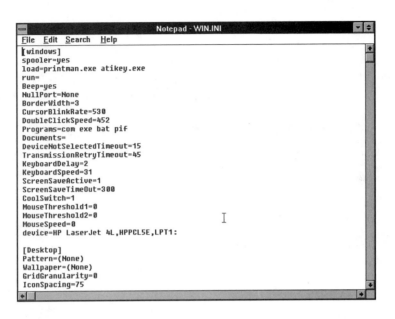

```
Notepad - WIN.INI
File   Edit   Search   Help
[windows]
spooler=yes
load=printman.exe atikey.exe
run=
Beep=yes
NullPort=None
BorderWidth=3
CursorBlinkRate=530
DoubleClickSpeed=452
Programs=com exe bat pif
Documents=
DeviceNotSelectedTimeout=15
TransmissionRetryTimeout=45
KeyboardDelay=2
KeyboardSpeed=31
ScreenSaveActive=1
ScreenSaveTimeOut=300
CoolSwitch=1
MouseThreshold1=0
MouseThreshold2=0
MouseSpeed=0
device=HP LaserJet 4L,HPPCL5E,LPT1:

[Desktop]
Pattern=(None)
Wallpaper=(None)
GridGranularity=0
IconSpacing=75
```

A sample WIN.INI file.

Backing Up Your System

Before you make any major changes to your system, it's a good idea to back up (at the very least) the key files we've been talking about: AUTOEXEC.BAT, CONFIG.SYS, WIN.INI, and SYSTEM.INI. Then if something goes wrong with these critical files, you can use the backup copy. Backing up is easy: you use a backup program to make a compressed copy of the files on one or more floppy disks or on a tape drive.

You shouldn't just back up when you make a major change. You should back up on a regular basis. Back up your data files daily, once a week, or once a month, depending on how valuable the information is. Back up your entire system a couple times a year.

To be safe, you should also back up the data and programs on your hard disk. What if you install something new and *poof!*, a puff of black smoke shoots out of the computer's disk drives? What if the only copy of your great American novel was on that disk drive? Well, I'll tell you. It went up in that black puff of smoke.

If you have the floppy disks to spare or can afford to buy them, it's a good idea to back up your entire system so that if something goes wrong, you still have your system on a collection of floppies. Depending on the amount of data you've accumulated on your hard disk, it could take anywhere from dozens to hundreds of floppies.

210

You can use a DOS command or a program to create your backup disks. For DOS versions 6.0 and above, use the MSBACKUP command and follow along with the boxes that appear. (For more information about using this program, pick up *The Complete Idiot's Guide to DOS,* by Jennifer Fulton.) For versions below 6.0, use the BACKUP command and follow the on-screen instructions. If you're feeling very ambitious, you can buy a special backup program (such as The Norton Backup) that has more features than the backup utility that comes with DOS.

For those who are considering skipping the backup, be warned! The computer *knows* when you haven't backed up! You'll be crying some big tears if something goes wrong.

Making an Emergency Startup Disk

Here's another step you don't want to skip: making an emergency disk before you start messing with your computer's setup. This simple step can save you a bundle of worries and technician bills.

Mini Hardware Lesson: How a Computer Starts Up

Do you ever wonder what that grinding sound is when you start the PC? Do you see the floppy disk light go on and wonder what's up? Well, when you hear that grinding and see the light, what you are witnessing is DOS looking for its head.

Remember the BIOS, the basic input-output system found on the ROM chip inside the system unit? The BIOS tells DOS, "Here's a tiny bit of what you need to run, and here's where to look to find the rest." Then the BIOS sends DOS off in search of the rest of the instructions.

When I say DOS is looking for its head, it's actually looking for the files IO.SYS, MSDOS.SYS, and COMMAND.COM. The first place it looks is on the first floppy drive in your system. (You'll understand in a second why it's important that DOS looks in drive A first for a bootable disk—one that contains the files it's looking for.) If there's no disk in drive A, DOS looks on the hard drive (usually drive C) for the file it needs. If it finds the files, DOS puts on its head and goes about its merry business.

If you see the error message **Non-system disk. Press any key to continue** when you start the computer, it means you have accidentally left a non-bootable disk in drive A. Take out the disk and press any key to continue.

How an Emergency Startup Disk Can Help

We all lose our heads once in a while, and the same is true of DOS. An emergency startup disk can give DOS a temporary head (from a floppy disk) so the computer can function while you're figuring out what's wrong with the permanent head (the one on the hard disk).

Sometimes a key file (such as COMMAND.COM, CONFIG.SYS, or AUTOEXEC.BAT) gets screwed up. When DOS tries to start up using the screwed up file, it chokes. Or, sometimes the hard disk goes kaplooey and refuses to start. In either case, you may get an error message, or you may get nothing at all—just deadly silence.

Obviously, the first thing you are going to do is panic; that's what everyone does. The next thing you are going to do is use your emergency startup disk to start up the PC.

If you think of not being able to start the PC as being locked out of your house, you can think of the emergency disk as a spare key.

To use your emergency startup disk, just put the disk in drive A and restart the computer (press **Ctrl+Alt+Del** or turn the computer off and then back on again). Lucky for you, DOS looks at drive A first. So if drive C is screwed up, you can still start the PC from drive A. If drive A contains the right files, the system will boot (start), and you can try to fix the problem.

Creating the Emergency Startup Disk

In order for the system to boot from a floppy disk, that disk must contain the system files. To put the system files on the disk, you use a special procedure when formatting the disk. You can use the following DOS command to format the files in that special way:

FORMAT A: /S /U

You can also use the Windows File Manager to make a system disk. To do so, use the Disk Make System Disk command.

Once you've created the system disk, you should copy your key files (CONFIG.SYS, AUTOEXEC.BAT, WIN.INI, and SYSTEM.INI) to this disk. You can use the Windows File Manager or the DOS COPY command to do this. You may also want to put some of the utility programs you use on the disk as well.

The Least You Need to Know

Before you decide to upgrade your PC, you should understand what's involved. You don't have to be a technical wizard, but you should be prepared.

➤ To upgrade, 1) know what you have, 2) take apart the system, 3) plug in the new component, and 4) run the software to set up the component.

➤ You should know the basic information about your processor, hard disk, floppy disks, and ports before you start.

➤ To find out the details of your system, you can look at your original invoice, run your setup program, use the DOS commands MEM, CHKDSK, and MSD, or use a special utility program.

If you have an already-formatted blank disk, you don't have to reformat it to make it into a system disk. Just use the SYS A: command. If you get the message **No room for system on destination disk**, go back and use the regular **FORMAT A: /S /U** command.

➤ When you start the computer, CONFIG.SYS and AUTOEXEC.BAT execute automatically to tell DOS about the various equipment you have.

➤ Before you make any changes, you should back up your entire system so that if anything goes wrong, you have an extra copy.

➤ You should create an emergency startup disk and include CONFIG.SYS, AUTOEXEC.BAT, WIN.INI, and SYSTEM.INI on it. If something prevents you from starting your computer from drive C, you can start from this disk and then fix the problem.

Opening the Box and Looking Around

Ever wonder what the inside of a PC looks like? This is your chance to find out. In this chapter, you learn how to open up the PC and do some exploratory surgery. You can see exactly what pieces and parts you have.

Most upgrades (with the exception of something simple such as plugging in a new keyboard) involve opening up the system unit. Even if you don't want to upgrade, you may want to open it up just to see what the inside looks like.

A Few Words of Caution...

Before you get out the scalpel—well, in the case of PC surgery, a screwdriver—read the following list of warnings:

➤ Don't ever, ever work on a PC that is turned on. It's worse than sticking a fork into a toaster. Not only can you damage the PC, but you can give yourself a quick trip through the ceiling.

➤ Static electricity can make your hair look like hell and can fry your computer's hairdo as well. Before you touch any component inside the PC, you should ground yourself. To do so, touch some piece of metal outside of the computer.

➤ Eating Cheetos, drinking a Big Gulp, and checking out the innards of your PC don't mix. You're not at the movies. Be careful not to spill or drop anything inside the system unit.

➤ Put the monitor, keyboard, and other stuff somewhere safe. To get at the system unit, you have to move the monitor, keyboard, and mouse. That doesn't mean stack them on the edge of the desk. Put them someplace where they won't be damaged.

➤ Put the screws someplace safe, too. When you put your system back together, you're going to need them. If you're adding new equipment, it might have screws too. To keep from mixing up the screws, put the system unit screws together someplace where you can find them later. Also, don't use a magnetized screwdriver. Magnets destroy data!

➤ Be sure you have an emergency startup disk and a back-up of your hard drive, as explained in Chapter 22. (I know—nag, nag, nag! But it's important!)

Opening the System Box

Have you read the warnings I just gave you? Do you understand them and agree to adhere to them till-death-do-us-part? Good. Let's get started.

Step 1: Turn Off the Computer

The first step in system unit surgery is to put the PC to sleep: exit all programs, remove any disks from the CD-ROM drive or floppy drives, and turn off the computer. You probably should unplug all of the components as well.

Step 2: Disconnect All the Other Plugs

Once the PC is unplugged, you can undo all the outside connections. Start by looking at all the connections and noting what each one looks like. Most of the connections on the back of the PC look different. (For example, you probably won't confuse the phone line for the modem with the power cord for the PC, but it's a good idea to take a look.) When you put your system back together, you're going to have to reconnect all the cords and plugs. If you think you won't remember, make notes. (And if you think you will remember, make some notes anyway.)

If your monitor sits on the system unit, unplug it from the PC and move it someplace steady. You can also unhook the keyboard and mouse. If you have speakers that sit on the system unit, disconnect and move them as well. Disconnect your printer and modem line, if necessary.

Another warning: don't work on a PC that is still plugged in. Doing so is dangerous—and not in a cool, action-hero kind of way. You could get killed!

How you unplug these items varies. Some are plugs: you simply pull them to unplug them. Some have thumb screens that you can loosen. Some have regular flat-head screws; use a small flat-blade screwdriver to unscrew them. Be sure to put the screws someplace safe.

The back of your computer should now be free from cords, and you should be able to easily access the back of the system unit.

Step 3: Unscrew the Screws

The PC is now free of its hangers-on. You can begin surgery. Look at the back of the system unit and note the screws that hold on the system case. Unscrew each of these screws and put them in a little cup or some other holder.

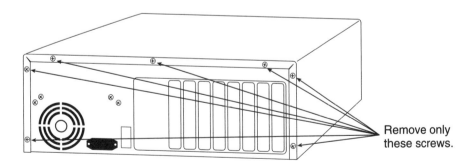

Remove only these screws.

Unscrew the screws on the system case.

Step 4: Remove the System Case

Next you need to slide the case off the system unit. It varies from model to model exactly how the thing comes off, and if you don't know how, this can be pretty frustrating the first time you do it. On some models, the case slides from the back forward and then lifts off. On others you slide the case from the front backward. You may have to give a good push to get the case moving. However, if it really won't budge, don't force it. You're either doing it wrong, or some screws still need to be removed.

 If you're having trouble getting your case off, check your system documentation. Sometimes the case is connected differently. For example, some IBM PCs have a cover latch, and some are connected with nuts instead of screws.

Place the case someplace where you won't trip over it and the dog won't mistake it for a new chew-toy.

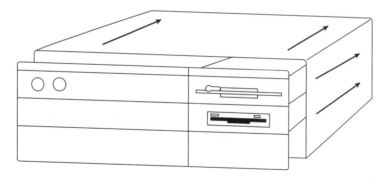

Most cases slide easily off the system unit after you undo a few screws.

Step 5: Do Your Work

Once the case is open, you can take a look around (covered in the next section) or make some changes (covered in the remaining chapters). When you are done, you need to reconnect the system case, as covered in the next step. Whichever option you choose, we've got you covered.

Step 6: Put the Case Back On

Putting the case back on is the reverse of taking it off. Makes sense, right? Slide the system case back in the opposite direction you used to take it off. If you slid the case forward and up to take it off, slide it down and back to replace it. (Some cases have these really frustrating little grooves that the sides must slide into.)

Once the case is on, find those screws that you put together someplace and screw the case back on. Finally, reconnect all the cables that you disconnected.

Identifying the Key Components

The inside of a PC is pretty colorful; most of the expansion boards (including the motherboard) are on bright green flat cards. The wiring is gold or silver, and the plugs are different colors such as red, yellow, and blue. Pretty, huh? Let's take the tour.

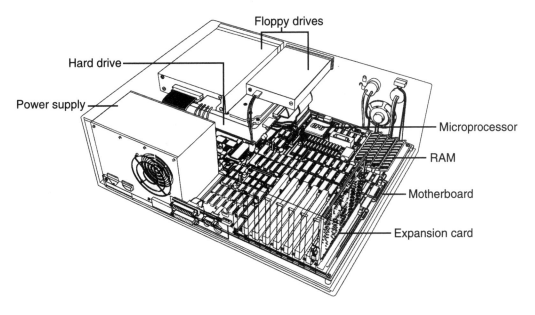

The insides of a PC.

Hello Mother! Finding the Motherboard

The biggest, baddest board in the PC is the motherboard. You can spot this board by its size. All other equipment inside the PC is somehow connected to the motherboard. For example, on the motherboard, you'll find the processor, RAM chips, and other key electronic circuitry.

Let's take a moment to locate a few important things on the motherboard. The processor? Look for a big square chip with the word Intel (if you have an Intel processor) or some other name (if you don't). For memory, look for one or two banks of four little circuit boards that are standing up at an angle.

The Bay Area: Shelves for Drives

If you are thinking about adding a new drive, check out the drive bay area, which is most likely near the front right side of the system unit. Notice that each drive sits in a shelf, called a drive bay. If you have an empty bay, you can add a drive there.

Also notice that the drives are connected to the controller card (or local bus) with a flat ribbon. You should also see a power cord running from the power supply (the big silver box) to the drive. When you add a new drive, you'll mimic these connections.

Checking Out Expansion Slots

In the back left area of the system, you'll find the expansion cards and slots. Some of the slots will already contain expansion cards. Notice how they are set up, plugged in vertically to the motherboard. Each one is secured on the top of the system unit with a screw.

 Can't find your processor? Rest assured, it's there. It may not be a flat square with writing on it, though. Instead of having a flat surface on top, it may have a bed of plastic spikes sticking up; those are called heat sinks, and they're used to keep some very fast processors cool as they work.

The connectors on the back of the card peek through the back of the PC so that you can plug in outside equipment to the card. For example, if you have an internal modem, your phone line will hook up to the back of the card, the part that peeks through the hole. If you have a sound card, your speakers will connect to the back of the card.

Some slots will be empty; you can plug in new components into these blank slots. You have to match the slot type and size to the card type and size. For example, you can only put a 16-bit card in a 16-bit (or larger) slot. For more information on card types and sizes, see Chapter 11. You'll learn the nitty-gritty details of installing a card in the chapters that follow.

The Least You Need to Know

Taking a look at the inside of the PC can be fun and educational, even if you don't want to make any upgrade changes. If you are upgrading, opening up the PC is the first step.

➤ Before you open your system case, turn everything off and disconnect all the power cords. When you are working inside the system unit, ground yourself (touch something metal) and don't spill or drop anything inside.

➤ To open the system case, unscrew the screws on the back of the PC and then slide and lift off the case. Be sure to put the screws someplace safe where you can find them again.

➤ The motherboard is the largest electronic board inside the PC. Look for a big green flat thing on the floor of the case. Notice the motherboard contains the microprocessor, RAM, and expansion slots.

➤ The drives and available drive bays are usually found at the front right part of the PC. If you have empty drive bays, you can add another disk drive.

➤ The expansion slots and cards are usually found to the back and left of the system. Some slots should be empty; if so, you can use them to add new features to your PC via an expansion card.

DOUBLING UP, BABY!!

Adding a Second Hard Drive

Why would you want to consider adding a new hard drive (or replacing your existing one)? Primarily for more space.

Think about your house or apartment when you first moved in. You probably thought you had plenty of room to keep your various collections (shoes, tools, baseball cards, books, clothes you're going to wear as soon as you lose 20 pounds, and so on). But after a few months, you probably filled all available closets, the attic, the garage, the basement, and any extra bedrooms. Anywhere you could store stuff, you did.

Instead of adding a new hard drive, you may want to consider purchasing a disk compression program, the most popular of which is Stacker. This utility uses trickery to shrink and expand your files so that you have more room. If you aren't desperate for hard disk space, a compression utility may be all that you need. See Chapter 21 for alternatives to upgrading.

That's how it is in a computer. At first, you may not have a lot of programs and files, but as you buy new games and other programs, your hard disk fills up fast. Plus, each document you create takes up room, too. After a while, you may find that you barely have room to save a short little memo. If this sounds like your situation, you may want to consider adding another hard drive.

You might consider replacing your current hard drive not only to gain more room, but also to get a faster hard drive. Just keep in mind that the computer's speed is determined by a lot of factors, not just one. Even if you upgrade to a faster hard drive, if you have a slow processor, you might not see that big of a gain in performance.

What's Involved?

Tired of **Disk Full** error messages? Tired of having to figure out which programs and files you probably won't need, so you can delete them to make some room? If so, you're ready for a new hard drive.

Adding a hard drive isn't that difficult. You just have to follow six basic steps:

1. Purchase the drive.

2. Assemble your tools.

3. Check out the available space.

4. Insert the drive.

5. Connect the drive.

6. Set up the drive.

If you don't want to install the hard disk yourself, you can pay someone to install it for you and can skip steps 2–4. When you are shopping around, ask about installation and service fees. You may find that you would rather spend the money to have someone else install the actual hard drive than take on the project yourself.

The rest of this chapter takes you through the six steps for adding a hard drive in detail.

Step 1: Selecting a Hard Drive

Hard drives are covered in detail in Chapter 7, so for complete information on the differences among hard disks, read that chapter. The following summarizes the key shopping points you need to remember:

Size   Remember that hard drives are measured in megabytes (MB) and gigabytes (GB), and the rule of thumb is the bigger, the better (and more expensive). You can expect to pay $250–$300 for a 420MB hard drive. Because you can always use the space, get the biggest drive you can afford. A gigabyte is no longer considered obscenely large—go for it if you can afford it.

> It's a good idea to purchase a hard disk kit, which includes most of the cables and screws you need to hook up the drive. If you purchase just the hard drive, you may have to buy the connectors separately. Read the packaging to find out what you're getting.

Speed   Speed is measured in milliseconds (ms). The lower the number, the faster the drive (and, again, more expensive). A good range is 12ms to 13ms.

Drive type   Select a drive type that is compatible with your existing controller card or motherboard. If you don't understand drive types, see Chapter 7 for an explanation.

Internal or External   If you don't have any open drive bays, and if you don't mind paying a little more, consider an external hard drive. (You'll need an expansion slot for the hard drive card.) If you have the room inside the computer and want to pay less, get an internal drive. This chapter covers installing an internal drive.

Manufacturer   You don't want to buy a hard disk from Crashes R Us hard disks, so be sure to buy from a reputable maker. Ask the salesperson for recommendations. Conner, Seagate, and Western Digital are popular hard drive manufacturers.

Dimensions   Like floppy disks, hard disks come in different dimensions. You can purchase a 5 1/4" drive or a 3 1/2" drive. (Get a 3 1/2" since that's the latest standard.) Be sure that the kit includes a mounting frame, which shelves the drive inside the drive bay.

You can shop for hard disks at any of the computer stores mentioned in Chapter 20. Compare prices and talk to the service reps if the store has them. Ask for recommendations on what type of hard disk to purchase.

Step 2: Assembling Your Tools

The hard disk is now sitting in its neat little box on your computer desk waiting to be installed. Before you take the plunge, it's a good idea to collect all the tools you will need. This prevents you from having to make several trips to the computer store for parts. (This happened to me. I went to the store for a part I already had because the kit said I didn't have it. Then I was missing a part that I should have had, but didn't. Arrgh!) It's also a good time to review the safety rules I spelled out for you in Chapter 23.

Here's the run-down of what you need for your tool kit:

The hard disk kit   This should include the actual hard disk, screws, an interface cable (flat, gray ribbon-looking thing), a mounting frame, and the installation manual.

Screwdriver   You'll probably need a regular size screwdriver, as well as one of those tiny ones to take off the system case and mount the new drive.

DOS manual   You may need your DOS manual for information on setting up the new drive, if the drive doesn't come pre-formatted.

Computer manual   Your computer manual should include some specific information about how your system unit is arranged, as well as information on how to run your system setup utility program (used to recognize the new drive).

An emergency startup disk   If you're replacing your old hard disk, keep in mind that you'll need something to boot from until you get the new hard disk formatted and the appropriate system files loaded. Chapter 22 explains how to create an emergency boot disk for this purpose.

Step 3: Checking Out the Inside

Ready to start? Okay, first let's go through the preliminaries that you learned in Chapter 23. (Turn back there now if you've forgotten.) Remove the case and take a look inside to see where the new drive will go.

Your computer might have originally come with extra drive rails. If so, I hope you didn't throw them away just because you didn't know what they were.

If you're replacing your old hard disk, you don't need an empty drive bay; the new one will take the place of the old. However, it's more likely that you're adding a second hard disk. I mean, why would you get rid of perfectly good storage space, when you could keep the original and add more? If you're adding a second hard disk, you'll need to make sure there's a drive bay available.

If you are installing a smaller disk into a larger bay, you also need to have a mounting frame, which should come as part of the kit. You may also need drive rails to secure the mounting frame inside the drive bay. (I was missing these and had to order them from my computer manufacturer.)

Finally, you need a free power connector on the power supply. You're looking for several colored wires strung together that have a 4-hole plastic socket on the end. Most power supplies have more than enough free connectors.

Installation Caveats

Here are some things to keep in mind as you work with the hard disk:

➤ It goes without saying that you should never, never work on a PC when the power is on. Unplug the PC and all its various attachments.

➤ Hard disks are hard on the outside, but that doesn't mean you should toss them around. Inside they are really, really sensitive. Don't drop, bang, or toss the hard disk, use it as a hockey puck, or otherwise jostle it.

Check out how your existing hard disk is hooked up and mounted. You simply want to mimic these connections.

➤ Beware of magnets. Magnets destroy data, so don't use one of those magnetized screwdrivers, and don't decorate the hard disk with refrigerator magnets.

➤ Static electricity is also damaging, so don't do any soft shoe routines on the carpet when you are installing the drive. Be sure to "ground" yourself first by touching something metal that's outside of the system. And keep your hard disk in its little anti-static bag when you aren't trying to screw it into the mounting frame.

➤ Don't get overzealous when screwing in the drive. Don't make your own holes, and don't screw in the screws too tightly.

Step 4: Inserting the Drive

Now you're ready for the fun part: surgery! Keep in mind that you'll have to refer to the hard disk installation manual and perhaps your computer manual for specific instructions on some of the steps.

Here are the basic steps you follow to insert the new hard drive. These steps assume that you're going to install a second drive and leave your original one in place, because that's what most people do. (See the last section for steps on replacing a drive.)

1. Take off the system case so that you can see the guts of your computer. (We covered this back in Chapter 23, remember?)

2. Check out the inside to make sure you have all the inside stuff you need (drive bay, mounting rails, and power supply cable). If not, stop and review your parts list again.

3. Decide which is going to be the primary drive and which is the secondary drive, or which is the master and the slave. (I'm not joking about master and slave; those are the terms used.)

The drive from which you boot is the master drive. You set the master and slave with the drive jumpers. It's easiest to keep the current drive as the master, and make the new drive the slave so you don't have to change the jumper pins on the old drive. If your old hard drive is really slow, though, you may want to change the settings: Make the old one the slave and the new the master. The placement inside the PC has nothing to do with the master or slave.

4. If you have to set jumpers, check your hard disk kit manual for instructions on how to set them for that particular drive. They vary, and you can't tell how just by looking at it. A jumper is a really tiny pin at the back of the drive. You sometimes place a shunt (a really tiny sleeve) over the jumper to change how the drive is configured. Or, you may use another method to set the jumpers; check your manual.

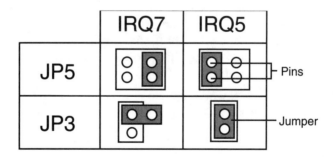

Jumpers are little pins that have movable rubber sleeves across them. Change the position of the sleeve to change the setting.

5. If necessary, mount the drive into the mounting frame. If you have a smaller drive, you should also have a mounting frame that came with the drive kit. This frame keeps the drive in place inside the drive bay. To mount the drive into the frame, match up the holes on the drive with the holes on the frame.

There are two kinds of holes on the frame: holes for attaching the drive to the frame and holes for attaching the frame to the drive bay. Hopefully, your hard disk manufacturer includes a nice drawing that shows you how to properly align the holes.

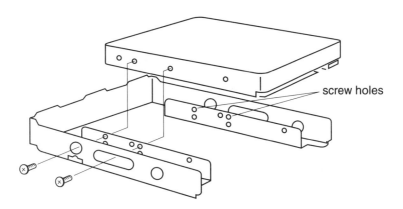

Attach the mounting frame with screws.

6. Mount the new drive into the drive bay. To do so, put the saddle on the drive and sing the theme to "Rawhide." Just kidding. How you do this will vary depending on the computer system and the drive. For my Gateway computer, I screwed the drive rails onto the drive and then slid the drive into the bay. Once the drive was in place, I secured the mounting rails with a screw.

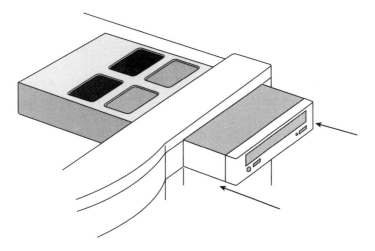

Slide the drive into the bay.

229

Step 5: Connecting the Drive

Two cables are used to connect the drive. The interface cable looks like a flat ribbon and connects the drive to the controller card or motherboard. The power cable has four different colored wires and connects the hard disk to the power supply. Follow these steps to make the connections:

1. Connect the interface cable to the drive by pushing the cable onto the little pins at the back of the drive. (See your hard disk manual for help if you aren't sure where to plug in the cable.)

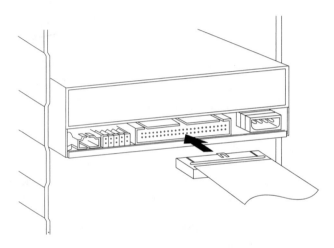

Connect the cable to the hard drive.

If you have two hard drives, you should have a cable with three connectors already. You can use this one. (The extra connector just wasn't used when you had only one drive.) If you don't have a three-connector cable, you can buy one at a computer store and use it to connect the two drives to the controller.

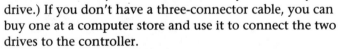 Be sure you put the drive into the bay with the connections facing toward the back, not the front. You'll need to use the connectors on the back to connect the power cable and interface cable, as covered in the next section.

The cable connects from the first drive to the second drive to the motherboard or controller card (next step). Connecting one item to another to another is called daisy chaining. Make sure that you hook pin 1 on the cable to pin 1 on the drive. Your hard disk kit manual should explain which is pin one on the drive, and the cable should be marked. (Mine was marked faintly with a thin red line.)

2. Connect the other end of the cable to the motherboard or controller card. Again, the cable should plug onto the pins on the controller card or motherboard. Your hard disk manual should show exactly how to make this connection.

Daisy chain The process of connecting one hardware piece to another to another.

3. Connect the power cable from the power supply to the hard drive. The power supply is the big silver box toward the back of the PC. You should see lots of power cables going from this box to other hardware elements (such as the other disk drives) in the PC. To connect the power cable, plug the four-prong connector into the back of the hard drive.

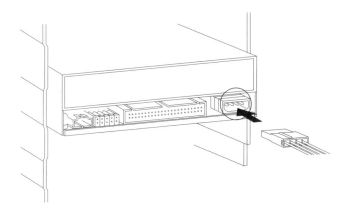

Connect the power cable.

4. Put the cover back on, but don't screw it on. You'll want to test the new drive before you tighten the screws. Plug in the power cord, connect the monitor, mouse, and keyboard, and turn on the PC.

You're done with the surgery part; on to the setup!

Step 6: Setting Up the Hard Disk

For the hard disk to work, the motherboard has to know certain things about the hard disk—technical stuff such as the number of heads, cylinders, and so on. Think of this as completing the hard disk's birth certificate.

Then DOS has to poke its ugly head in: you have to format and partition the drive. Start the computer and get your DOS disks and hard disk installation manual handy.

Introducing the Hard Drive to the Motherboard (Mom)

The next step is to introduce the hard drive to the motherboard, for which you can choose one of three methods.

The easiest way is to use your computer setup program to automatically configure the drive. Check your computer manual for instructions on running your setup program. Sometimes you press some set of keys (such as Ctrl+Alt+Esc or Ctrl+Alt+Insert) from the DOS prompt. On other machines, a message such as **Press F2 to Enter Setup** will appear at startup. Do what it says.

There should be a message somewhere on the setup screen that tells you how to make changes. For instance, in mine, I use the up and down arrow keys to move to the item I want to change and press the Spacebar to toggle through the available settings for that item. When I'm done, I press F10 to exit and save my changes. Info lines on the screen tell me all this.

Once you're in the setup program, go to the Hard Disk part of the screen (you can usually move around with the arrow keys) and enter the settings for the new hard disk. How do you know the settings? It varies. A setup program usually comes with presaved settings for 50 or so types of drives. If there's a drive type written on the casing of your hard disk, you've got it made: just select that drive type, and all the other technical specs will fall into place. To make it even easier, some setup programs have an AutoConfigure option that checks out the drive for you, decides what type it is, and adjusts the tech settings automatically. You simply select AutoConfigure, and the setup program does the rest.

The next way is to use a software program, such as EZ-Drive. Your hard disk kit may include a copy of this program, or you can purchase it separately. You just boot your computer from the software disk and follow the instructions on-screen. Again, check with your manual for information on running and using this program.

The hardest way is to enter the hard disk information manually using your computer setup program and the hard disk specs included with the hard disk kit. This is the last-resort method; only use it if the other two won't work for some reason.

If you're forced to go the hard route, it can be a little scary. You'll have to enter the number of heads and cylinders and other techie stuff. Ask for help from a computer repair tech or a friend who knows how to deal with the nitty gritty details of a computer's innards.

DOS Makes Its Hellos

The final step in installing a new hard drive is to let DOS make its marks on the hard disk (that is to partition and format the drive). Partitioning the drive divides it into sections and marks which drive you boot or start from. Formatting erases all information and gets the disk ready for storing data. Think of formatting as painting parking lines on a parking lot (the hard disk) so that the operating system knows where your data is parked.

The following steps walk you through formatting your hard disk. Refer to your DOS manual for complete instructions.

1. To partition the drive, use the FDISK command. For example, to set up drive D, type **FDISK D:** and press **Enter**. If you are adding a second drive, it will most likely be named drive D. Keep in mind that partitioning a drive erases all the information on that drive; you want to do this only for a new drive!

    When you are adding a new drive, you already have a primary DOS partition on the current drive. You just need to partition the second disk as an ordinary hard disk, called a logical DOS partition. Select this option and follow the on-screen steps.

Partition A section of the hard disk.

Partitioning The act of breaking the drive into those sections. The primary DOS partition is the disk that you want to start from, usually drive C. This partition will contain the key DOS files you need to use the computer.

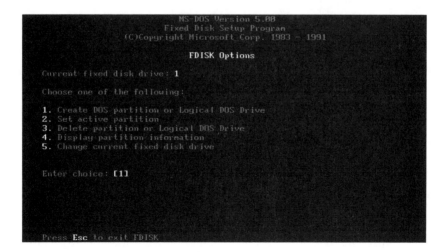

```
                        MS-DOS Version 5.00
                     Fixed Disk Setup Program
                (C)Copyright Microsoft Corp. 1983 - 1991

                           FDISK Options

Current fixed disk drive: 1

Choose one of the following:

1. Create DOS partition or Logical DOS Drive
2. Set active partition
3. Delete partition or Logical DOS Drive
4. Display partition information
5. Change current fixed disk drive


Enter choice: [1]




Press Esc to exit FDISK
```

Running the FDISK command.

2. To format the hard disk, use the command **FORMAT x**, where *x* is the drive letter. For example to format drive D, type **FORMAT D:**. Formatting may take a few minutes.

Once the drive is partitioned and formatted, you can take it on a test drive.

Testing the Drive

Now you can restart your system and, if all goes well, access your new drive. Try changing to the drive from DOS. Run the CHKDSK command to check for errors (or use SCANDISK if you have DOS 6.0 or above). Try accessing the drive from Windows.

Enjoy the free space while you can, because you know that before you can say "Disk Space" your programs and your spouse and you and your data files and your kids will be hogging up all the new space.

Troubleshooting

If you try to change to the new drive and get an error message, or if you can't start the computer, you need to find out what went wrong. Turn off the power, take off the system case again, and check the following things:

➤ Make sure the cables are connected tightly.

➤ Make sure your cables are connected correctly. Check your hard disk manual for illustrations on how to connect the drives.

➤ Make sure you partitioned the drive correctly. Check your DOS manual on exact instructions for partitioning the primary and secondary drive.

➤ Make sure you formatted the drive. You can't access the drive until it is formatted.

➤ Make sure the boot drive contains the system files (the files needed to start DOS).

➤ Make sure you are accessing the right drive letter.

➤ If you still can't get the hard drive to work, call the technical support line for the hard disk company. There should be a phone number in the documentation.

Replacing a Drive

Although it's less common, you might want to replace your old hard drive with the new one. For instance, you might do this if the old one uses an older controller technology, is really slow, or doesn't work. You follow a similar procedure to the one you just learned, but note the following differences:

➤ Be sure to back up all the data on the old drive first. (We talked about backing up in Chapter 22, remember?)

➤ Before you start, copy the FDISK and FORMAT commands to your emergency startup disk (the one you created in Chapter 22). You'll need those commands to set up the new drive.

➤ You'll need to disconnect the old hard drive and take it out of the drive bay. To disconnect the cable, just pull the connector for the cable (not the cable itself). To remove the drive, unscrew the mounting screws, which are usually found on the sides, and slide the drive out of the drive bay. You may have to give the drive a good tug to get it moving.

➤ Your new drive will need to be set up as the master drive. Check your hard disk manual for instructions on setting the jumper pins.

➤ Because the new drive hasn't been formatted or partitioned, you won't be able to start from drive C after the installation. Instead, boot from your emergency startup disk and then use the FDISK and FORMAT commands to partition and format the drive.

➤ Be sure to partition the new drive as the primary DOS partition and format the drive with the system files. Use the following format command to format the drive and include the DOS system files:

FORMAT C: /S

The Least You Need to Know

Installing a new hard drive isn't as difficult as it sounds. You need to be able to operate a screwdriver, hunt through a few manuals for some help, and run a few programs.

➤ When purchasing a new hard drive, consider the capacity, the speed, and the controller type. Also, consider purchasing a hard disk kit, which should include all the hardware and software you need to install the new drive.

➤ Inside the PC, you mount the drive into the drive bay and make the connections. You need to connect the hard drive to the motherboard using a flat gray cable.

➤ You also need to connect the hard disk to the power supply. If you don't have extra power supply cables, you can purchase some.

➤ Before you can use the hard disk, you have to configure, format, and partition it. Use your computer setup programs or a software program included with the hard disk kit to configure it. To format and partition the drive, use DOS.

Chapter 25

Multimedia Magic: Installing a CD-ROM Drive and Sound Card

In This Chapter

➤ What's involved?

➤ Step 1: Selecting a multimedia kit

➤ Step 2: Assembling your tools

➤ Step 3: Inserting the sound card

➤ Step 4: Inserting the drive

➤ Step 5: Making the connections

➤ Step 6: Setting up the software

➤ Troubleshooting

Many new systems come bundled with the whizz-bang of multimedia—basically a CD-ROM drive and a sound card. With these components, you can explore a mysterious island, have a book read aloud to you, race an Indy 500 car, and take advantage of all the other cool multimedia titles on the market.

If you didn't buy a system that had these components, you can add them to your PC. The best way is to buy a multimedia kit that includes the CD-ROM drive, sound card, and software. This chapter tells you all about it.

What's Involved?

Here's a quick overview of the steps involved in upgrading a PC and adding multimedia equipment:

1. Purchase the kit.

2. Collect your tools: multimedia kit, software, screwdrivers.

3. Insert the sound card.

4. Insert the CD-ROM drive.

5. Connect the pieces.

6. Set up the software.

Remember that you can hire someone to install the multimedia components for you. Before you decide to do this, ask about the installation prices; you may decide to save yourself some money and do it yourself.

Step 1: Selecting a Multimedia Kit

If you remember, the first PC was cobbled together with different parts from different companies. This left the door open for PC makers other than IBM to create and manufacture PCs, which meant more competition, more innovation, and more competitive pricing. That's the great part of how PCs were created.

The nasty part is that there's no standard on how the different pieces work together. Ideally, a sound card from one maker should work with a video card from another manufacturer. Ideally.

Plug and Play Puffery

You may hear the term "plug and play" touted a lot in the press. This refers to the computer makers' promise to make it easy to add any component ("plug") and run it with any other equipment ("play"). The system can understand and automatically configure different cards from different companies so that all you have to do is sit back and watch. Unfortunately, there's no playground attendant, so things can get ugly.

You may find that a sound card won't work with your video card or that you can't use a certain CD-ROM drive with your microprocessor. Figuring out where the conflict lies can be difficult. This is one area that is *supposed* to improve, but has a long, long way to go.

So the first thing to look for when adding multimedia components is compatibility. How do you ensure compatibility? First, instead of buying a sound card from one source and a CD-ROM drive from another, purchase a drive kit. When you do, you can be sure that the drive and sound card work together at least.

Second, know the type of controller your PC supports. Many CD-ROM drives are designed to work with the IDE or SCSI type of controller. Check your invoice or ask your salesperson to find out what kind you can use in your system.

Finally, insist on a money-back guarantee. If you cannot get the system to work, you will want to return the equipment without being charged a restocking fee.

Watch for specials! When I bought my multimedia kit, the store was running a special where they installed certain multimedia kits for free. I decided to do it myself because I didn't want to lug my computer up to the store, but you should ask your computer store if they do free installations.

Checking Your Sound Card

Chapter 12 covers how to check out the components of a multimedia PC in detail, but here is a quick summary of the points to check for when purchasing a sound card:

➤ The current standard is 16-bit stereo, so you want at least that.

➤ Check out the speakers that are included as part of the package. Some offer dinky speakers that will be okay for most sounds. If you want true stereo sound, you will want better speakers.

➤ Look for a sound card that is SoundBlaster-compatible. Many games and other software programs were written to work with the SoundBlaster card. If your card is SoundBlaster-compatible, you'll be able to run the software without any trouble.

➤ If you are interested in using the PC to play music, look for a sound card that has a MIDI interface.

➤ If you want to hook up a joystick to play games, make sure the sound card has a game port (if your PC doesn't already have one).

➤ If you want to record sounds, make sure the sound card comes with a microphone or that a microphone can be plugged into it.

Checking the CD-ROM Drive

Here's a quick reminder of the features to look for when selecting the CD-ROM drive. (Remember that Chapter 12 covers multimedia PCs in more detail.)

First, check out the speed. The fastest CD-ROM on the market now is a quad-speed. If you want top-of-the-line, purchase this type of drive. If you are watching your budget, you can get by with a double-speed drive. Stay away from the really cheap single-speed drives. They are too slow by today's standards, and you'll be sorry you bought it later.

Don't get a triple-speed CD-ROM drive. The price you pay isn't worth the minimal performance edge you get with this type of drive.

To verify the speed, find out the transfer rate and access time. The access time tells you how fast the drive can find the data you want. A good access time is in the range of 300 milliseconds. The transfer rate tells you how fast the drive can transfer the information to the PC. Look for a CD-ROM drive in the 350+ kilobytes per second range.

You can purchase an internal drive or an external drive. The internal drive is housed in a drive bay in the system unit. If you have an extra drive bay, you'll probably want to get an internal drive. The external drive sits on the desktop and is a little more expensive.

What's the Total?

Depending on the quality of the components, you can expect to pay $200–$700 or more for the multimedia kit. If you purchase the components separately, you can expect to pay in the range of $100–$300 for a sound card, $20–$200 for speakers, and $150–$500 for a CD-ROM drive. You can shop at any of the places mentioned in Chapter 20.

Goodies Make the Difference

When comparing systems, you'll find that price makes a difference. Some kits will be much more expensive than you are willing to pay. However, you may find more than one that are similar and in the price range you want. How do you make a choice?

Read the list of software carefully. Sometimes you get only a demo version of the game or software, which isn't really worth anything more than a free test drive.

Check out the software. Many kits come with multimedia titles, an encyclopedia, games, kids' educational software, and more. You can make your choice based on these goodies.

However, keep in mind that you are really paying for that *free* software. For example, suppose that you are Mr. Top-of-the-Line, and you gotta have the best. You buy the most expensive multimedia kit on the market. When you are bragging about your new kit to your neighbor, you find out that your systems are comparable in power and speed. The difference is that he got a few choice CDs where you got 50—and you paid $150 more.

Before you decide which kit to buy, look closely at the software and decide what you will use and what you won't use. Tally up the value of the package accordingly. Also, use the software to compare one system to another. If one system has MYST, MegaRace, and SimCity (all popular games) as well as Home Medical Advisor and Compton's Encyclopedia, and the other system has Leonard Nimoy Sings Show Tunes, which one sounds more appealing?

Step 2: Assembling Your Tools

Inside your PC, you need an available expansion slot for your sound card and an available drive bay for your CD-ROM drive (if you bought an internal CD-ROM drive). To power the new components, you need an available power adapter. (If you don't have a free power adapter in the system, you can purchase one at your computer dealer.)

Your multimedia kit should include the following:

➤ CD-ROM drive

➤ sound card

➤ data cable (flat gray cable like the one used to connect hard drives)

➤ audio cable (skinnier cable)

➤ speakers

➤ installation software

From your tool kit, retrieve a small flat-head screwdriver and a Phillips head screwdriver. Make sure neither screwdriver has a magnetic tip.

Step 3: Inserting the Sound Card

When you are installing a kit, you are adding two new components. You can start with the sound card. Follow these steps:

1. Take off the system case. (If you need help with this step, turn back to Chapter 23.) Make sure you have all the inside stuff you need (drive bay, free expansion slot, and power supply cable). If not, stop and review your parts list again.

2. Take off the slot cover for the expansion slot you want. To do so, unscrew the slot cover and lift it out. Keep the screw; you'll need it for step 4.

   Remember that the expansion slot has to be the same size as or bigger than the card. If you have a 16-bit card, you need a 16-bit expansion slot.

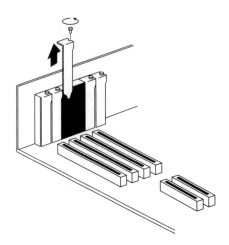

The connectors of an expansion card.

3. Insert the sound card into the expansion slot. If you look at the bottom of the card, you'll notice the connectors, which look kind of like a comb. To plug in the card, align the connectors with the expansion slot and push straight down. On some PCs, you have to press pretty hard to lock the card into place.

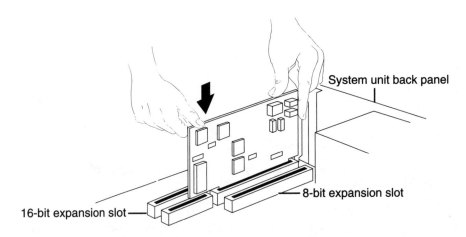

Inserting the card.

4. Using the screw you saved from the slot cover, screw the card into place at the top.

Now that the sound card is in place, you can move on to the next step: inserting the drive.

Step 4: Inserting the CD-ROM Drive

The second part of installing the multimedia kit is inserting the CD-ROM drive. This is a lot like inserting a hard drive—or any drive. You might want to review Chapter 24 before you get started.

Unplug the PC and disconnect the power cable before you remove the system case. Remember never to work on the PC when the power is on. Also, handle the components carefully. Static electricity can damage the sensitive electronic components, so ground yourself before handling the equipment. (Touch something metal outside the computer to ground yourself.)

1. Figure out which bay the new drive will go into, and then pop out the plastic cover in the computer case for that bay. (Some of them slide out instead of popping.)

2. Slide the CD-ROM drive into the drive bay. Some drives will slide right in and be secured directly to the system unit (see next step). On others, you may have to use drive rails (I did). In this case, you attach the drive rails to the drive with screws and then slide the drive into the drive bay.

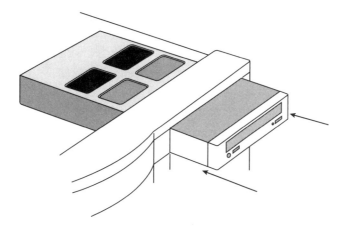

Inserting the drive bay.

3. Secure the CD-ROM drive in the bay using the screws provided in the kit. For this step, you can check the picture in the CD-ROM installation manual. If the picture doesn't look like your system and you can't figure out how to secure the drive, try mimicking the way your hard drive is connected.

After these three steps, you are ready to make the connections.

Step 5: Making the Connections

In order to get everything hooked up, you have to make some inside connections and some outside connections. On the inside, you need to connect the CD-ROM drive to the power supply and connect the sound card and drive using a data cable and an audio cable. On the outside, you need to connect the speakers (and the microphone if your kit came with one).

Inside Connections

Look at the back of the drive. You should see three areas for connections: the audio connection, the data connection, and the power connection.

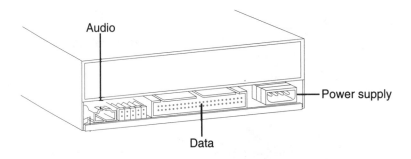

The connections on the back of the CD-ROM drive.

Follow these steps to make the inside connections:

1. Plug in a power adapter from the power supply to the power outlet on the back of the CD-ROM drive. The power adapter will have four colored wires hooked to it and will run from the power supply to the drive. The outlet for the CD-ROM drive should have four connectors to match the drive and is probably marked DC Input.

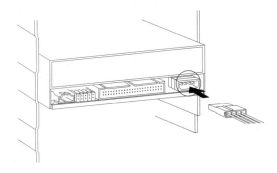

Connecting the power cable.

244

2. Take the data cable (flat gray ribbon-looking thing) and connect one end to the sound card and one end to the CD-ROM drive. You have to be sure that pin 1 on the drive aligns with pin 1 on the cable. On the other end, you have to align the right pin on the cable with the right connector on the card.

   Usually the proper alignment is marked in some way. The cable may have a tab, or the card and cable may have a colored mark. Check your installation manual.

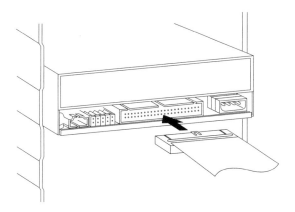

Connecting the data cable.

3. Connect the audio cable to the CD-ROM drive (look for an outlet marked AUDIO). Connect the other end of the audio cable to the sound card.

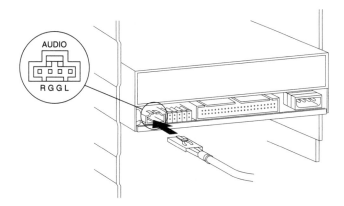

Connecting the audio cable.

Outside Connections

Once the inside stuff is done, you can replace the system case and reconnect the system. Don't screw the case's screws down yet because if something isn't working, you'll have to check the connections. Plug the speaker cord into the sound card out plug, and then turn on the PC.

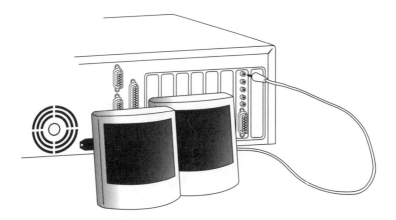

Plug the speakers into the sound card, just as you would plug into a stereo receiver.

The final step in the installation process is to run the installation software to set up the new components.

Step 6: Setting Up the Software

Before your system can take advantage of these new features, you have to introduce the new components to your system. You do this by running the installation software included with the kit. This software will set up your sound cards and your new drive.

Check your installation manual for the software installation steps. The program will install the files it needs onto your hard disk and make any changes to your CONFIG.SYS and AUTOEXEC.BAT files in order to load the drivers (the programs that control the hardware). The program may also ask whether you have Windows and may make changes to the Windows system files as needed. The installation program will also select an IRQ and DMA channel (see the next section) automatically, or you can set them manually if you prefer.

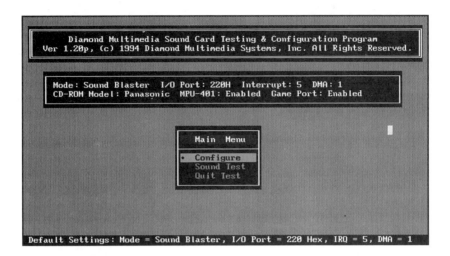

An installation program for a multimedia kit.

IRQs, DMA Channels, and Other Technical Stuff

One of the most frustrating things about adding a new piece of equipment is figuring out which DMA channels and IRQs are used and which piece of equipment is using each one. If you're lucky, you can just accept the default settings or let the setup software determine the right settings to use. But in some cases, you have to figure it out on your own.

An IRQ is an interrupt request. It's the hardware components' way of calling 911: "Hey! I need help!" Some IRQs are reserved for certain components. For example, line 1 is usually reserved for the keyboard. Some are free and can be used for new equipment you have, such as a modem or a sound card. The problem occurs when you use the same line for different components.

In addition to managing IRQ conflicts, you have to make sure you keep your DMA channels straight. DMA stands for direct memory access and is a high-speed direct path between the component and memory that bypasses the microprocessor. Like IRQs, DMAs are often reserved for special purposes; DMA 2 is usually used for transfer information between a floppy drive and memory. Some DMA channels are free, and some can be used by new components.

Unfortunately, there's no easy way to determine which IRQs and DMAs are used and which are free. Your system documentation may give you a list of which IRQs and DMAs are used initially. But in order for that list to do you any good, when you add new components, you have to be meticulous in keeping track of which IRQ and DMA channels are taken. Write them down! Some system diagnostics programs, such as DOS's MSD program, can tell you what your IRQ settings are—in case you didn't write it down initially.

What happens when you have a conflict? Sometimes you can change the IRQ or DMA channel that's being used by running software and making a different selection or by manually switching the jumpers on the cards. Check your documentation.

Debugging IRQ and DMA conflicts can be a nightmare. If you run into this problem, try calling the technical support company for the new device.

Testing 1, 2, 3

Once the sound card and CD-ROM drive are set up, try testing them. Your kit may have come with some free programs, such as a Talking Clock. Try that to make sure the sound works.

To test the CD-ROM drive, insert a CD into the drive and try to access that drive from the DOS prompt or from File Manager. It should act just like a regular hard or floppy disk. Next, try running a game that includes sound to be sure the sound feature works. Many kits come with games on a CD-ROM. Install and run one of these games to test both the drive and the sound card.

Finally, if you're interested in this capability, try running a program (one probably came with your sound card) that plays audio CDs. Windows comes with a program, Media Player, that will do if you don't have something better. Pick your favorite audio CD and settle back for a good listen.

Introducing Sound to Your Applications

In addition to hardware introductions, you may also need to make some software introductions. That is, you need to let your applications know that you have a new sound source. Some programs will recognize the new kid on the block and automatically start using the sound card and its features. For example, once you've set up a sound card in Windows, most Windows applications will use the sound card. (The installation program you ran when you set up the sound card probably told Windows about the sound card.)

With other programs, you have to reconfigure the software yourself. Run its setup or installation program again (check your software documentation) and select the sound card and sound card settings you are using so that your program can sing!

Troubleshooting

Does your sound card play really loudly? Or not at all? Can't access any disks in the CD-ROM drive? If you had problems in the installation, check the following trouble-shooting list:

➤ If your sound card plays too loudly, too softly, or not at all, check the volume control. You may find the volume control on the back of the sound card, on the speakers, or on the CD-ROM drive.

➤ If you aren't getting any sound out of your speakers, make sure you hooked up the speakers correctly. In my installation manual, the steps said something different than the picture showed. I messed around with all kinds of technical settings (see the next item) before I found out the problem was something simple. The speakers were plugged into the wrong outlet.

➤ If your sound card doesn't work or only works sometimes, you may have trouble with your IRQ or DMA channels. You can try different settings, or you can call tech support for the kit and ask for their help.

➤ If you can't access the CD-ROM drive, be sure you have a disk in the drive (face up). If you do, make sure that you made all the connections. Check your kit manual and verify that you made the connections as described.

➤ If you hear computer sounds from your speakers but you can't hear your audio CDs, try plugging headphones into the headphone jack on the front of the CD-ROM drive. If you hear the CD playing there, the problem is that the audio cable isn't properly connected between the CD-ROM drive and the sound card. Open up the case and check that out.

The Least You Need to Know

If you want to take advantage of some of the funnest, coolest games and educational software on the market, you need to equip your PC with multimedia equipment. Basically, you need a sound card and a CD-ROM drive.

➤ It's a good idea to buy a multimedia kit. That way you are sure the sound card and CD-ROM drive work together. Be sure that you have a money-back guarantee in case the kit won't work with your system.

➤ Look for a kit with a 16-bit sound card that is SoundBlaster-compatible and includes speakers. The CD-ROM drive should be a double-speed or quad-speed. Don't get a triple-speed drive.

➤ When comparing multimedia kits, look at the software included as part of the kit.

➤ The multimedia kit should include the CD-ROM drive, sound card, data cable, audio cable, speakers, and installation software.

➤ After you take off the system case, remove one of the expansion slot covers (take off the screw). Then insert your sound card into the slot. Secure the card with the screw at the top of the card.

➤ Take off the drive bay cover and insert the CD-ROM drive into the drive bay. Check your manual for instructions on how to secure the drive in the bay.

➤ Use the flat data cable to connect the CD-ROM drive to the sound card. You'll also use the audio cable to connect these two pieces. Connect the CD-ROM drive to the power supply using an available power adapter.

➤ Put your system case back on and plug in the speakers. Run the installation program to set up the drive and the sound card. Then test the drive using the utility programs that came with the kit or by installing and playing a game that uses sound and the CD-ROM drive.

Chapter 26

More Memory!

In This Chapter

➤ What's involved?

➤ Step 1: Buying memory

➤ Step 2: Installing the memory

➤ Step 3: Configuring the memory

➤ Troubleshooting

Everyone could use more memory: you, your spouse, your mom, your dog, and most importantly, your PC. Memory on a PC is the all-important working area. The bigger the working area, the more information the PC can store in its "head." That basically means you can work faster (in most cases) and run more complex programs.

If you have 4MB (megabytes) of RAM or less, you should definitely consider upgrading to at least 8MB. If you have 8MB and use a lot of Windows programs or graphics-intense programs, you may benefit from having even more memory, up to 16MB or 32MB. This chapter covers the ins and outs of adding memory.

What's Involved?

Here's a quick overview of the steps you follow to add more memory to your PC:

1. Buy the memory. This is the hardest step, believe it or not. The rest of the steps get easier as you go.

2. Insert the memory.

3. Configure the memory.

The rest of this chapter explains each step in full detail.

Step 1: Buying Memory

What are you shopping for when you are adding memory? Capacity and speed. For the first shopping spree feature, you need to know how much you have and how much you can add.

How Much Do I Have?

If you don't remember how much memory your system has, don't fret. Just because you can't remember doesn't mean you're a complete idiot. I mean, how often does it come up in conversation? About as often as your shoe size.

You can find out how much memory you have in a couple of ways. First, if you have your invoice for the system, check that. It should tell you. If you don't have the invoice or can't find it, you can have the PC tell you how much memory you have.

When you turn on the PC, watch the PC tally up the system memory. The power-on self-test (POST) does a quick flip through the memory to make sure it adds up. You'll see each chunk of memory tallied up as the PC checks it out. The last number you see is the total amount of memory you have. If you aren't fast enough to catch this figure, you can use a DOS command to find out how much memory you have. At the DOS prompt, type **MEM** and press **Enter**. DOS displays on-screen the amount of memory you have.

```
C:\>mem

     655360 bytes total conventional memory
     655360 bytes available to MS-DOS
     436432 largest executable program size

    7340032 bytes total contiguous extended memory
          0 bytes available contiguous extended memory
    5177344 bytes available XMS memory
            MS-DOS resident in High Memory Area

C:\>
```

Use the DOS command, MEM, to find out how much memory you have.

It doesn't look like 8MB! When you are watching a computer tally memory, remember that a computer uses a binary numbering system. One byte isn't 1,000KB; it's really 1,024KB. Because that's too many digits for most people to remember, we round up or down to the nearest thousand.

If you have 8MB, you actually have the standard 640KB of conventional memory, 384KB of reserved memory, and 7MB or 7,168KB of extended memory. That's why you don't see an even 8MB on-screen during the POST or in the results of the MEM command. (For information on the types of memory—conventional, extended, and reserved—see Chapter 6.)

How Much Can You Add?

You can add as much memory as your system will hold (which should be the first limit) or as much as you can afford (which should be the second limit).

How much memory your system can hold depends on how much you have now and how much your motherboard allows. Most motherboards support up to 16MB, 32MB, 64MB, or 128MB of memory (way more than you'll ever need). You can check your system documentation to find out how much memory your motherboard can support. If you can't figure it out by looking at the documentation, call technical support for your PC manufacturer to find out. If you call tech support, have your computer model number and serial number ready.

If your computer's capability for memory is already maxed out and you still want to add more, there are some ways to finagle it. However, they involve adding special expansion boards to hold the memory. It's best to consult a computer professional (such as the tech support department of the manufacturer) before you try to buy such a board yourself. These boards vary widely and don't work with all computers.

What Type of Memory?

While you're scouring around in your manual, look also for the type of memory your motherboard can take. To help set the stage, here's a short history lesson.

The earliest type of memory on the market was a single memory chip, called a DIPP (dual in-line pin package). If you put nine DIPPs together in a row, you had a bank of memory. Adding these types of chips was indeed dippy because it was easy to bend and break the pins. These days, only old computers use DIPPs; they're all but obsolete for PCs.

The slightly better package that came next was the SIP (single in-line package). This type of memory connected to the motherboard via little pins on the edge of the card. You may still find these available today, but they're rather dated.

Today, most memory is packaged as an entire bank of memory on a little rectangular circuit board called a single in-line memory module or SIMM. You just plug the SIMM board into the available memory slot on the motherboard, and you have more memory.

Types of memory.

If your computer is relatively new, you will most likely be purchasing SIMMs. You plug the SIMMs into the available memory slots on your motherboard.

The sockets into which you plug the SIMMs are organized into banks. The motherboard decides how many sockets equal a bank—sometimes two, sometimes four. On most motherboards built today, there are two banks (Bank 0 and Bank 1) of four sockets each, for a total of eight sockets.

If your computer uses DIPPs or SIPs, it's worth the money to have a computer store or repair shop insert the chips. Because it's so easy to bend and break the pins, inserting this type of memory chip isn't really for the novice upgrader. We won't be covering DIPP and SIP upgrades in this book.

Sub-Types of SIMMs

The number of actual memory chips on the SIMM will vary. You may find some SIMMs with eight chips, some with nine, and some with three. Check with your computer manufacturer to see which type of SIMM you can install. Also, some computers will accept only proprietary memory—that is, memory purchased from the computer manufacturer.

How Fast Is the Memory?

The second factor to consider when selecting memory is the speed. Memory speed is measured in nanoseconds (ns). One nanosecond is equal to one billionth of a second. Try timing that! You can find memory chips that range from 20ns (really, really fast) to 200ns (not as fast).

The speed you should buy depends on the speed of your current chips. The memory that came with your computer is probably the correct speed for your motherboard, so use it as a guide. You can buy chips that are the same speed or faster (although you won't get a performance edge by adding faster chips). Don't buy slower chips, though; they won't be able to keep up with the motherboard, and you'll have problems.

You can check your manual (yes, again) for your chip speed, or you can open up the system case and look for secret code numbers on the existing memory. The chip usually has a number on it. Look for the number at the end after the hyphen, and add a zero to get the speed. For example, if you see –7, the chip speed is 70ns. If you see –12, the chip speed is 120ns.

The Match Game

Are you with me so far? You also have to match the following: the type of memory chip to the type the motherboard likes, and the speed of the memory chip to the other chips.

Remember, the mother-board determines how many slots make a bank. It should tell you in your computer's documentation what the motherboard considers a bank.

And there's one last match: All the SIMMs in a bank have to be identical. You can't have different size SIMMs in one bank. (On most computers, you can have different memory-capacity SIMMs in different banks.) You can't have one 1MB SIMM and three 2MB SIMMs in a bank of four sockets, for example. Think of a cash register drawer, where you're supposed to keep all the money of the same denomination together. The same is true for memory banks.

Do You Have To Do the Memory Shuffle?

Depending on the amount of memory you have and how that memory is packaged, you may not have any available SIMMs. For example, if you have eight 1MB SIMMs, you won't have any open sockets. You'll have to remove four of the SIMMs to make room for the newer, larger capacity SIMMs—for example, 4MB SIMMs.

What's the Cost?

You can expect to pay around $400 for 8MB of memory, around $200 for 4MB, and around $100 for 2MB. I would highly recommend buying as much memory as you can afford. This is not an area to skimp on.

Step 2: Installing the Memory

The hardest part is figuring out what kind and how much memory you need. The rest is fairly easy and painless. You simply open up the system case and plug in the memory. Can't get any easier. Follow these steps:

1. Open the system case, as covered in Chapter 23. Be sure to turn off and disconnect the power before you start working on the PC. Put the screws for the case in a safe place, and touch something metal outside of the computer to ground yourself.

2. Locate your memory area. Look for a little board of chips inserted at an angle on the motherboard. Some of the memory slots will be filled, but you should also have some empty ones. You will want to use the first available empty spot. Look for a number on the SIMM slot and select the one with the lowest number.

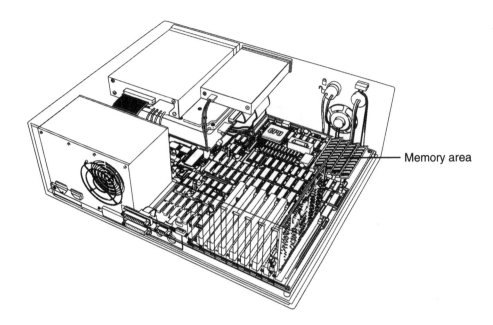

Finding the RAM (memory) on your motherboard is easy; look for the parallel rows of angled boards sticking up.

3. If necessary, remove any of the SIMMs you are replacing. Check your computer manual for which bank to remove. Usually the bank numbers appear next to the slots so you can tell which is which. To remove the SIMM, unclip each end; it should spring forward. You can then take the SIMM out of the slot.

4. Position the SIMM so that the notch on the corner corresponds to the slot. Hold onto the top of the SIMM and insert it at an angle in the SIMM slot. Push the SIMM into the slot.

5. Rock the SIMM backwards to lock it into place.

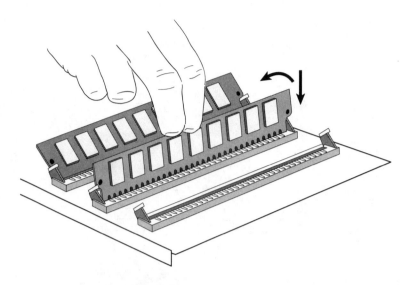

Inserting the SIMM into the slot.

6. Some computers will recognize the new memory automatically; some will require that you set a DIP switch on the motherboard. If necessary, set any DIP switches on the motherboard to tell it how much memory is installed. Check your computer manual for instructions on this step.

You're finished! Now you can put the system case back on (don't tighten the screws), connect the monitor and other pieces, and turn on the system.

Step 3: Configuring the Memory

Depending on your system, all you may have to do to configure the new memory is turn on the PC. The PC may detect the new memory and automatically make it available. Watch the PC as it starts and does the POST (power on self test). You'll see 256KB, 512KB, and so on displayed on-screen as the PC checks all the memory. If the PC goes past the original memory amount and starts checking the new memory, you are set. Lucky you!

If the PC doesn't check the new memory, or if you see an error message, you need to change your memory settings. To do so, run the setup program for your PC. If there's a problem, you may get a message on-screen such as

Memory parity error - press F2 for Setup

or some such thing. It may tell you how to enter Setup to correct the problem, or it may dump you into setup automatically. Check your system documentation to find out how to start the setup program.

In the setup program, you can change the amount of memory installed to the new amount in the CMOS. Exit the setup program and reboot the system.

Troubleshooting

Having trouble? Check the following troubleshooting list for common problems and solutions:

➤ Are you sure you bought the right type of memory? It may be worth a call to your PC's manufacturer to make sure. All SIMMs are not created equal.

➤ Can't get the computer to recognize your memory? Make sure you installed the chips correctly. Also, be sure you did everything your computer's documentation said to do (such as setting DIP switches or running the setup program).

➤ There are two banks on the motherboard, and the PC is very particular about which is which. Check your computer's documentation to make sure you have the right SIMMs installed in the right banks. For example, my motherboard requires that Bank 0 always be full (although Bank 1 can be either full or empty).

The Least You Need to Know

Computer programs gobble memory like popcorn at the movies. The more powerful the program, the hungrier it is. You can add more memory to your PC to make the computer operate faster.

➤ Find out the type (DIPP, SIP, or SIMM), the amount, and the speed of memory your system can accept.

➤ The memory speed is measured in nanoseconds in a range from 20ns to 200ns (the lower the number, the faster the memory). You want to purchase memory chips that are as fast or faster than your current chips.

➤ SIMMs come in different capacities. You can purchase the amount you need, but you can't mix sizes in a single bank.

➤ To install the SIMM, open up the system case, align the SIMM to the slot, and press it in.

➤ Some systems recognize the new memory right away, but on other systems, you have to run your setup program and enter the amount of new memory in the CMOS.

Chapter 27

Connections Made Easy: Adding a Fax/Modem

> **In This Chapter**
>
> ➤ What's involved?
>
> ➤ Step 1: Selecting a fax/modem
>
> ➤ Step 2: Assembling your tools
>
> ➤ Step 3: Connecting the modem
>
> ➤ Step 4: Testing the modem
>
> ➤ Troubleshooting

If you are interested in cruising the information superhighway, sending e-mail to President Bill, making plane reservations, or playing chess with someone in Paris, you will want to add a modem to your computer setup. (Or you might even want one for something as boring as accessing your office PC from your home PC.)

With a modem, you can take advantage of all the communication stuff discussed in Chapter 15. If you didn't purchase a modem as part of your original system, you can add one inside the system unit or as a desktop unit. Just read on.

What's Involved?

Adding a modem is a fairly straightforward upgrade. Unlike adding memory, you don't have to determine your motherboard's modem likes and dislikes. Here's a quick overview of the steps involved:

1. Buy a modem. You can purchase just a modem or a combination fax/modem.

2. Get your tool kit together.

3. Connect your modem.

4. Set up the modem.

If you don't want to fuss with the upgrade, you can just follow step 1 and then have your computer dealer connect and set up the modem. However, before you fork out that extra cash, check into the price for upgrade installations and read through the steps. You may find that all you really need is some skill with a screwdriver. Installing a modem (especially an external one) is very easy and straightforward.

Step 1: Selecting a Fax/Modem

Chapter 15 covers all the nitty-gritty details of what you can do with a modem and what you want to look for. As a quick reminder, here are the important things to keep in mind when shopping.

Communicating in the Fast Lane

Modem speed is measured in bits per second (bps). The higher the number, the faster the modem. Why is speed so important? Remember that when you and your online beau across the country are sending e-mail love letters, you are racking up long distance charges. Also, some commercial online services tack on a fee on top of the long distance charge. The faster you can get online and offline, the less expensive communicating is going to be.

The fastest modem is now 28,800 bps. If you want top-of-the-line, select a 28,800 bps modem. If you don't need top-of-the-line, buy a 14,400 bps modem at the minimum. You may be tempted to buy the less expensive 2400 and 9600 bps modems, but try to resist. You'll be sorry later and will eventually upgrade to at least a 14,400 bps.

Internal or External?

You have two types of modem to choose from. You can purchase an internal modem that plugs into one of the expansion slots inside your system unit or an external modem that sits on your desk. Internal modems are less expensive than their external counterparts, don't take up desk space, and don't occupy a power outlet (the power supply inside the PC provides the power).

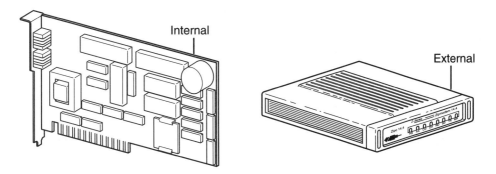

Internal

External

Modems come in internal and external models. Take your pick.

If you aren't an innie person, you can purchase an external modem. This modem sits on the desktop and has little UFO-type flashing lights that let you know when the modem is working. If you want to spend a little more to watch the light show, you can purchase an external modem. An external modem is easier to set up, and it doesn't take up one of your expansion slots.

What's the Price?

You can expect to pay $100–$200 for a 14,400 bps modem. For a faster modem (28,800 bps), expect to pay $200–$400.

However, the bucks don't stop there. When you're tallying up the total upgrade price, don't forget the cost of communications software. To use the modem, you'll need one kind of communications program, and to use the fax feature of the modem (if you get a fax/modem), you'll need fax software as well. Sometimes a "lite" version of a program is included with the modem. If this software isn't powerful enough for your needs, you may want to purchase a stand-alone communications program. Add this cost to your budget.

Finally, although you can use your current phone line, you'll have to coordinate the phone's dual personality. Is it a modem now or a phone? If you don't want to deal with the Sybil-esque aspect of managing the phone line, you can install a separate modem line —another cost for your budget (if you choose to go that route).

Step 2: Assembling Your Tools

To hook up and use the modem, you need the following:

➤ The modem (duh!)

➤ A flat-head screwdriver and a Phillips-head screwdriver

➤ A phone line and jack. The phone cable will be provided with the modem, but you need a phone jack near the modem to make the connection

➤ A serial cable (external modem only)

➤ Communications software

Collect all your equipment and get ready to join the electronic village. On to the next step!

Step 3: Connecting the Modem

Did you get an external modem? If so, read the following section on hooking up an external modem. Did you opt for the internal modem? Well, you can skip a few pages and read the section on hooking up an innie.

Hooking Up an External Modem

Hooking up an external modem is easier because you don't have to take apart the PC. You just have to plug in a few connections.

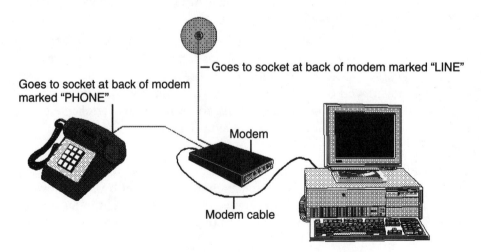

Goes to socket at back of modem marked "LINE"

Goes to socket at back of modem marked "PHONE"

Modem

Modem cable

Here's how to connect an external modem.

Follow these steps:

1. Take a look at the back of the modem. You should see connections for the power, the serial port cable, your telephone, and the phone line.

The connections on the back of an external modem.

2. Start by connecting the serial cable to the serial port on the back of the PC. Connect the other end of the cable to the serial port on the modem.

You may have received a serial cable as part of the modem package. Check the package carefully to see if one is included. If you don't have one, you'll have to buy one separately. Look at the back of your PC to see what kind of serial port you have. The port should be labeled either COM1 or COM2 and will have a different number of pins. Buy a cable with the same number of pins as the port you want to use.

3. Plug the phone cord into the wall jack. Connect the other end to the jack marked LINE or LINE IN on the back of the modem. If you are using the same line for your telephone, connect your telephone line to the jack marked VOICE, PHONE, or OUT on the back of the modem.

4. Plug one end of the power cord (included with the modem) into the back of the modem. Connect the other end to your power supply.

Ta da! You're done! Skip ahead to the section on testing the modem.

If you find two modems similar in price and performance, see what extras are included as part of the package. Some modems come bundled with communications and fax software and even limited free connection time on popular online services (such as PRODIGY, America Online, and CompuServe). Pick the one that offers the best software.

You can also compare the warranty and tech support offered by each one to see which one provides better service.

Hooking Up an Internal Modem

If you purchased an internal modem, when you open the box you'll see an electronic expansion card. Pretty cool, huh? For this type of modem, you'll have to expose the guts of your PC. Get your screwdriver and follow these steps:

1. Open the system unit. If you need help with this step, see Chapter 23, which covers how to open and take off the system case. Once the system unit is open, look near the left rear of the system to find expansion slots.

2. Decide which COM port you're going to set the modem for. You have to assign the modem a COM port number (COM1 through COM4). You can't use numbers that are already in use, so if your computer has two built-in COM ports (COM1 and COM2), you'll need to set your modem to be either COM3 or COM4.

 Here's a good way to decide between COM3 and COM4. If you have a serial mouse (a mouse attached to a COM port), see which COM port the mouse is connected to. If it's connected to COM1, choose COM4 for your modem. If it's connected to COM2, choose COM3 for your modem.

The reasoning behind this has to do with system interrupts (IRQs). Odd-numbered COM ports use IRQ 4, and even-numbered COM ports use IRQ 3. If two COM ports try to use the same IRQ at the same time, there may be a conflict.

Don't worry about the technical definition of IRQ; just follow the recommendation here and you should be fine.

3. Find out how to specify the COM port on your modem, and do whatever you need to do. This varies, so you'll have to look at the documentation. There may be switches on the back panel or jumpers on the circuit board. Set whatever is needed to specify the COM port you want.

4. Find the expansion slot that you want to use. You have to find a slot that is as big or bigger than the card. For example, if you have an 8-bit card, you can plug it into an 8-bit or a 16-bit expansion slot.

5. Take off the slot cover. Use a screwdriver to unscrew the securing screw. Keep the screw! You'll need it later. Don't forget to ground yourself by first touching something metal outside of the computer.

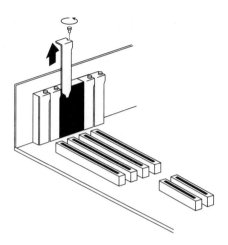

Find an expansion slot and take off the slot cover.

6. Hold the board at the top and get the connectors along the bottom aligned with the slot. Push the board into the slot. On some PCs, you can push the card in fairly easily. On others, you have to press pretty hard.

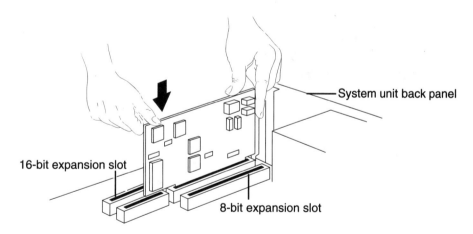

Insert the fax/modem board into the expansion slot.

    If the card won't go in and you are thinking about hammering it in, don't. Make sure you have the card and slot aligned properly. You have to press pretty hard on some, but you shouldn't have to STAND on the card to get it to go in. Try seesawing it back and forth to wedge it into the slot.

7. Secure the board at the top with the screw you saved from step 5.

8. Put the system cover back on, but don't turn on the power. You have some external connections to make.

9. If you look at the back of the system unit, you'll notice that part of the card sticks out. That's where you make the external connections. Plug your phone cord into the line marked LINE (or something similar). If you are using the same phone line for your modem and your telephone, connect your phone to the jack marked PHONE, OUT, or something like that.

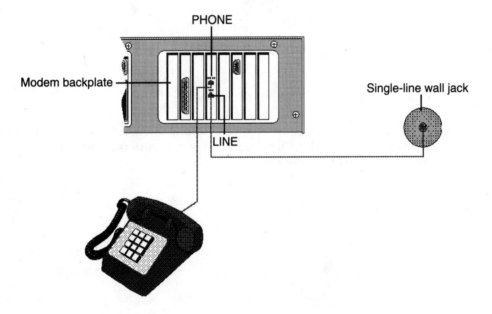

Hooking up the phone line.

10. Hook the other end of the phone cord into the wall jack for the phone. You're ready for the next big step: testing the modem.

Step 4: Testing the Modem

To be sure your modem works, test it out. To do so, you'll need some kind of communications software. Sometimes the modem includes a communications program and fax program as part of the package. If not, you can purchase the software separately. If you have Windows, you can also use its communications program called Terminal to test the modem (and even make some calls).

Start the PC and then start Windows. For our testing purposes, let's try using Windows Terminal. Start the program, set it up for your particular modem (see your modem instructions or Windows documentation), and type the following command:

atz

Press **Enter**. You should see a message that says **OK**.

You can also try calling the modem's technical support bulletin board and registering your modem. Many modems offer a BBS number and enable you to both test your modem and register your modem by calling the BBS. Check your modem manual.

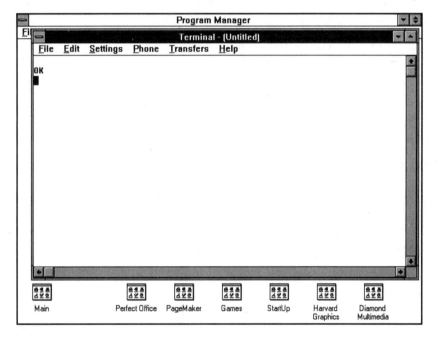

A communications program

Another way to test your modem is to call an online service. Many modems come with introductory offers for online services such as America Online. Follow the instructions that come with the modem to hook it up.

If you purchased a fax/modem, you can install the fax software by following the instructions in the fax software manual. Once the software is installed, try faxing someone a note that says, "I'm hip, I'm cool, I'm online!"

Troubleshooting

Does your software give you a **No Dialtone** error message? Or does it not respond at all? That means the connection between the modem and the phone line isn't getting through. Check the following potential problem areas:

The phone jack   Check this by plugging in a regular phone and seeing if you get a dial tone.

The cable   Try plugging your regular phone into that jack using the modem phone line.

The modem   If it's an external model, make sure the power is on. If it's internal, make sure it's firmly seated in its expansion slot.

The cable connection   Sometimes the jacks on the back of the modem aren't marked. You have to guess which one is for the phone line and which is for the telephone. If you can't get the modem to work, try switching the lines.

The COM port (software end)   Did you tell your communications software which COM port you are using? Most programs assume COM1 unless you specify other-wise. Check the software documentation to find out how to specify this.

The COM port (hardware end)   If you're using an internal modem, did you follow the directions that came with the modem to specify which COM port you wanted to use? And did you pick one that wasn't already in use?

The Least You Need to Know

Your modem is your passport to cyberspace. With a modem, you can hook up to other computers across town, across the country, or even across the world. If you bought a PC that didn't have a modem, you can add one so that you can take a journey far away without ever leaving your desk.

➤ When buying a modem, the most important spec is the modem speed. The fastest modem on the market is a 28,800 bps (bits per second) modem and costs $200 or more. The minimum modem speed you should buy is a 14,400 bps modem, which will cost you $100 or so.

➤ An external modem costs more but is easier to hook up. An internal modem is housed inside the system unit. It's less expensive but harder to connect.

➤ To hook up a modem, you need a flat-head screwdriver, a Phillips-head screwdriver, the modem, a serial cable (external modems only), an available phone line near the modem, and communications and fax software.

➤ To connect an external modem, connect one end of the serial cable to the modem and the other to the serial port on the back of the PC. Connect the phone line and the power cord, and you are set.

➤ To connect an internal modem, take off the system case and plug the modem card into one of your available expansion slots. Close the system case, and then hook up the phone cord to the back of the modem card (the part that sticks out of the back of the system unit).

➤ You can test your modem by installing your communications software and trying to call someone. Try your modem's bulletin board system if they have one.

BRAIN, PLEASE.

Brain Transplants: Upgrading Your Processor

Is your computer slow, slow, slow? Are you limited in what you can do because you have an old or slow processor? Have no fear. In some cases, you can upgrade to a faster, spiffier processor. Yes, you can get a brain transplant for your PC. Will miracles never cease?

What's Involved?

The hardest part in upgrading your processor is the first step, knowing whether you can or not. The rest of the steps get easier. Here's a brief rundown of the process:

1. Find out whether you can upgrade.

2. Purchase the upgrade chip.

3. Insert the new chip.

If you don't think you can do brain surgery, you may want to have this upgrade done at your computer dealer or superstore. They'll make sure the upgrade is going to work, take care of the details, and return your system; you won't have to worry about a thing. However, If you think you want to do it yourself, read on. The rest of this chapter explains the steps in detail.

Step 1: Finding Out Whether You Can Upgrade

To prevent your computer from becoming obsolete the second you unpack, many manufacturers thought it might be a neat concept to sell upgradable PCs. With an upgradable PC, you can replace the processor to keep your PC current a little longer.

If you have a 386 chip, you may be able to upgrade to a 486. If you have a slower 486 chip, you may be able to upgrade to a faster 486 chip. And if you have the fastest 486 chip, you may be able to upgrade to a Pentium. Depending. "Depending on what?" you ask. Depending on a lot of factors.

Is It Possible?

Before you start dreaming of all the power from your new processor, you need to find out whether you can upgrade. The best way to do this is to check your system documentation or, easier than that, call Intel. Intel is the major manufacturer of PC processors. They can tell you whether there is an upgrade chip (called an OverDrive chip) that is compatible with your system. And they can tell you which upgrade chips are available.

For example, you can purchase an upgrade chip that will turn a 386 into a 486 or can upgrade a 486SX/25 processor chip to a 486DX2/50 chip for double the performance.

The phone number for Intel at the time of this publication is (800) 538-3373. You can also use the fax number (800) 525-3019.

Or you can upgrade a 486SX/33 chip to a 486DX4/100Mhz chip. Ideally, you should also be able to upgrade a 486 to a Pentium, but the chips to do so have been promised and promised and promised. They should be available at this book's publication time.

There are other chip manufacturers besides Intel, such as AMD and Cyrix. You also can check with these companies for details about buying an upgrade chip for your computer.

Is It Difficult?

The answer to that question depends on your PC. On some PCs, the chip is soldered onto the motherboard. Sorry, but you can't upgrade this type of processor unless you replace the entire motherboard, which is really, really difficult. On some PCs, you can yank the chip out, but it's also difficult. Intel provides a chip-pulling tool with some of its upgrades. You can use this rake-shaped chip puller to take out the chip.

However, some motherboards have an extra processor socket especially for upgrade chips. To upgrade to a new processor, you simply insert a new chip in the blank socket. On other PCs, you have to replace the chip, but the PC uses what is called a zero insertion force (ZIF) socket (such a fancy name for such a simple concept). This type of socket has a handle. To take out the chip, you simply lift the handle.

How do you know which type of socket you have? You can check your documentation or call your manufacturer. Or you may just have to wait until you open it up.

Is Upgrading Worth It?

It depends. How much are you willing to spend, and what do you hope to get in return? Here's the breakdown in current chip prices:

386 to 486	Around $250
486 DX2/50	Around $200
486 DX/4 OverDrive	Around $650

Keep in mind, though, that when you upgrade the processor, your other components may get PC envy. Do you also need to add more memory? Is the power supply adequate for the new chip? Check with a computer dealer to be sure you won't need any other changes when you upgrade the processor.

You may also have to get a new BIOS if your version is old. You can check the BIOS date using the MSD command from the DOS prompt. If you have a BIOS that is more than one year old, check with Intel to see whether you have to upgrade the BIOS.

Step 2: Purchasing the Chip

Go to the computer dealer of your choice and buy the chip that works for your system. Not too much more than that for this step! As a reminder, don't forget to check the prices at some reputable mail-order catalog houses. You can find them listed in the back of most computer magazines.

Step 3: Upgrading the Microprocessor

So you want to be a brain surgeon. Before you begin, keep in mind the upgrade rules. Be sure to turn off and unplug your PC before you start working on it. Handle the processor with care; it's an expensive and sensitive piece of equipment. Finally, be sure to ground yourself. (No TV and no friends over for one week. Just kidding.) Touch something metal outside of the computer to ground yourself.

Be sure to get a money-back guarantee on the new chip. If you get it home and it won't work, you want to be able to return it. Otherwise, you'll have this $700 computer chip that might make a neat necklace for some computer chick, but for $700 you could do better in the jewelry department.

Here are the steps you follow to install your new processor:

1. Open the system case following the steps in Chapter 23. Put the screws some place where you can find them again.

2. Find the big green motherboard inside the system unit, and find the processor. Look for the word Intel (or some other manufacturer's name) on a chip about the size of a cracker. You may have to look around because this chip can appear in different locations depending on the size and orientation of your system unit.

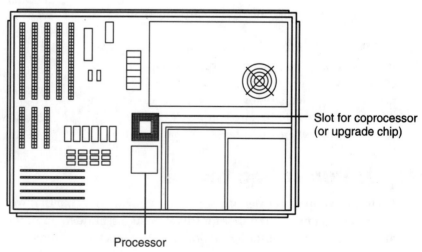

Slot for coprocessor
(or upgrade chip)

Processor

The processor.

3. If necessary, take your current chip out of the socket. (Remember, if you have an upgrade socket, and the chip you bought is designed to go into it, you don't have to remove the current processor.)

If you have a ZIF socket, lift the socket's lever and gently pull out the chip. Easy as pie.

If you don't have a ZIF socket and your replacement chip included a chip puller (it looks like a little rake), use it to take out the chip. Slide the raked edge under one side of the chip. Push the handle *toward* the chip. Do this on all sides to loosen the chip. Then lift it gently out of its home.

If you don't have a ZIF socket or a chip puller, you can use a small flat-head screwdriver. Slip the edge under one side of the chip. Move the blade back and forth to gently pry this side. Do the same on all sides until you can pry the chip out of the socket and take it out with your hand.

In some cases, you may have to remove some of the other equipment to get to the processor. For example, you may have to move the housing that holds your disk drives. Ugh! If you have to do some rearranging, be sure to keep the screws in a safe place. You may want to take a Polaroid snap shot so that you can remember exactly how the stuff was arranged. Remember: you're going to have to put it back just the way you found it!

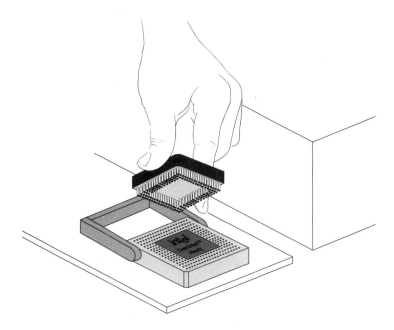

Taking out the old chip.

4. Align the new chip with the socket. The chip should have a notched or rounded corner that enables you to align the chip in the proper position. (The socket should have a similar rounded corner.) Make sure the pins on the processor are aligned with the pins in the socket.

5. Gently press the new chip into the socket from the sides, not the top. Don't expect to hear a confirming click when the chip is all the way in. Just press until the processor is in the socket.

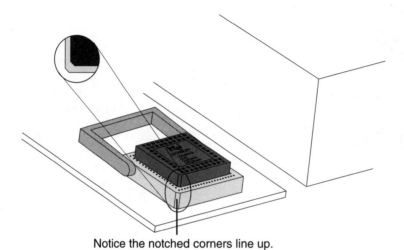

Notice the notched corners line up.

Placing the new chip into the socket.

Don't twist the processor to get it out. Also, don't use pliers or a magnetic screwdriver. And no matter how frustrated you get, don't yank it out. Handle with care! When you are pressing in the new chip, you shouldn't have to press hard. The chip should go in easily. If you are thinking about pressing really hard, at least make sure the pins are aligned.

6. If you have a ZIF socket, push the lever back down to lock the PC into place.

7. Set any jumpers or switches. With some motherboards, you have to mess around with the motherboard in order to use a faster processor. You may have to flip one of the switches or set a jumper. Check your processor installation and your system documentation for help with this step.

8. Reconnect your system and start it up.

When the computer starts, you should see the new processor on the information that flashes on-screen. Now you are in OverDrive!

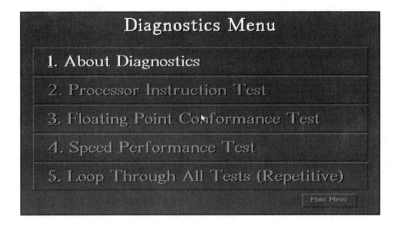

Run the diagnostics program to check out the new chip.

Intel provides a diagnostic program with its chip upgrades. You can install and run this diagnostic program following the instructions in the manual to test your new processor. If you purchase another brand of processor, that chip may also come with diagnostic software. Check your manual.

Troubleshooting

Didn't get what you expected when you turned on the PC after the upgrade? Check the following troubleshooting list:

➤ You turn on your PC expecting a powerful new machine, and nothing happens. Not a thing. What's wrong? Turn off the power and take off the system case. Make sure the new chip is aligned in the socket and is firmly in place.

➤ The chip is in place, but still nothing. For some motherboards, you have to make some changes to the motherboard: flip a tiny switch or set a jumper. Check your processor manual for help with setting the right switch or call for technical support.

➤ You turn on the PC and it starts all right, but now you can't access your hard drive, or your sound cards don't work, or something else goes wrong. Probably something came loose when you were doing the upgrade. Turn off the PC, take off the system case, and check all the connections to your other internal components. Make sure the hard drive data cables are connected, check the power supply, and check the other connections.

➤ Still no luck? I don't mean to panic you, but maybe you didn't buy the right chip for your system, or maybe the chip is defective. Place a call to your PC manufacturer's technical support department.

A True Upgrade Horror Story

As part of the research for this book, I thought it would be a good idea to upgrade my processor. I had already added a fax modem, installed a new hard drive, and added multimedia capabilities. So I figured why not upgrade the processor? Here's what happened:

Just as Intel suggested, I called and found out my system was upgradeable. I purchased the chip they suggested and got it installed perfectly. That part was easy!

When I started using my system, I noticed intermittent weirdness with my monitor and printer. The problems weren't damaging, just annoying. I called Intel support for help.

During the first call, they recommended I upgrade my BIOS and sent me off on my own to track down the BIOS for my system. I had to call my manufacturer, who referred me to the BIOS company, who charged me over $80 for a new BIOS.

Back to work on the PC. The steps for installing a new BIOS aren't difficult, but upgrading a BIOS is scary because it's so critical. (Remember that the BIOS is the tiny bit of information that wakes up the computer. I didn't want to goof up and have my computer end up thinking it was a toaster.) I did successfully upgrade the BIOS. What a relief—but the problem still wasn't fixed!

I called Intel back and got a helpful tech support guy who knew nothing. After I insisted to speak to a manager (they were all at lunch), the tech guy said he'd "red flag my folder" and promised an immediate callback.

I waited a week. Then I mailed a letter. Then I put a message on CompuServe. No response. Then I called back. The tech support office was closed because of bad weather. Yes, it's true.

I finally got through to a manager, and she now says to take apart my system, put my old chip back in, repackage the new chip, and send it at *my expense* to Intel, where they will test it and possibly send me a new one that will work better. How will this end? I don't know. I'm waiting on my new chip.

What can you learn from this? A few things. First, understand that upgrading can be frustrating. If you aren't prepared to deal with this, consider having your upgrade done at a computer dealer or superstore. Realize that you are investing your time and your money when you make an upgrade. Second, be prepared to do some troubleshooting if something goes wrong. Call tech support immediately. If you can't get an answer, ask to speak to a manager. If you don't get a response, write to the president of the company. Be persistent. Third, save all your receipts and packaging. If necessary, you can insist on returning the entire upgrade for a full refund.

The Least You Need to Know

If you have an older, slower PC, you may want to upgrade the processor to breathe new life into your computing life. Whether you can upgrade or not depends on the type of system you have and the type of processor.

➤ To find out whether you can upgrade, check your system documentation or call Intel. You can also purchase an upgrade chip from other manufacturers. Check with your local computer dealer.

➤ Expect to pay from $200 to $700 for the new chip, depending on what type of chip you are purchasing. Be sure to get a money back guarantee in case the chip won't work in your system.

➤ To replace the chip, start by taking out the old chip. Open the system case and gently take out the old chip.

➤ If you have a ZIF socket (one with a lever), you can easily take out the chip. Lift the lever and take out the chip.

➤ If you have an older system without a ZIF socket, use the chip rake provided in the upgrade kit to gently pry the chip out of the socket.

➤ To put the new chip in, align the notched edge on the chip with the notched edge on the socket. Be sure the pins are aligned, and then press the new chip into the socket.

➤ When you turn on the PC, you should see the new chip name flash on-screen during the POST.

➤ If nothing happens, turn off the PC and make sure the processor is securely in place. Check your documentation to see whether you have to do anything else, such as set a switch or jumper on the motherboard.

Speak Like a Geek:
The Complete Archive

3 1/2-inch disk   A size of floppy disk used to transfer data to and from the hard disk. This type of disk comes in a hard plastic case and doesn't seem floppy. Currently, the 3 1/2-inch disk size is the standard.

5 1/4-inch disk   A larger size floppy disk used to transfer data to and from the hard disk. This type of disk is actually floppy. The 5 1/4-inch disk was once the standard, but now the 3 1/2-inch is the standard.

386   Pronounced "three-eighty-six." Nickname for the 80386 microprocessor, which is now outdated.

486   Pronounced "four-eighty-six." Nickname for the 80486 microprocessor. This processor is probably the most popular processor sold today. It is not as fast or as high-powered as the Pentium. See *Pentium*.

access time   The average time it takes a disk to access a particular piece of information.

adapter   Another name for an expansion card you can plug into an expansion slot inside the system unit to add additional features to the PC.

application   A program designed for some application (for instance, to create documents, work with numbers, maintain data, and so on).

AT command set   The standards set by Hayes and followed by most modem manufacturers. When shopping for a modem, you want to look for one that uses the AT command set.

AUTOEXEC.BAT   A special file containing commands that are executed each time you start the computer.

backup   The process of making an extra copy of your data and/or program files. If something happens to the original, you can use the backup copy.

baud   A measure of how many changes per second a modem can make. Compare to bits per second.

binary   The numbering system used on computers. The system has two digits: 0 (off) and 1 (on).

BIOS   Stands for Basic Input/Output System. The software permanently recorded on the ROM chip that enables the computer to start itself.

bit   Short for binary digit. The smallest amount of information a computer can process.

bits per second (bps)   A measurement of the speed of a modem (the number of bits of information transferred per second). Sometimes mistakenly called baud.

Bulletin Board System (BBS)   A communication system that's usually set up by an individual and usually dedicated to a hobby or interest. You can connect to a BBS to chat with other participants, download files, and more.

bus   The electronic pathway that connects different components of the system.

byte   8 bits, or roughly one typed character.

cache   A method of speeding up the computer. The computer makes assumptions about what data it thinks you will need and stashes the instructions in the cache.

CD-ROM   Stands for Compact Disc-Read Only Memory. A storage device that stores a lot of information, such as an entire set of encyclopedias. You can only read information from the disk; you cannot write information to the disk.

CGA   Stands for Color Graphics Adapter. An outdated monitor standard.

characters per second (cps)   A measure of how fast a dot-matrix printer can print.

chip   Usually a square-shaped wafer about the size of a cracker that is made of silicon and includes thousands of transistors (electronic circuitry). Nickname for the micro-processor.

CISC   Stands for complex instruction-set computing. The type of architecture used in Intel-based chips.

clock speed   The operating speed of a microprocessor, measured in megahertz.

clone   See *compatible*.

cluster   The smallest allocated unit for storage on a hard disk.

CMOS   Stands for complementary metal-oxide semiconductor and pronounced "see-moss." This type of computer chip stores configuration information about your PC, such as the type and size of the hard drive and the amount of memory. You can make changes to the CMOS by running your setup program.

COMMAND.COM   The program that handles the DOS interface.

compatible   A type of computer that is the same as an IBM PC, but is manufactured by someone other than IBM.

CONFIG.SYS   A file with commands that control different devices, such as the mouse. This file is read and executed each time you start the computer.

convergence A measure of how accurately the three beams on a monitor align to create an image.

CPU Stands for central processing unit. The main computer chip or set of chips. CPUs are named mostly with numbers (8088, 8086, 80286, 80386, 80486, Pentium). Also called the microprocessor.

database A type of application program used to work with sets of information such as an inventory, client list, and so on.

defragmentation The process of rearranging files stored on a hard disk so that the files are stored in clusters next to each other.

desktop publishing program A type of application program used for page layout.

DIPP Stands for dual in-line pin package. A type of individual memory chip that you can plug into the motherboard to add more memory.

disk compression A program designed to squeeze (compress) the files on your hard disk so that you have more room.

DMA Stands for direct memory access. A high-speed direct path between the component and memory that bypasses the microprocessor. DMAs are often reserved for special purposes.

DOS Stands for Disk Operating System and pronounced "doss" (rhymes with boss). The most common operating system for IBM and compatibles. The most current version is DOS 6.22.

DOS prompt The on-screen prompt you see when you start the computer or have exited all programs. The DOS prompt usually looks like this: C:\>.

dot-matrix printer A type of printer that creates characters by striking a series of dots (which combine to create a character) against the ribbon.

dot pitch A measurement of how close the holes are placed on a monitor. The closer the hole, the better the image. Dot pitch is measured in millimeters (mm).

dots per inch (dpi) A measurement of the quality of a printer or monitor. The higher the number, the better quality the output.

double-density (DD) A lower-capacity floppy disk. Double-density 5 1/4-inch floppies can store 360KB. Double-density 3 1/2-inch floppies can store 720KB.

download The process of copying a file from a BBS or online service to your computer.

DRAM The most commonly used type of memory. Stands for dynamic random access memory.

DX   A suffix added to a microprocessor number. DX chips are faster than SX chips.

EGA   Stands for Enhanced Graphics Adapter. An outdated monitor standard.

EIDE   The latest enhanced version of the IDE controller. Stands for Enhanced Integrated Drive Electronics.

EISA   Stands for Extended Industry Standard Architecture. A 32-bit bus used in some computers. See *bus*.

electronic mail   Messages sent from one PC to another over a network, BBS, or online service.

ESDI   Stands for Enhanced Small Device Interface. A fast, acceptable type of hard drive controller.

expanded memory   A type of memory on an expansion card that enables DOS programs to gain access to more memory. Extended memory can also be configured as expanded memory.

expansion card   An electronic card that you insert in an expansion slot to add capabilities to your system.

expansion slot   A slot in the back of the computer that enables you to add and connect expansion boards (sometimes called cards). These boards provide additional features such as sound.

extended memory   The memory above 1MB in a computer. To use this type of memory, the computer uses a special program called a device driver.

FAT   Stands for file allocation table. The table on the hard disk that keeps track of which clusters are used to store your files.

fax/modem   A combination fax and modem. You can use this type of modem to send faxes from your computer to another computer or to a regular fax machine. You can also receive faxes.

flatbed scanner   A type of scanner that works much like a photocopier. You can use the scanner to turn a paper copy of an image into a digital copy.

floating point unit (FPU)   A section of the processor designed to handle complex math calculations. Also called the math coprocessor.

floppy disk   A portable storage device. You insert a floppy disk into the floppy drive to gain access to the information on the disk. Disks come in two sizes (3 1/2" and 5 1/4").

floppy drive   A slot on the front of the system unit into which you insert a floppy disk to access its information.

floptical   A high-capacity disk drive that uses a combination of laser and magnetic technology to store data.

font   One set of characters in a particular typeface and size.

footprint   The amount of desk or floor space that a PC takes up.

format   The process of preparing a disk for use.

game port   A connection, usually found on a sound card, for a joystick.

gigabyte   Approximately 1 billion bytes.

graphics adapter   The video card inside the system unit that determines the quality and features of a monitor display.

graphics program   A type of application program for creating graphic images. There are different types of graphics programs, such as presentation programs for creating visual presentations, CAD programs for creating architectural and manufacturing drawings, paint and draw programs for creating pictures or logos, and so on.

hand-held scanner   A type of scanner that you use by dragging the scanner over the image.

hard disk   A storage device for files and programs. Hard disks come in different capacities, measured in megabytes and gigabytes.

hardware   The physical components, such as your monitor, keyboard, and system unit, that make up a computer.

hertz (Hz)   Cycles per second, used to measure frequency for monitors.

high density (HD)   A higher-capacity type of floppy disk. High-density 5 1/4-inch floppies can store 1.2MB. High-density 3 1/2-inch floppies can store 1.44MB.

IDE   Stands for integrated device electronics. A popular, fast type of hard drive controller.

inkjet printer   A type of printer that creates characters by spraying ink through tiny jets.

integrated programs   A type of application program that combines the most common applications (word processing, spreadsheet, charting, database, communications, and graphics) into one package.

Intel   The manufacturer of microprocessor chips used in IBMs and IBM-compatibles.

IRQ   An interrupt request made by one hardware component to the microprocessor. Certain interrupt lines are reserved for certain components. Some interrupt lines are free and can be assigned to new hardware that you add.

ISA   Stands for industry standard architecture. A 16-bit bus used in many computers.

joystick   An arcade-style input device often used to play games. The joystick hooks up to the game port.

keyboard   A computer component with alphanumeric characters and other special keys, used to communicate with the system unit.

kilobyte (K or KB)   1,024 bytes, usually rounded to 1,000 bytes. Abbreviated KB or K. Memory and file size are measured in kilobytes.

kilohertz (kHz)   A measure of 1,000 cycles per second. Used to measure a monitor's scanning frequency.

laptop   A type of portable computer that weighs approximately 9–12 pounds.

laser printer   A type of printer that creates an image in a way similar to a photocopier machine. Laser printers provide the best quality for printouts.

local area network (LAN)   Two or more computers connected via some type of cabling. The connected PCs can then send messages, share files, and share equipment such as a printer.

local bus   A direct high-speed connection between an electronic card (such as the video card) and the microprocessor.

magneto-optical drives   Disk drives that store a lot of data using a combination of laser and magnetic technology.

math coprocessor   A chip added to speed up arithmetic functions. All 486DX machines and Pentiums have a built-in math coprocessor. Also called the floating point unit (FPU).

MCA   Stands for MicroChannel Architecture. A 16-bit or 32-bit bus used in IBM computers. See *bus*.

megabyte (M or MB)   1 million bytes. A byte is a measure of computer information. Memory and hard disk space are measured in bytes, usually megabytes. Abbreviated M or MB.

megahertz (MHz)   The measurement of the speed of the microprocessor. Speeds range from 25 MHz to 100 MHz.

microprocessor   The main chip or "brain" of the computer. Sometimes called the CPU.

Microsoft Windows   An operating environment that runs on top of DOS and provides a graphical interface.

MIDI   An interface that enables you to hook up musical equipment to your sound card and record music. Also the file format used to store the music files.

millisecond (ms)   One thousandth of a second. Some times, such as a hard disk's access time, are measured in milliseconds.

modem   Stands for MOdulator-DEModulator. A peripheral device that enables you to communicate with other computers through the phone line.

monitor   The essential output device. The monitor displays what you type.

motherboard   The main board inside the system unit. The motherboard contains the microprocessor chip and other key electronic components.

mouse   An input device that you can use to issue commands.

multimedia   The combination of text, graphics, and audio used to present a message.

Multimedia PC (MPC)   A multimedia PC usually includes a CD-ROM drive, a sound card, and speakers. Multimedia applications can play sounds and display animation and video.

multisync   A monitor that can operate using different video display standards.

nanosecond (ns)   One billionth of a second. The speed of memory is measured in nanoseconds.

notebook   A type of portable computer small enough to fit into a briefcase and weighing around 4–6 pounds.

OEM   Stands for original equipment manufacturer. A company that uses other companies' parts to create a product with their own name.

online service   A professionally run BBS system that you can hook up to using your modem. You can review information (current events, sports scores, stock prices), send messages to other users, shop, make travel arrangements, download files, and more.

operating system   The software that directs your computer, telling it where to find a file, how to display a file, and so on. The most common operating system for IBM computers is DOS.

optical character recognition (OCR)   The software used to translate scanned text from an image into characters.

palmtop   A portable computer about the size of a checkbook that is usually limited in function.

parallel port   A connection on the back of a PC that can transmit and receive 8 bits at a time. Most often, you connect a printer to the PC using the parallel port.

partition   A section of a hard disk that appears as a single, separate drive. DOS boots from the primary partition.

PCI   Stands for Peripheral Component Interconnect. A 32-bit bus type introduced in 1993. This bus offers more features and more power than other bus types.

PCMCIA (Personal Computer Memory Card International Association)   A slot and/or card you can use to add functions to a portable computer (for example, to add more memory).

pen computer   A portable computer that uses a pen as an input device.

Pentium   Basically, a 586 computer. The latest, most powerful, and most expensive microprocessor.

peripheral   Extra equipment, such as a printer or scanner, that you can connect to the PC.

pixel   Short for picture element. The smallest unit that can be used to create an image. Resolution for monitors is measured in pixels (for example, 600×480).

port   A connector on the back of the computer that enables you to hook up a device such as a printer to the computer. There are two types of ports: serial and parallel.

POST   Stands for power on self test. A series of tests and checks executed by the PC to make sure everything is working okay.

PowerPC   A type of microprocessor introduced in 1994 jointly by IBM, Apple, and Motorola. This chip uses a RISC-technology for working with computer tasks. See *RISC*.

ppm   Stands for pages per minute. A measurement of how fast a printer can print.

processor   The main chip or "brain" of the computer. Sometimes called the CPU.

protocol   The set of rules that govern communication.

RAM   Stands for random access memory. A temporary storage space for information you are currently working on.

resolution   A measurement of the crispness of a monitor image or a printed image.

RISC   Stands for reduced instruction-set computing. The type of design used in the new PowerPC chip. This type of chip breaks down tasks into smaller tasks, is more powerful, and is cheaper than CISC chips. (The CISC chip tries to handle the entire task at once.)

ROM   Stands for read-only memory. A type of memory that has instructions (such as the BIOS) hard-coded on the chip. You cannot change the instructions in ROM.

scanner   An input device that converts a printed image to an electronic image. Often used when working with graphics.

scanning frequency   A measurement in hertz or kilohertz of how quickly the electron beam can scan the monitor horizontally and vertically.

SCSI Stands for Small Computer Systems Interface and pronounced "scuzzy." A type of controller. You can chain different SCSI devices together.

serial port A type of connection on the PC that can transmit bits serially. This type of device can be used to hook up mice and other equipment, such as a scanner.

shareware Software that is distributed freely for users to try. If you like the shareware, you then pay a fee to register the copy with the shareware creator.

SIMM Stands for single in-line memory module. A chip that you can plug into your computer to add more memory.

SIP Stands for single in-line package. A type of memory chip with connectors on the side. You connect the SIP to the motherboard.

software Instructions that tell your computer what to do. Also called a program or application. There are different types of software, including system software and application software.

sound card An electronic board you can add to your computer to provide sound capabilities.

spreadsheet A type of application program used to work with numbers—calculating a budget, tracking sales, and so on.

static RAM (SRAM) A type of memory that's faster than DRAM.

subnotebook A smaller version (2–3 pounds) of a notebook computer.

SuperVGA (SVGA) The newest monitor standard. Can display 256 colors simultaneously.

SX A suffix added to a microprocessor number. SX chips are slower than DX chips. This type of chip does not have a math coprocessor.

system bus The series of electronic wiring that enables different expansion cards to communicate with the microprocessor.

system unit The case that houses the electronic parts (motherboard, memory, power supply, hard disk, floppy disk) of the computer.

tower computer A style of system unit that sits upright on the floor.

trackball An input device (like an upside down mouse) used to issue commands. Many notebook computers use a trackball.

transfer rate The amount of time it takes a disk to transfer data to memory.

utility A type of application program used to maintain and tweak your computer system.

VESA   Stands for Video Electronics Standards Association. A 32-bit bus type introduced in 1993. This bus is an inexpensive bus type that provides more power than the ISA bus. Also called the VL bus.

VGA   An acceptable monitor standard that can display 256 colors simultaneously.

VRAM   Memory used for processing video images. Stands for video random-access memory.

word processing program   A type of application program used to work with words and create documents (memos, letters, reports, and so on).

Index

video accelerator cards,
  monitors, 85
video cards, 78-79, 84-86
voice recognition software,
  163
VRAM (Video Random-
  Access Memory), video
  cards, 85

W-Z

warranties, 190
weight, portable PCs,
  124-125
WIN.INI files, 209
Windows 95, Microsoft, 17
word processing software,
  10, 292
Wozniak, Steve, Apple
  computers, 29
wrist pads, keyboards, 170

zero insertion force (ZIF)
  socket, 50, 275
ZIP drives, 155

More
Fun Learning
from
Alpha Books!

If you liked this *Complete Idiot's Guide*,
check out these other completely helpful books!

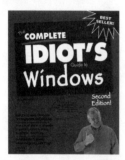

**The Complete Idiot's Guide
to Windows, Second Edition**
ISBN: 1-56761-546-5
$16.95 USA

**The Complete Idiot's Guide
to PCs, New Edition**
ISBN: 1-56761-459-0
$16.95 USA

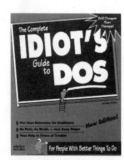

**The Complete Idiot's Guide
to DOS, Second Edition**
ISBN: 1-56761-496-5
$16.95 USA

**The Complete Idiot's Guide
to the Internet,
Second Edition**
ISBN: 1-56761-535-X
$19.95 USA

*Look for these books at your favorite
computer book retailer, or call
1-800-428-5331 for more information!*

Also Available!

Okay, so you finished this book and now you can do all the basic stuff that gets you through the day. Congrats!

But what about those other cool features you never get to use? Welcome to the perfect follow-up to *The Complete Idiot's Guide!*

The Complete Idiot's Next Step!

The *Next Step* books begin where *The Complete Idiot's Guides* leave off. You learn how to use all those powerful features that make life easier. And it all comes in the same lighthearted, beginner-style format that the *Idiot's Guides* are famous for!

Plus, the *Next Step* books come with a free disk full of software to make your work even more impressive! Get full-powered results without all the work!

You too can do things like an expert—without actually being one!

Don't Let Everyday Life Make You Feel Like An Idiot!

Whatever the topic, there's a Complete Idiot's Guide ready and waiting to make your life easier!

The Complete Idiot's Guide to Getting into College
ISBN: 1-56761-508-2
$14.95 USA

The Complete Idiot's Guide to Buying & Selling a Home
ISBN: 1-56761-510-4
$16.95 USA

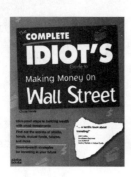

The Complete Idiot's Guide to Making Money on Wall Street
ISBN: 1-56761-509-0
$16.95 USA

Also Available!

The Complete Idiot's Guide to Managing Your Money
ISBN: 1-56761-530-9, $16.99 USA

The Complete Idiot's Guide to Starting Your Own Business
ISBN: 1-56761-529-5, $16.99 USA

The Complete Idiot's Guide to Cooking Basics
ISBN: 1-56761-523-6, $16.99 USA

The Complete Idiot's Guide to the Perfect Vacation
ISBN: 1-56761-531-7, $14.99 USA

The Complete Idiot's Guide to the Perfect Wedding
ISBN: 1-56761-532-5, $16.99 USA

The Complete Idiot's Guide to VCRs
ISBN: 1-56761-294-6, $9.95 USA

Look for these books at your favorite bookstore, or call 1-800-428-5331 for more information!

Down-to-ea
answers
to comple
question

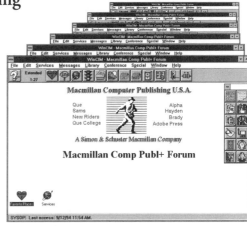